BLOODSWORTH

ALSO BY TIM JUNKIN

The Waterman, a novel
Good Counsel, a novel

BLOODS|WORTH

The True Story
of the First
Death Row Inmate
Exonerated by
DNA

TIM JUNKIN

A Shannon Ravenel Book

ALGONQUIN BOOKS
OF CHAPEL HILL

2004

ℝ

A SHANNON RAVENEL BOOK
Published by
Algonquin Books of Chapel Hill
Post Office Box 2225
Chapel Hill, North Carolina 27515-2225

a division of
Workman Publishing
708 Broadway
New York, New York 10003

This is a true story. At the request of Kirk Bloodsworth, and for both privacy
and security reasons, the names of a number of individuals with minor roles
in the story have been changed.

Library of Congress Cataloging-in-Publication Data
Junkin, Tim, 1951–
    Bloodsworth : the true story of the first death row inmate exonerated
by DNA / Tim Junkin.
        p. cm.
    Includes bibliographical references.
    ISBN 1-56512-419-7
    1. Bloodsworth, Kirk Noble, 1960–.   2. Death row inmates—
Maryland—Biography.   3. DNA fingerprinting—Maryland—Case studies.
I. Title.
HV8701.B56J85 2004
364.66'092—dc22
    [B]   2004045819

10 9 8 7 6 5 4 3 2 1
First Edition

for my children

Contents

BLOODSWORTH

PART I

A STAIN LIFTED

And so, to the end of history, murder shall breed murder, always in the name of right and honor and peace, until the gods are tired of blood and create a race that can understand.

—GEORGE BERNARD SHAW

ONE

IN THE LATE AFTERNOON of April 27, 1993, Bob Morin sat in his law office located near the city courthouse in Washington, D.C., and stared out his window at the new Olsson's bookstore across the street. There were books in there he'd wanted to read for years but couldn't find the spare hours. Morin had been up most of the night assisting lawyers in Austin on an emergency petition for a stay of execution on behalf of a Texas inmate scheduled to die by lethal injection. For weeks, he'd been immersed in preparing to defend a man at trial facing a possible death sentence in Maryland. He'd also been assisting lawyers in Georgia and South Carolina on numerous postconviction strategies in capital cases in those states. And he'd been preparing pleadings opposing the federal government's first attempt to apply a new death penalty law in a military tribunal. That April afternoon, Morin had just returned from a meeting with the federal prosecutors at the Department of Justice. His khaki suit was creased, his tie undone. He wanted to change into the blue jeans, pullover shirt, and sandals that he usually wore in the office and that lay in a heap on the floor, but he felt too tired to move.

Morin looked over a desk piled high with files. His gaze stopped on the dream catcher tacked to his office door. It was an authentic Navajo relic, presented to him by a grateful client. Raised a Boston Catholic, he preferred the simple Native American spirituality to any institutional religion. He studied the dream catcher on his door and made a wish for the one client whose image he couldn't shake, the one client who was haunting his thoughts. He took a deep breath, looked up a number on his Rolodex, picked up the phone, and dialed long distance.

At forty years old Bob Morin had devoted most of his legal career to assisting people facing the death penalty. By age thirty he had walked away from both a lucrative position in private practice and a promising academic career at Georgetown University to join the Southern Center for Human Rights in Atlanta in an effort to fight the swelling tide of death sentences being imposed and carried out in nine southern states. From there he'd gone on to become a public defender in Maryland, specializing in death penalty cases, and then in the nation's capital he formed a small law firm dedicated to helping death row inmates. Morin had long believed that the way the death penalty was being imposed in the United States was unjust. Now, having spent years battling executions in state after state, he'd become certain of something else—that there were inmates facing execution or serving life terms in prison who were innocent. One such person, in whose innocence Morin had come to believe strongly, was Kirk Bloodsworth.

Kirk Noble Bloodsworth had been sentenced to die in Maryland's gas chamber for the 1984 rape and murder of a nine-year-old girl. After being granted a new trial by a Maryland appellate court, Bloodsworth had been convicted a second time. His appeals to the higher courts in Maryland had all been exhausted. In February 1989 Morin had received a call from Gary Christopher in the state public defender's office, asking him to meet with Bloodsworth. "Every lawyer who's touched this case believes the kid is innocent," Christopher had said. Morin had been reluctant. He knew that Bloodsworth's sentence after his second trial had been changed from death to two consecutive life terms. Morin was swamped with death penalty cases and felt like a triage doctor at a disaster site. He had so many clients scheduled for execution that he couldn't afford to spend time trying to help one facing only a double life sentence. But when Christopher called a second time, Morin, as a favor to a colleague, agreed to visit this kid Bloodsworth. He had no intention, though, of becoming his lawyer.

A month later, in late March, Morin and his partner, David Kagan-Kans, had driven to the Maryland Penitentiary to meet with another client. They figured they'd briefly interview Bloodsworth while at the prison. The plan was to hear the man out, then politely tell him that they just didn't have the time or the resources to take on his case. Over the years Morin had interviewed hundreds of incarcerated prisoners seeking a lawyer's help and knew all too well the typical convict rap.

"Kirk came into the interview room all pumped up," Morin recalls. "He was a big kid, and he'd been lifting weights. His hair was long and shaggy, wild looking. He had bushy sideburns and a Wyatt Earp mustache running down his face. He wore mirrored sunglasses and had a pack of Kool Filter Kings rolled up in his sleeve. The classic biker con. I figured the interview would be short . . ."

Bloodsworth immediately took off his sunglasses. His eyes were teary. He shook hands with the two lawyers. "The first thing I want to do is apologize for the way I look," he said. "This is not me. This is not who I am. But this is the way I have to look to survive in this place. This is what I've had to become . . ."

Morin had never had a prisoner come on to him like this before. They talked further. Bloodsworth seemed interested in the little girl who had been killed. As though he had a connection to her. He wanted more than just to get out of prison. He stressed not only that he was innocent, that he didn't commit the crime, but that he wanted to find out who did. "For the sake of the little girl," he kept emphasizing.

Morin began trying to explain the legal difficulties to Bloodsworth. He told him there were immense hurdles to overturning his conviction a second time, particularly as his appeals were over. Even if a legal basis to further contest his conviction could be found —a constitutional violation previously overlooked or significant new evidence unknown at the time of his second trial—no judge, state or federal, would be eager to put the victim's family through the ordeal of a third trial. And even if a new trial were granted, how would they go about convincing a jury that there was reasonable doubt?

"Mr. Morin, I appreciate what you're saying," Bloodsworth interrupted him, "but this is not about reasonable doubt. If you're going to be my lawyer, you need to understand this. I did not do this. I am innocent. This is what we must prove. I am not here to get a lawyer to raise a reasonable doubt. If you take this on, it is not to raise a technicality—I am innocent. We must prove that. We must prove who really did this."

Morin was amazed. He'd never heard an inmate talk like this. But he did know some things about this one that were extraordinary. He'd learned that Bloodsworth had written hundreds of letters from prison proclaiming his innocence, that every day this man woke up thinking of a new person to write. Every day, seven days a week, for five years . . . A guilty man, Morin figured, just wouldn't have the energy, the perseverance, the will.

"Kirk," Morin responded. "You say you are innocent—"

Bloodsworth interrupted him again. "Mr. Morin," he said, "if you're going to be my lawyer you just can't use phrases like that. It's not that I'm just *saying* that I'm innocent. I *truly am* innocent. And we have to find the person who really did this."

Bob Morin and David Kagan-Kans walked together out of the prison without saying a word. Morin was frustrated, angry. They stood together on the stone curb outside the penitentiary walls. The sky was overcast, the air chilly. Traffic whizzed by. Morin slammed his file down on the hood of his old Chevy. The last thing he needed was this—an innocent client with no money, with almost no hope or chance. While the public defender's office might provide some small stipend for the representation, it would be a major undertaking involving hundreds of hours, a case his small firm would probably have to fund, and one that would further exhaust resources that were already stretched thin. He looked at his partner. They were thinking the same thing. "You know we have to do this," Morin said.

"I know," Kagan-Kans answered.

"It's going to be a bear. I mean, how are we ever going to prove he's innocent? I'm just not sure we can do anything for this kid."

"Right," Kagan-Kans answered. "Right."

Two prison guards in brown uniforms walked by. Kagan-Kans stretched out his arms and looked up at the low sky, which had begun to spit. He lowered his head and watched his partner. "But isn't this why we became lawyers?"

Morin smiled and nodded. He picked up his file and got into his car.

TWO

OVER THE FOLLOWING THREE years, from early 1989 through early 1992, neck deep in dozens of other pressing death penalty cases and trying to help his wife raise their two young sons, Bob Morin devoted every spare minute to the details of Kirk Bloodsworth's life, his case, the circumstances of the crime, the manner of the police investigation, and the actual trials. All of this and particularly Bloodsworth himself—his background, his natural dignity—further convinced Morin that he had an innocent man for a client. The dilemma was how to prove it.

Trying to find some basis on which to make a case, some edge, however slight, Morin exhausted every available legal remedy. Building on what other lawyers representing Bloodsworth had done before him, he hired investigators to pursue leads concerning other suspects dismissed by the police, searching under every rock from Maryland to California to try to find evidence that would establish the identity of the real murderer. The information pointing to a different killer that he amassed was disturbing, even convincing, but not legally sufficient to clear Bloodsworth. Morin tried to locate the child eyewitnesses, witnesses who'd since grown up whose testimony convinced two juries to convict his client, to see if they'd admit to error or a change of mind. He prepared and filed a habeas corpus petition, known as a collateral attack, a way to challenge the conviction on federal constitutional grounds never raised before. He even tracked down evidence of two murders that occurred after Bloodsworth's incarceration, murders that bore features strikingly similar to the crime for which his client was convicted. He was hoping to establish that a killer with the same modus operandi was still at large and that Bloodsworth thus was innocent. Again, this information, while unsettling, was not legally sufficient to compel his client's release. Morin had come up empty on all counts. Every effort led to a dead-end. He had nearly lost hope and given up when Kirk Bloodsworth's own reading and bullheaded obstinacy convinced Morin to reconsider the use of an emerging forensic tool, one unheard of just seven years earlier, in 1985, when Bloodsworth was initially tried.

Kirk had been reading everything he could get his hands on in the prison library—newspaper articles, magazine pieces, legal treatises and appellate cases from old law books, as well as other secondhand books donated to the prison by local civil rights groups, churches, and charities. He read with a purpose, looking always for a door, a hook, anything to help prove his innocence. He had come across a recently published work of nonfiction, a true crime story by Joseph Wambaugh titled *The Blooding,* that described how in England a scientific technique called genetic fingerprinting was first used to solve a double murder. A young scientist there, Alec Jeffreys, had discovered a way to identify and compare DNA patterns extracted from blood or semen samples, patterns that like fingerprints are unique to each individual. In the village of Narborough, near the city of Leicestershire, two teenage girls had been raped and killed three years apart. The assailant had left semen on the body and clothes of each victim. By using his genetic fingerprinting,

Jeffreys determined that the killer of both girls was the same man. The Leicestershire Constabulary, relying on this new science, had then undertaken to obtain a blood sample from every sexually active male living in the vicinity and to compare the DNA from each with that left by the killer. Incredibly, over a period of several years, police "blooded"—drew and tested the blood from—over three thousand men. Alec Jeffreys's technique worked. In late 1987 the investigators found the DNA match. They arrested the killer, who confessed to both crimes. Kirk Bloodsworth read the book in one sitting and excitedly contacted Morin.

In 1989, when Morin had first accepted Bloodsworth as a client, DNA testing was still in its early stages, though it was starting to generate interest in the legal community. Few people, however, seemed to understand its applications, how it worked, or how to interpret its results. It had never been used defensively in a capital case or to clear a convicted murderer. Nonetheless, Morin had considered whether a DNA test might help Kirk. He'd contacted a leading DNA laboratory in the country, Cellmark Diagnostics, to learn what would be needed to pursue a DNA analysis. Morin had reviewed all of the forensic reports in the file. The FBI had analyzed the crime scene evidence and reported that there had not been any spermatozoa or foreign blood specimens detected or preserved. Though cotton swabs had been used to gather fluid samples from the victim at autopsy, which were then smeared on glass slides, no semen had been found by the FBI. Morin had written to Bloodsworth's prosecutors, requesting that any fluid specimens of the assailant be tested. They'd written back, reiterating that no such fluid specimens existed. According to Cellmark Diagnostics, even if the slides had contained identifiable semen, Cellmark's testing techniques in 1989 could not analyze trace specimens preserved on glass slides. Moreover, any attempt to test them would probably completely destroy any existing DNA sample.

But Kirk, fired up after reading *The Blooding,* blew over all these old "details." He wanted a DNA test pursued. He called Morin repeatedly and pestered him about it. He wanted the evidence sent to a private DNA lab for testing. Morin knew that the science was changing fast. DNA technology was in a dynamic state. Scientists around the world were experimenting with improved methods for identifying, extracting, and testing DNA from a variety of sources. Breakthroughs probably would be forthcoming. If his client would be patient, Morin believed, the techniques might improve. The risks of an unsuccessful test destroying any remaining DNA might diminish. Morin cautioned his client to wait, to be patient. But Kirk was done with waiting. He was the one rotting away in a cell. "My life's not worth living in here," he told his lawyer. "Guys get jammed here every week. Black Smoky last month—somebody tied his neck to an overhead steam pipe. Guards called it suicide. And he was decent. One of the few."

They sat in the visiting room of the penitentiary surrounded by inmates. A March snow fell outside the barred window. Next to them a couple kissed while a guard pretended to look away. In the corner, another inmate, watching the couple kissing, played with himself.

Kirk was quiet, but unyielding. "And it's more than that. Living with what they've done to me I'd rather go for broke. It's my call now. You told me that. And I want it tested."

Bob Morin, despite three years of effort, knew he had run out of options. Although he believed the attempt would prove futile, he agreed to revisit a DNA analysis for Kirk. Initially, he wasn't even sure where to begin. The road turned out to be as twisted as the bizarre facts surrounding Kirk Bloodsworth's convictions.

THREE

ACCORDING TO THE FBI, the physical evidence collected at the murder scene in 1984 had yielded no useful information. In an effort to look for a possible blood type back then, cotton swabs had been used to capture fluid specimens from the victim's vagina and rectum at autopsy. Residue from these swabs was then smeared on glass slides and stained with a preservative. While the state medical examiner, using a microscope, had noted some spermatozoa on the slides, the FBI had analyzed the cotton swabs and determined that no semen was present. The FBI also reported that no semen traces and no foreign blood had been found on the victim's clothing.

Morin had first to determine whether this crime scene evidence still existed, and if so, where it was stored. If he could locate the evidence, he'd have to then persuade both the prosecutors and the court to permit him access to the evidence to send it off for testing. He'd have to further research testing facilities—find the laboratory with the most advanced techniques in DNA analysis, one that would be willing to take on the challenge. If all this could be accomplished, and even in the unlikely event that traces of sperm were found, he didn't know whether DNA could be retrieved and analyzed from such traces, particularly after the passage of so much time.

When Bob Morin first agreed to represent Bloodsworth, he'd obtained a court order requiring the state to preserve all of the existing evidence. He learned that the cotton swabs were still available at the FBI. Through persistent calls and interviews, he discovered that the state medical examiner's office had kept the glass slides preserved in a freezer. By personally rummaging through the court clerk's office, Morin also found the victim's clothing, the murder weapon, and the other physical evidence taken from the crime scene in a cardboard box. This was a start.

Morin understood that most efforts to lift preserved specimens of DNA off glass slides still were unsuccessful. The stain used to preserve the specimens on slides back in 1984, before genetic fingerprinting was even heard of, tended to degrade the DNA, and the most widely used technique for analyzing DNA—the one employed by Cellmark and most other labs—usually consumed the sample, leaving nothing left to test. Morin discovered, though, that a laboratory in Richmond, California, was employing an advanced technology that was capable of extracting and analyzing DNA from a very small amount of biological material. Forensic Science Associates was run by Dr. Edward T. Blake, a leading scientist in the developing field of forensic use of DNA for criminal identification purposes. Blake's lab, employing this new technique for amplifying DNA, known as PCR—polymerase chain reaction—was capable, under some circumstances, of identifying and reproducing tiny amounts of genetic material so that it then could be successfully analyzed. Given the FBI's findings, and believing that the slides and swabs were probably of no help, Morin asked if Blake's lab could examine and test *all* of the crime scene evidence, including the girl's clothing, the scrapings underneath her fingernails, the murder weapon as well. If he was going to take a last shot, he figured he'd at least put everything in the hopper. If any semen could be found or blood that was not the victim's, and DNA retrieved, it could be compared with a DNA sample from Kirk Bloodsworth. Dr. Blake's lab was willing to test it all, provided it got paid. The cost, the lab estimated, could run between $10,000 and $12,000.

Fortunately for Bloodsworth, his conviction and imprisonment had remained controversial. Questions occasionally still surfaced in the press about the quality of the evidence against him—that most of it was circumstantial, that no scientific proof tied him to the crime scene, and that the two key identification witnesses against him had been a seven-year-old and a ten-year-old. The prosecutors who tried and convicted him were cocksure that Bloodsworth was the murderer, but they were rankled by the lingering doubts. While skeptical that a DNA test would shed any light on the crime, they were certain that if it did, it would resolve any question about Bloodsworth's guilt. Consequently, they cut a deal with Morin. Provided Morin was willing to pay for the test, they'd agree to release the crime scene evidence to Morin to be sent to the laboratory. If any DNA could be retrieved and identified, it would be matched against Bloodsworth's. The results would then be made public, whatever they showed. The prosecutors told Morin that they looked forward to scientific confirmation that Bloodsworth was the murderer.

Morin talked it over with his partners, Gerry Fisher and David Kagan-Kans. The three were seated at a card table they sometimes used for conferences in their office. Morin told them that the test would probably yield no new information. The lab expense was steep, and there was little likelihood they'd be reimbursed. Still, he needed to be able to tell Kirk Bloodsworth that he had done everything in his power to help him.

"I'll just have to find another couple of fee cases," Gerry Fisher said, leaning back. "Beat the bushes a bit."

"Yeah," David Kagan-Kans said. "Me too."

In August 1992, after months of negotiations and wrangling over arrangements with the prosecutors, Morin obtained the evidence and sent it, along with a sample of Kirk's blood, to the California lab. Three months passed with no word. He was not surprised. He had no expectations.

The day before Thanksgiving, Morin received the strangest and most unexpected of phone calls. A lab technician working for Dr. Blake called late in the evening. She said they'd found a stain of semen on the girl's underpants. Morin was astonished. Back in 1984 the FBI lab had reported that there wasn't any identifiable semen on the panties.

"Are you sure?" he asked.

"I'm looking through the microscope at the little sperm heads right now," she answered.

She wanted to know if Morin wanted the semen found on the girl's panties lifted and tested. She cautioned him. Utilizing the PCR technology, a DNA test could only exclude about 90 percent of the population. Morin's client could be grouped in that other 10 percent, she advised. There was a significant risk that DNA from the sperm might be compatible with Kirk Bloodsworth's, even if he weren't the actual donor. And Morin remained concerned that the test might compromise the sample, that there might not be the opportunity to test the semen again. Did he want to take the risk?

Morin drove to Baltimore and met with Kirk on Thanksgiving Day. Kirk had just finished a plate of turkey and watered-down mashed potatoes. Morin told him the good news and the bad. He explained that if the DNA from the sperm stain was found to be consistent with Kirk's DNA, while not probative of anything, Kirk's effort to free himself would be over.

Kirk, when he heard they'd found a trace of semen on the girl's panties, started crying. It took him several minutes to compose himself. He listened carefully to Morin's cautionary warnings, nodding the entire time. "Test it," he said, as tears streamed down his large, flushed faced. "Test it. It's there for a reason. It's my ticket out of here. Test it . . ."

But by April 1993 the results were long overdue. It had been eight months since the lab had first received the evidence and five long months since the semen had been discovered. Kirk was scared and anxious. He called Morin almost daily. Morin tried to calm him, to reassure him. With each passing week, though, Morin had grown more worried himself. What test could possibly take so long to complete? Had the semen stain even yielded a testable DNA sample? Would the results ever come? And what might they show?

It was the telephone number of Dr. Edward Blake that Morin dialed late on the afternoon of April 27, 1993. He'd run out of excuses to give Kirk, run out of his own wick of patience. The phone rang just once. Morin was taken aback when Dr. Blake answered it personally. Morin introduced himself. He asked about the Kirk Bloodsworth test results.

"Bloodsworth?" he heard Dr. Blake say. "Bloodsworth? Yes, Bloodsworth . . . Yes, yes, I have him right here." Morin could hear Blake rustling through papers on the other end of the line. The DNA scientist seemed to take forever. Morin closed his eyes, held his breath, and waited.

FOUR

AT ALMOST THE SAME MOMENT, about fifty miles away, Kirk Bloodsworth entered a room in the Maryland Penitentiary designated as the prison library. He'd been lifting weights with Stanley Norris, known as Bozo because he had hair like the clown's, and Big Tony, who had once been a Hell's Angel and could bench press 500 pounds. Kirk, himself, had pressed 380 that day. He was burly, overweight from the prison food, wore a bandanna around his head and his dark sunglasses. His faded purple T-shirt was damp with sweat from his workout. On his way to the library, he'd been listening to his Walkman radio through the earphones. The disc jockey had been playing hard rock and heavy metal hits from the past. Kirk had listened to one of his favorites, Guns N' Roses playing "Welcome to the Jungle." Music that touched on his world, that sought to reflect or capture his mean existence, had become an important source of both solace and escape in the prison. A few years before, when inmates had rioted and taken over Dormitory C, near where his cell was located, and he'd heard the incessant screams of an inmate who was beaten and raped sixteen successive times, he'd played a Guns N' Roses tape over and over to drown out the terrible sound.

The DJ that afternoon followed up with a song by Ozzy Osbourne, known as the grandfather of heavy metal. The song was called "Mama, I'm Coming Home." Hearing it, Kirk had stopped in his tracks and leaned against the tier wall. Kirk considered himself a religious man, but in a waterman's way—drinking, smoking pot, womanizing—these were just part of his life as a Chesapeake Bay crabber. Along with his faith in God, he also believed in portents, dreams, and mysticism. He'd been born on Halloween and was convinced that spirits inhabited an invisible world connected to this one. In prison he'd converted from Protestant to Catholic. He liked the ritual, the symbolism, the mystical side of the Catholic Church. Hearing Ozzy Osbourne that afternoon sing "Mama, I'm Coming Home" gave him a jolt. He had always liked and admired Osbourne's music. He'd only heard this song a few times, but its refrain was the wish and hope of his life. Kirk felt it might be a sign. Hearing the song made him both hopeful and afraid.

Once in the library, Kirk sat at a steel table in the center of a small windowless room around which a couple of hundred books were stacked on institutional shelving crumbling with rust. The books were all secondhand, old law books mostly, some dime store mysteries, some true crime accounts; a few were hardbacks with their covers still intact but most looked ragged and dog-eared. Kirk had spent thousands of hours in this room. He believed that he had read nearly every book on the shelves. For a waterman's son, he thought to himself humorlessly, he'd become damn well read.

He had entered the library to begin drafting yet another of the hundreds of letters he still wrote and sent out regularly protesting his innocence in the crime of raping and murdering Dawn Venice Hamilton. He signed each and every one "Kirk Bloodsworth— A.I.M.—An Innocent Man." He set a sheet of paper on the table and started writing a letter, this one to Lou Ferrigno, the Incredible Hulk. Kirk tried to write to everyone he admired. He began each letter with a description of who he was and where he'd come from. Halfway through this letter he stopped and set the pen down. Writing about his past made him think of his mother, Jeanette. Kirk had lost her to a massive heart attack three months earlier, the day of President Clinton's first inauguration. Kirk had been taken—in handcuffs, a waist chain, and leg irons—to view her body for five minutes alone in a closed room, though he had been refused permission to attend her funeral. He'd convinced himself that she'd died of a broken heart over what had happened to her son, over what he'd gotten himself into. He thought of her as his angel and knew if spirits ever helped people, she would help him. Since her death, he'd thought of her constantly, missing her with a physical ache. He could see her there, in their home in the small town of Cambridge, Maryland, where he grew up. He shut his eyes to picture her more clearly. And then without meaning to, he drifted off.

Kirk would remember later that he dreamed that day of himself as a boy, free on the marsh, running his skiff on a silver river, a dream that was both momentarily peaceful yet troubling. In the dream he was at first small, just five or so, wearing the snowsuit his mother had sewn for him and helping his father tong for oysters on the broad Choptank River. The near shore was pocked with ice and foam, the gray green waves chased by the wind, and his father smiling as the boy culled the oysters, his father strong and the white workboat safe and sturdy. Then he was maybe ten and was in cut-off waders, sloughing through the gum thickets off Blackwater Marsh, setting his muskrat traps in the predawn quiet, the air expectant, the horizon glowing lilac in the flat oval of his water-bound world, the waves lapping the marsh grass, the first sound of the birds. And then he was nearly full size, the year he first started crabbing. He saw his silhouette in the mist, rowing a boat on water that was flat and smoky. His mother was there standing on a dock. She waved to him, then beckoned. His dream was interrupted by a tug on his arm. A prison guard, Sergeant Cooley Hall, stood over him.

Sergeant Hall, a dark Trinidadian with a wide grin and a penchant for whistling, had always been friendly to Kirk. Hall had a message for him written on a piece of scrap paper. He waited for Kirk to wake fully and adjust himself and then he handed it to him. It was from Kirk's lawyer, and it was marked urgent. Kirk focused more closely. He read the word *urgent* again and read that Bob Morin wanted him to call immediately. Kirk's eyes opened wide and he sat up straight. He looked at Hall, then back at the message. Then he placed a hand over his face to hide his emotion, to keep himself from shaking.

Kirk Bloodsworth was thirty-two years old and would ever after remember the date and the time he got that message. The offspring of generations of Chesapeake Bay waterman, he'd grown up crabbing and fishing the rivers and creeks on the Eastern Shore of Maryland, and trapping the Dorchester marshes, as befit the descendant of an independent, free, and proud breed. His ancestors had emigrated to Maryland from Great Britain and Ireland in the 1600s and an island in the Chesapeake Bay just below Cambridge, Maryland—Bloodsworth Island—had been named for his forbearers. A high school graduate, he'd been a marine and a champion discus thrower. But for the past nine years he had lived a nightmare that he could not understand, account for, or articulate.

For nine years of his life he'd been locked up in prison, most of it in the hellhole known as the South Wing of the Maryland Penitentiary—nine years of eating inedible food, shivering in a dim cold cell in the winter or sweltering in what became an unventilated sweatbox in the summer; nine years of being cursed as a child rapist and killer, of being threatened daily by other inmates, of having to lift weights with the Pagans and the Hell's Angels in order to stay fit and able to fight for survival in the shower, of having to fend off shanks and clubs made of batteries crammed into socks, of hearing at night toothbrushes being sharpened into knives on the prison floor; worst of all, nine years of being despised by the outside world, of being mistrusted by his family, of being embarrassed about what he'd become and the way he had to live. Nine years of this before the afternoon Sergeant Hall tapped him on the shoulder and gave him the message.

The first time Kirk had met Sergeant Cooley Hall, back in 1985, he'd told him that he was being held hostage, that Hall was holding an innocent man. When Hall heard this he laughed aloud. He had a deep bass laugh that he seemed to exhale like a shout. He was one of the few people who Kirk ever heard laugh inside the prison. "Everyone in the pen is innocent, mon, don't you know?" Hall had told him. "You just one more innocent lamb, Mister Bloodmon. One more innocent lamb . . ." And he had continued to laugh as he walked away. But Kirk had reminded Hall nearly every day of the fact that he was innocent and that he was being held hostage. "You know you got an innocent man, here?" Kirk would say when Hall would walk with him to the commissary. "You holding an innocent man hostage, now. I just want you to know it." Sometimes Hall, in that accent of his, would say quickly, "No, no, no! I don't hold you nowhere! Da' government got you, not me." Kirk had repeated his claim of innocence, though, so often and so regularly through the years, that Hall had stopped laughing about it and stopped denying it. And then Kirk had stopped repeating it. It had become an un-spoken token between them. Hall was just one of many in the prison who thought Kirk might be speaking the truth.

While Hall had been standing there, the blood had drained from Kirk's face as he'd reread the piece of scrap paper, then stared at it as if mesmerized. Kirk's hand trembled as he asked Hall if he could use the phone. Hall smiled. His grin was gleaming white against his dark face. "Sure, mon," he said. "Maybe your crab boat done finally come in this time, Mister Bloodmon."

Kirk could hardly see as he walked down the tier. The world seemed to squeeze itself into one small circle of gray, the place he had to step next. He rounded the corner, got to the phone, dialed the operator, and asked to make a collect call. He had the number memorized. He'd called it enough. The telephone rang and rang and finally Bob Morin's secretary answered. When Bob Morin got on the phone Kirk asked him for the test results.

"How are you, Kirk?" Bob asked first.

"For christsakes, Bob, tell me the goddamn news."

Morin paused.

"Please, Bob. What did the test say? It is back, ain't it?"

"It came back, Kirk, yes."

"Well, what did it say?" Kirk braced himself. His life had become one terrible disappointment after another.

"The sperm stain on Dawn's underpants, though small, was good enough to use. The new test worked, Kirk." Morin couldn't hide his own emotion. His voice was cracking. "They found the DNA, Kirk. The DNA said it couldn't have been you. You're excluded. The man who raped and killed that little girl could not have been you." Morin felt the tears well up in his own eyes. "The DNA said it's not you," he repeated.

Time passed. Several seconds of silence. "Well, I told you so, didn't I!" Kirk finally shouted into the phone. He felt a rush of blood. "Goddamn it, of course it ain't me! Didn't I tell you? Ain't I been telling you?" Kirk felt a flood sweep through his head. "Didn't I tell you? Over and over? But no one believed me? Didn't I . . ." Kirk stopped speaking because he realized that his hand shook so hard he could barely hold the phone. He felt lost suddenly and began to cry. He tried to control himself. Down the tier an inmate had stopped his mopping and was watching. Kirk had learned never to show weakness in front of other inmates in the prison. He tried to hold the phone still and steady to his ear and speak again. "Didn't I tell you?" And then he couldn't anymore. He just broke up, let the phone drop, and began to weep both with shame and without shame, covering his face to hide himself at first and then just letting himself be seen. Down the row of cages, three or four more inmates were peering out their cell doors watching him. Kirk no longer cared. The phone dangled on its aluminum cord. He stood then and whispered, "It's over, it's over . . ." Then he repeated it louder to no one in particular: "It's finally over, ain't it?" Then he raised up on tiptoes, threw his hands high in the air mimicking a touchdown, and started screaming it: "Sweet Jesus, it's over! It's goddamn over, Bob!" He leaned down and yelled it into the dangling phone. "It's over, Bob! This is fucking great! It's finally over, man!" He raised up on tiptoe again, his arms stretched high. Tears streamed down his face. He started hopping in place, then started running down the tier, his arms still up, turning one way and then another, jumping, crying and screaming. "It's over! It's over!" He kept hollering it. "The DNA says it ain't me! It ain't me! The DNA says it ain't me. It's over . . ."

Bob Morin could hear all this through the phone. As he listened, he shivered with emotion. What would happen next to Kirk, how long would it take to actually free him, would the real killer ever be caught? He bowed his head thinking about how such an injustice could occur.

Sergeant Cooley Hall was not surprised. He just leaned back against the tier wall shaking his head and whistling over this strange inmate, his friend, this Mister Bloodmon, in whom he'd come to believe.

PART II

A CRIME
IN FONTANA
VILLAGE

May the bad not kill the good
  Nor the good kill the bad
I am a poet, without any bias,
  I say without doubt or
    hesitation
There are no good assassins.
—Pablo Neruda

FIVE

THE MARYLAND PENITENTIARY, the oldest continually operating prison in the Western world, sits like a medieval castle high on a promontory at the intersection of Madison and Forrest Streets in the city of Baltimore. Its grimy walls have incarcerated generations of convicts including "Negro Bob" Butler, who was reputedly the first to enter the institution upon its completion in 1811, as well as the celebrated "Tunnel Joe" Holmes, who chiseled through slate, concrete, and seventy feet of earth and clay to escape. For two centuries it has housed the state's most violent and incorrigible criminals. Its walls enclose men who live by brute force, who seethe with anger, who are pitiless. Kirk Bloodsworth spent nearly a decade in the Maryland Penitentiary, much of it on death row.

This mausoleum was built at an elevated altitude, supposedly to benefit from the breezes off the water. Beneficent city officials believed that the disorders that seemed to habitually infect prisoners—smallpox and dysentery—might be alleviated by fresh air. Initially, there were few buildings nearby. No one had ever heard of a skyscraper. As its population of convicted criminals grew, as time passed, this prison witnessed the dramatic growth and transformation of a society.

The first settler of the city of Baltimore is reputed to be David Jones, who in 1661 surveyed about 380 acres of prime land along the eastern bank of Jones Falls and then built himself a house on what is now Front Street. Irish immigrants and German-speaking settlers from Pennsylvania had already begun farming the rich Susquehanna sediment covering the rolling hills of Baltimore County near where the city eventually sprang up. Easy access to a port was essential to the farmers looking to trade with England, Europe, and the West Indies. Baltimore's natural harbor, gouged deep by a glacial trowel, fit this need.

Throughout the eighteenth century, schooners laden with corn and tobacco sailed from Baltimore, down the wide Chesapeake into the Atlantic, and returned loaded with sugar, rum, and slaves to sell. In 1784 Baltimore City's first police force was formed. By 1790 the population of the city had grown to over thirteen thousand and had become a favored destination for immigrants sailing to America. Greeks, Italians, Jews, Lithuanians, Poles, Ukrainians, and others found their own neighborhoods and settled into city life or moved into outlying Baltimore County to farm or trade. In 1876 Johns Hopkins University opened its doors. And on August 16, 1893, Oriole pitcher Bill Hawke threw the first modern major league no-hitter defeating rival Washington 5 to 0.

Inevitably, as the new industrial century took shape, as Baltimore grew into a major international port, its population rapidly increased and swarms of new neighborhoods pushed the city's boundaries away from the water, westward, northward, and eastward. Passenger steamers, ferryboats, cargo ships, oyster dredgers, and sailing clippers filled the harbor. Trolley cars careened up the city streets and railroads expanded their networks of tracks. Roads and highways crisscrossed the landscape. Outlying towns were swallowed up and absorbed by the urban spread. Crowded city neighborhoods gradually blended into crowded suburbs. In 1957 the Baltimore Harbor Tunnel opened, burrowing beneath the Patapsco River and Baltimore Harbor. Heralded as a marvel of modern construction, it allowed automobiles to travel from Washington, D.C., and points south directly north toward Philadelphia and New York on Interstate 95, without having to navigate the narrow streets and bottleneck traffic in the city. Interstate 95 was followed by Interstate 695, the Baltimore Beltway, which encircles the city with high-speed lanes. These roadways have become the conduit for millions of travelers. They also provide easy access to the many localities along their edges, places previously somewhat insulated from the outside world.

One such area of Baltimore County, known as Essex, sits not far from the junction of these two major arteries, I-95 and I-695. Just a few miles east of the Baltimore City line, slightly north, and not far from the headwaters of Back River, this area contains a congestion of shopping centers, malls, roadways, small industrial buildings, and a host of working-class communities with names such as Rosedale, Rossville, Overlea, and Bluegrass Heights. Sandwiched between I-695 and Rossville Boulevard, and just north of Pulaski Highway and the Golden Ring Mall, sits a sprawling apartment complex of 356 units of squat, flat-roofed, two-story squares, all joined and running together in long, identical rectangular rows. These units border Bethke Pond and a low-lying wooded area, dense with thornbush and vine. The complex is known as Fontana Village. In the summer of 1984 Fontana Village received much unwanted notoriety as the scene of a terrible and brutal murder—a crime that spawned a statewide manhunt, led to one misstep after another by both the hunters and the man they accused, and rekindled a national debate over the propriety of the death penalty.

• • •

OUACHITA TECHNICAL COLLEGE

THE MONTHS OF July and August can be hot in Baltimore. Temperatures routinely run into the nineties and the humidity turns the air clammy, making it seem even hotter. These dog days, as they're referred to locally, send adults inside seeking air-conditioning or window fans, and kids searching for swimming pools, broken hydrants, or shaded parks. The southern flank of the city that sits on the Patapsco River benefits from the prevailing breeze skimming off the Chesapeake Bay. But the crowded neighborhoods spiraling around the city to the north feel little relief. Late afternoon thunderstorms sometimes cool the air sending swaths of steam rising from the burning, pervasive, asphalt, but the heat soon returns. At times it is unrelenting.

For the residents of Fontana Village the summer of 1984 was no different from most in regard to the weather. It had been hot and sticky. Folks living in and around that area were taking it easy. Some rose early, as the hours before and after the sun got high were the most bearable. Ladies sat outside on their adjoining front stoops and fanned themselves to feel a breeze. People put off their outdoor projects, waiting for a break in the temperature. Most families felt reasonably safe in Fontana Village. Children played around Bethke's Pond or on swings shaded by the stands of oaks, maples, and elms that bordered the woods dense with underbrush. Mostly occupied by low-income tenants, the apartments housed plenty of kids and young parents.

After dark on July 24 of that year, television screens could be seen flickering from some of the apartment windows in Fontana Village. News shows reported that Ronald Reagan and his running mate, George Bush, were likely to win a second term against Walter Mondale and Geraldine Ferraro; the summer Olympics were about to start in Los Angeles; movies like *Beverly Hills Cop* and *Police Academy* were popular in area theaters; a company called Apple had recently introduced a home desktop computer called the Macintosh; and there was to be a break in the weather: the next day, Wednesday, July 25, 1984, was to be cooler and less humid, with temperatures in the low to mid-eighties, a day to enjoy the outdoors.

It was around 11 A.M. that Wednesday morning that Dawn Venice Hamilton, a pretty nine-year-old child with sandy bangs and a page-boy haircut, left the apartment in which she was staying to find some friends outside. She stopped by Bethke's Pond and saw two boys she knew, Christian Shipley and Jackie Poling, fishing for bluegill, and noticed that one had caught a turtle. While she examined the small creature, a man approached and asked her what she was doing. She told him she was looking for her friend Lisa. By one account the man told her that he was playing hide-and-seek with Lisa and asked her if she wanted to play. By another account he simply offered to help her search. She was last seen alive walking into the nearby woods with this strange man. The border of the woods was in shadow. As Christian Shipley and Jackie Poling watched, the figures of the man and little girl traversed a culvert, crossed into this line of shadow, and quickly disappeared.

When Dawn failed to return home a short while later, Elinor Helmick, who was watching over her, went searching. When her search proved unsuccessful, she called the police. Within ninety minutes, over one hundred Baltimore County police officers and cadets were canvassing the area where Dawn had last been seen. It was around two thirty that afternoon when Dawn's body was spotted in the woods. She was lying on her stomach, naked from the waist down, her head bloody, her skull crushed. She had been terribly brutalized, sexually assaulted, and murdered. The residents of Fontana Village and its environs were horrified. The police, who suddenly seemed to be everywhere, vowed to find the fiend who could perpetrate such an unthinkable atrocity on a child.

• • •

TONI HAMILTON, DAWN's mother, worked as a dancer in a club on North Point Boulevard, something she'd done for a while, a way to make a living. Thomas Hamilton, Dawn's father, had worked many different jobs, mostly as an electrician. Toni was just seventeen at the time of Dawn's birth. Neither parent had wanted to stay married, and neither felt they could handle raising a child. As a result, when she was just an infant, Dawn Hamilton was given away by her parents to a friend and neighbor, a gentle forty-one-year-old woman of Philippine descent named Casimira Escudero Sponaugle, who went by the nickname Mercy. Mercy raised Dawn in a frame house on Hilltop Avenue in Rosedale, a neighborhood about three miles from Fontana Village. She obtained legal custody of Dawn through social services and later tried to adopt her. Mercy had lost her own teenage daughter to a car accident in 1982, and Dawn had become her baby girl. But Thomas Hamilton, who was intent on maintaining a close relationship with his daughter, objected to the adoption, so it never occurred.

That July Mercy had arranged for Dawn to attend a Catholic summer camp near Annapolis where the kids could swim in the river and learn to canoe and sail. The camp was supposed to have begun on July 16. In June, though, once the school year had ended, Thomas had taken Dawn to visit her grandparents in Pennsylvania. Mercy thought Thomas knew about the camp schedule and that he had dropped Dawn off at camp. Mercy thought Dawn was at camp on July 25. Thomas claimed he had never been told about the camp. He was staying with friends at their apartment in Fontana Village for the summer and had Dawn there living with him. Unbeknown to Mercy Sponaugle, Dawn was staying that week with her father; his friends, Gary and Elinor Helmick; their two children, Lisa and Gary; and some cousins at the Helmick's apartment at 8749 Fontana Lane.

Had she known this, Mercy Sponaugle probably would not have

worried. Dawn had a good relationship with her father and enjoyed being with him. And Mercy thought of Dawn as quite self-sufficient. Dawn was, after all, a leader of her fourth-grade class at Rosedale Elementary School. Mercy called her the "big Mama." She described her as a confident and cheerful girl, and as a trusting child, unafraid of strangers. Dawn was about four feet nine inches tall and weighed ninety-nine pounds. After her body was found, police interviewed Mercy Sponaugle at her home in Rosedale. Sponaugle was distraught. "She was the same as my child," she cried. "Her books are in my house, her beautiful artwork is here. What did they do with my baby? Why wasn't she in camp? First my daughter, and now Dawn. What am I going to do?"

SIX

ON THE MORNING OF July 25, 1984, at a little after six o'clock, Thomas Hamilton kissed his daughter, who was sleeping on the couch, and left Fontana Village for work in White Marsh, an industrial area about five miles to the north. The morning was cool, and the day promised to be clear and fine. He drove with his window rolled down and listened absently to the radio during the trip. It was around noon that he got a call from Elinor Helmick telling him that Dawn was missing. His first concern was that maybe she'd fallen into the pond. He left work and rushed straight back to Fontana Village.

Elinor Helmick had a houseful of children that morning. In addition to her own kids, Lisa (age four) and Gary (age six), and Dawn Hamilton, she was looking after her sister's two kids, Missy and John-John. She'd spent the morning in typical fashion, making breakfast for the children and doing household chores while the kids watched the *Facts of Life* on television. At ten thirty, when the program ended, Elinor shooed the children outside to the back field where just through the trees there was a playground. Dawn Hamilton was wearing a pair of blue shorts, a peach-colored pullover shirt, and sneakers; she was carrying the gray shoulder bag that she took with her everywhere. A little while later, Dawn and Missy, Elinor's niece, returned to the back door and called for Elinor. Elinor came halfway down the steps from the upstairs and was told by them that little Lisa and John-John were in the woods. Elinor told Dawn and Missy to go to the fence and call the two children to come back to the house. The kids weren't supposed to be in the woods. Elinor didn't want them near the pond. Dawn and Missy left, and Elinor went back upstairs for a cigarette. A few minutes later she saw out the window Missy, little Lisa, and John-John all walking up the path to the house. Looking past them she saw a bunch of kids on the playground. Elinor came downstairs and began to scold the children for going into the woods when Missy told her that Dawn had gone into the woods and not come out.

Elinor went out back to the fence and called for Dawn. When she got no answer, she walked down the trail, past the playground, and into the woods, calling her name. She reached the pond and saw Christian Shipley and Jackie Poling fishing. She questioned them and they told her they'd seen Dawn go into the woods with a man they described as white, around thirty, with blond hair and a blond mustache. Elinor, more worried now, walked farther into the woods and up a hill, calling for Dawn but heard no response. She walked back to her apartment, called the police, and reported Dawn missing. Elinor also called Thomas at work and told him what was going on. She then got in her car and drove up to the farm store where the kids often went to buy candy or gum. Dawn hadn't been there. She drove up Rossville Boulevard, circling the woods near where the trail runs out. In an isolated spot, back where the road dead-ends, a car had pulled over and parked. A man got out of the car, and Elinor asked him if he'd seen Dawn. She described her to him. When he said no, she drove back to her apartment where she met the three policemen who had arrived. She told them what she'd done and seen. The man she'd met on the dead-end road was wearing camouflage pants and had long dark hair, she reported. Later she learned that his name was Richard Gray.

Thomas Hamilton had just started his lunch break at the Coastal Modular Corporation when he got the call from Elinor Helmick. He told his supervisor that he had to leave and drove quickly back to Fontana Village where police had set up a command post just outside the Helmick's apartment. He waited around for a few minutes, asking questions, but the officers seemed to be avoiding him. He then decided to look for Dawn himself. He ran down the field past the pond and walked into the woods where he began searching, calling her name. He walked through some brush to an isolated area near a creek, when he heard a whistle. A man wearing camouflage pants and carrying a nightstick stood across the stream. Hamilton recognized him as the *News American* delivery man. The man told Hamilton that he was helping in the search and that he had found something. Hamilton later learned that this man was Richard Gray. Gray led him farther into the woods and away from the path. He then pointed about twelve feet up a tree where there were some clothes hanging on a branch. Hamilton immediately recognized them as Dawn's blue shorts and underpants. His fear turned to dread. He climbed up the tree, retrieved the clothes, and hurried back to where the police were stationed.

THE FIRST POLICE to arrive at Fontana Village were Officer Paul Merkle, Corporal Barry Barber, and Officer Kevin Keene of the Baltimore County Police Department. Elinor Helmick's call had been received at 11:49 A.M., and they arrived at Fontana Village just twelve minutes later. After interviewing Elinor, they conducted their own search of the area. At Bethke's Pond, Chris Shipley and Jackie Poling repeated the information they had given to Elinor Helmick, that Dawn had gone off with a tall, thin stranger with blond curly hair. The boys, curious now, and impressed by these uniformed policemen, followed the officers into the woods.

When their initial sweep of the area proved unsuccessful, Officer Merkle became worried. He notified his district sergeant, William O'Connor, and told him the situation was bad, that he suspected foul play. District Lieutenant Paul Lowe then drove to the scene arriving at about 12:40 P.M., and commenced operations for a full-scale search. The department went all out. Four different K-9 units, uniformed officers, homicide detectives, youth services detectives, and nearly forty-five cadets from the sixty-sixth police academy class arrived and were dispatched to conduct a field search. A police helicopter scanned the scene from the air. Reporters from local media, hearing about the lost girl over police scanner airwaves, began showing up. An official police department spokesman, Jay Miller, arrived in Car No. 8 just before 2 P.M. Both the district captain and district major were on the scene by 2:30.

At around 1:50 P.M., while assisting in the assembly and coordination of such manpower, Officer Merkle saw Thomas Hamilton coming toward him, ashen-faced, and holding out some clothes — a pair of blue shorts and a pair of white cotton underpants. Hamilton told Merkle that they belonged to his daughter. He choked back sobs as he tried to describe where and how he found them. Everyone around stopped what they were doing. They all knew what this meant. Merkle placed the items in an evidence bag and then huddled with other officers discussing how to proceed.

Detective Mark Bacon, experienced in child molestation cases, had arrived at the command center about twenty minutes earlier and had been assisting in organizing the search. He questioned Hamilton, then took him along with several other Youth Services detectives to his police car and drove them to the wooded area near where Hamilton had retrieved his daughter's clothes. There they encountered Richard Gray who led them to the tree limb where he'd found the shorts and underpants. Bacon thought it all seemed too awful, too bizarre. He radioed in their position so that the search could be coordinated to concentrate on the immediate area. Detectives Bacon and Joseph Leitzer then walked down a path about two hundred feet searching for Dawn. Within a few minutes Bacon saw her, lying facedown, about twenty-five feet to the right of the path and maybe eighty paces from the tree on which her clothes had been found.

Bacon first checked for a pulse, but there was none. Dawn's body was still warm to the touch, and had normal skin color. Bacon sat back on his knees, reeling from the sight. The blood over her face had not coagulated. A terry-cloth top covered her torso, and a purse was still slung across her shoulder. Her head was a bloody mess. Except for white socks and blue tennis shoes, she was naked below the waist. A stick protruded about six inches from her vagina. Blood had pooled there. A rock lay a few feet from her head. A Big Red gum wrapper was crumpled on the ground alongside her. A swarm of flies buzzed around the corpse. Bacon radioed for crime scene technicians and homicide detectives to assist. Crime lab detectives Carroll Sturgeon and James Roeder were there within minutes. Homicide Detective William Ramsey arrived shortly thereafter, followed by his partner, Detective Robert Capel.

William Ramsey was a homicide vet. He could read a crime scene. Sturgeon and Roeder were experts too. They could pick it clean. They were all experienced professionals. Each thought they'd known the worst. Still, this little girl's body, broken and destroyed, mutilated, covered with flies, was a hard thing to see.

Together, they went about their job. They surveyed and processed the area. About twenty feet away from the body, waist-high weeds were bent down, indicating a possible path angling in a southerly direction back toward the dirt road. Photographs of the body and surrounding area were taken and sketches of the scene made. A footprint in a mound of dirt was observed and photographed. Detective Sturgeon tried to lift latent fingerprints from the victim's body using magna brush powder, but was unsuccessful. Later, because Chris Shipley thought the stranger might have touched his tackle box, Sturgeon dusted it for prints, again without success. The Big Red gum wrapper, with possible blood on its underside, was removed to a plastic bag; dirt and blood samples from around the body were taken; a navy blue belt loop, a red fiber from near the body, and a strand of human hair found nearby were all carefully stored. A piece of concrete found near the victim's head, with a possible spot of blood on it, was also bagged. Detective Ramsey assumed this was the murder weapon. He cautioned everyone on the scene that this one piece of information was to remain confidential. It was not to be revealed to the public or press. Ramsey noted a strange mark or bruise on Dawn's neck, like the imprint of a shoe's sole with a herringbone pattern. One was on her back as well. Close-up photographs recorded these markings. Dr. Paul Guerin arrived, and officially pronounced Dawn dead at 5:03 P.M. When the crime scene analysis was complete, her body was wrapped in a sheet and taken to the morgue. During the autopsy, as reported by the medical examiner in the autopsy report, semen was found in both her vaginal and anal cavities. She had died, the medical examiner determined, from both strangulation and traumatic brain injury.

While the area around Dawn's body was being picked over by investigators, Detective Capel radioed Detective Howard Hessie, who had been instructed to stay close to the two key eyewitnesses, the boys Shipley and Poling, and asked Hessie to escort them down to Youth Services where he would meet them. Capel figured that the people who had the best opportunity to view the probable killer were these two boys, Chris Shipley and Jackie Poling. Though Chris was only ten at the time, and Jackie just seven, Capel felt that they might be best able to provide the clues needed to find the murderer, and he wanted to interview them while their memories were fresh and untainted by suggestion. He remained at the crime scene for only about twenty minutes before he left to meet them.

PART III

A COMPOSITE, A PROFILE, A GAMBIT

A little neglect may breed mischief: for want of a nail the shoe was lost; for want of a shoe the horse was lost; and for want of a horse the rider was lost.

—BENJAMIN FRANKLIN

SEVEN

THERE ARE COPS AND then there are murder cops. Homicide investigators. The crème de la crème. The ones who've made it to the top.

They have to work their way up. First they're on patrol, walking a beat, cruising through neighborhoods, ticketing speeders, handling shoplifters, drunks, domestic fights. The good ones make detective: vice, fraud, robbery. Only the very best, the ones who prove their mettle, are promoted to homicide. Robbery, burglary, rape — they're ugly enough. But murder beats all.

Detectives Ramsey and Capel were not newcomers to death. They'd both pretty much seen the whole underbelly of Baltimore County. Bad and really bad. But this crime was in a category of its own. Dawn Hamilton was just a kid and the way she was abused and killed made them certain they had one sick and dangerous perpetrator on the loose out there.

Ramsey and Capel had been given control of the case as the lead detectives, the ones put in charge. It was their job to run the investigation, supervise the others, make the important decisions, solve the crime. Their peers were watching. The world was watching. The community was afraid. The community *needed* an arrest.

A nineteen-year veteran of the police department, with nine years of experience as a homicide detective, Robert Capel in 1984 was a tall, bearlike man, with salt-and-pepper hair and an inquisitive but courteous manner. He and Ramsey worked well as a team. It's a cliché, the Mutt and Jeff routine, but Capel came across as easygoing and naturally friendly. Ramsey could employ a cold, tough demeanor. People tended to trust and open up to Capel, if only to avoid Ramsey's rough questions and icy stare. Capel was probably the best suited of the two to deal with children.

Ten years earlier, Capel had attended a three-day seminar on the art of working with witnesses to create composite drawings of suspects, and since that time he had prepared around two hundred such sketches, most during his tour as a robbery squad detective. Since Chris Shipley was the older of the two boys and seemed to be more certain of what he'd seen, Capel decided to work with him first in an effort to arrive at a likeness of Dawn's probable killer. He took Chris into a room alone and gently asked him some questions about his age, school, family life, even fishing, trying to put the boy at ease.

Capel learned that Chris had been in the fifth grade at Park Elementary School, that he liked to watch cartoons in the summer such as *He-Man* and shows with motorcycles such as *Knight Rider*. Chris particularly enjoyed fishing and spent hours at the pond. He had his own pole and also used a hand string and had sometimes caught smallmouth bass in the pond as well as the bluegill that were always taking the worms he used as bait.

When Capel felt Chris was comfortable, he asked him to remember carefully the man he'd seen at the pond and to provide the most accurate description he could. Chris reiterated that the person was a white male, six feet five inches tall, slim to medium build, dirty blond, very curly hair with a light brown mustache, tanned skin, and spoke with no accent. He said he was wearing an Ocean Pacific short-sleeved T-shirt with three stripes around the upper chest: orange, red, and purple. He wore light tan shorts, calf-length socks, and tennis shoes. Chris mentioned that he had an uncle who was six foot five and that the man by the pond was the same height as his uncle. When Capel opened the door and motioned for another detective who was six foot three to come inside, Chris said the man at the pond might have been a little bit shorter than the detective. Even upon hearing that the detective was six foot three, though, Chris insisted that the man he'd seen with Dawn was six foot five. This experiment, along with the other available evidence, convinced Capel that the assailant was closer to six feet tall than six foot five. Chris Shipley said nothing about seeing orange or reddish hair. He also said nothing about the man being muscular or about seeing sideburns.

Capel then brought out a book of drawings of black and white facial parts to show Chris, explaining that by using the drawings, they would try to create a likeness of the man who went into the woods with Dawn. He told Chris, in order to further relax him, that the composite wouldn't be used to identify anyone but only to eliminate potential suspects. Capel had been taught to create composites by using a series of facial parts previously drawn on clear foils by Walt Disney Studios. Each transparency contained representations of different facial characteristics: facial outlines, noses, eyes, hair, chins, lips, cheeks, and facial hair. The foils could be placed on top of one another to form a complete face.

Capel began by showing different facial outlines to Chris. Was the face round, oval, angular, fat? There were a set number to choose from. Eventually, Chris selected the one he thought most closely resembled the facial outline of the man he had seen with Dawn. Capel then showed him various hairstyles. Chris picked a hairstyle but was never completely comfortable with it. He thought the man's hair was more unruly and lighter than the drawing reflected. He chose a chin line that seemed right but again could not find a pair of eyes that he thought was accurate. He settled for a pair that seemed closest to what he remembered, but he told the detective that the man's eyes were different, weird. Chris also pointed to a mustache but told Capel it was too thin and asked him if it could be thickened up. Capel said no. The thicker mustaches on the foils looked liked Fu Man Chu mustaches and weren't right, and Capel didn't want to bring in a freelancer. He hadn't gotten good results from using freelance artists in the past and was skeptical of their value. Also, the office wanted to get the composite out to the public quickly, and there wasn't time to bring in a police sketch artist. When the composite was completed, Chris was not altogether satisfied with it. In retrospect, why would he have been? He had been dissatisfied with the hair, the eyes, and the mustache. Capel asked him what could be done to make it more resemble the suspect, but Chris couldn't say. Chris Shipley, ten years old, finally agreed that it was a decent resemblance of the man he'd seen.

Then Capel brought in Jackie Poling. Jackie gave a slightly different description. He remembered the man at the pond as looking twenty to thirty years of age, about six feet tall, skinny, with light brown curly hair, and wearing tan shorts and a tan T-shirt. Again, no mention of reddish hair or sideburns. Capel considered making another composite with him and started the process, but Jackie seemed so unsure of the different features that Capel gave up. Instead, Capel showed the composite Chris had helped create to Jackie. When seven-year-old Jackie seemed satisfied with the likeness, Capel concluded it was reliable.

Later, Detective Mark Bacon, who had first discovered Dawn's body, would criticize this protocol. He had received the same training in working with witnesses to create composite sketches that

Capel had; they'd attended the same program at the same time. "Showing a composite made by one witness to another is totally against all principles taught in identity school," he said. "You never put two witnesses together at the same time. You do one composite with witness *one,* and you do another composite with witness *two,* and you hope that the two composites look alike."

That evening, Capel tried to develop another composite likeness, this time with an adult eyewitness, Fay McCoullough. McCoullough had lived on Fontana Lane for ten years and had worked for the Social Security Administration for sixteen years. She'd reported seeing a strange man standing by the woods that morning as she drove out of the complex on her way to work. She'd slowed down as she passed him and gotten a good look at the man. She remembered him as being five foot seven to five foot eight, slim, with curly blond hair, and wearing khaki shorts, a sleeveless pullover shirt, and tennis shoes. No mention of a strawberry tint to the hair. No mention of sideburns. Capel worked with her for two hours trying to arrive at a satisfactory composite. But neither was happy with the result. Fay kept shaking her head that the sketch just wasn't right. The eyes were wrong, she insisted. Finally, Capel gave up. He threw the composite in her trash can, concluding that she just wasn't a reliable witness. After he left her house, she retrieved it.

After Capel finished with McCoullough, the detectives decided to run with the composite put together by Chris Shipley. It was too late to make the newspapers and television news shows the next day, so they arranged to have the composite drawing disseminated to all media outlets for broadcast on Friday.

EIGHT

The murder of Dawn Hamilton created front-page headlines in all the local papers, including the *Sun,* the *Evening Sun,* the *News American,* and the *Times* of Baltimore County. Television news channels covered the crime in detail, and for several days Dawn's picture appeared everywhere. Thomas Hamilton, Toni Hamilton, Mercy Sponaugle, the Helmicks, and their neighbors in the apartment complex were all sought out by reporters. During one interview, Thomas Hamilton held in his hand a Ziggy cartoon Dawn had drawn for him. She had scribbled *I love you for all the world* in the corner. Hamilton leaned against the apartment wall heaving sobs. The words "pain . . . sorrow . . . hate . . ." came through. He covered his face with his free hand. He waved the cartoon at the sky. "If he wants to pick on a little child," he cried, "let him pick on me . . ."

The funeral was held July 28. Sympathy and support poured in from the community. Afterward Thomas Hamilton wrote that Dawn's death was the most horrifying thing that a person could live through. He went into a deep depression, developed a drinking problem, and tried to find new friends. Hamilton found it difficult to be around anyone who knew what had happened.

Dawn's mother, Toni, spoke to reporters outside her flat in Baltimore City. Fighting back tears, she cursed her daughter's killer, saying he should be tortured and slowly killed. "She couldn't even fight back," she cried. "I just hope she didn't feel any pain . . ."

Parents in communities all around Fontana Village huddled with their children indoors in fear. The Baltimore County Police Department promised to spare no resource in tracking down the monstrous person responsible. Five two-man teams of homicide detectives and numerous teams of police officers from the Fullerton precinct were assigned to assist in investigating the murder, and the FBI would lend its expertise both in forensic testing and psychological profiling. Officers going door to door interviewed every resident of Fontana Village. Neighbors from adjacent communities; merchants from nearby Golden Ring Mall; employees from the local 7-Eleven, the Dunkin' Donuts, and other eateries on Rossville Boulevard; representatives of Essex Community College; and the manager of the Trailways bus station all were questioned. Even before the composite sketch was broadcast on Friday, the leads were substantial in number. Once the picture of the killer was shown on television and in the newspapers, calls flooded in. A hotline was set up for tips, and Metro Crime Stoppers offered a $1,000 reward for information leading to the arrest and indictment of the murderer. By Monday, July 30, the police department had received over two hundred telephone reports. Over the following week, the number would more than double.

Neighbors gave varying accounts of seeing strangers in the area with descriptions running from short to tall, stocky to thin, men on foot, men in cars, men wearing long pants, men in shorts. Some tips coming from different sources seemed to point to the same suspect; sometimes the reports seemed random, isolated, unhelpful.

On the day of the murder Officer Lionel Weeks interviewed William Adams of Fontana Village, who reported that a man named Bob, six feet tall, with blond curly hair, wearing a black cowboy hat and western clothing, and possibly driving a cream-colored Chevy van, had two weeks before been offering money to the neighborhood children to buy ice cream. Donna Hill, of Gemini Court, had seen a heavyset man in a cowboy hat hanging around the complex. Once the composite was released, Shannon Wooden, of Capella Court, said that the sketch resembled the man she'd seen wearing a cowboy hat and giving out money to children. He was driving a green-and-white car. And Robert Krue told Detective Ramsey of a man named Bob, six feet two inches tall, with blond curly hair, who resembled the composite.

The afternoon of the murder, Patricia Ruth claimed to have seen a man in light-colored shorts come running out of the woods at half past eleven that morning. He appeared exhausted and gave her an angry look.

Patricia Logan, of 8860 Fontana Lane, told Detective Ramsey that she'd seen a white male on the path near Fontana Village early that morning. She described him as six feet tall and in his midtwenties. He had light curly blond hair, a thin mustache, and was wearing cream-colored shorts and a gold T-shirt. She particularly remembered his eyes, which she said protruded strangely, like he was on drugs.

On July 30 Mary Ann Freeland told Detective Ramsey that on July 25 at about 2 P.M., she'd observed a white male, about five feet eight inches tall, of medium build, with curly hair and a blond mustache, and wearing a white T-shirt and jeans, walking alone along Ridge Road near the woods where Dawn had been killed. Mrs. Freeland stated that she'd be able to recognize the suspect if she saw him again.

Mrs. Sarah Nelson, on Trimbleway, reported that around eleven o'clock or eleven thirty on the morning of July 25, she'd seen a white male, six feet tall, with dirty blond hair and a slender build, wearing a short-sleeve shirt and old jeans, standing by a car near the back of the woods off Bethke's Pond. She later saw police cars all over that area.

Thomas Jackson, of Serpens Court, told officers that he saw a six-foot-tall white male with a stocky build at 6:10 A.M., wearing purplish shorts, a purple striped shirt, and white tennis shoes. The man had a mustache. He seemed to be loitering.

Debbie McNamara, of 26 Orion Court, said that between ten and eleven o'clock she had seen a white male, twenty-five to twenty-six years old, a little over six feet in height, weighing 180 pounds, with sandy blond hair and a mustache, sitting on the electric box out front of her place. The electric box was dusted for fingerprints but no prints were recovered. McNamara would later be asked to attend a police lineup.

Nancy Hall, of 18 Orion Court, was first interviewed by Officer Charles Moore and later by Detective Robert Castagnetti. She told them that around nine thirty that morning she'd seen a white male sitting on a transformer box on Orion Court wearing black khaki pants and a maroon pullover shirt. He had dark brown hair that was curly in the back and had a thin build. She said that her friend, Donna Ferguson, had seen him too. Two days later, this same Nancy Hall approached an officer and told him that the composite looked like a man she knew named Mickey Manzari. She reported that Manzari had been hanging around the complex, had been recently released from prison, and had brown curly hair. On July 31 officers arrested Manzari at Nancy Hall's apartment but later released him when his alibi checked out. Despite her error in fingering Manzari and despite the fact that the strange man she saw was wearing black pants as opposed to the tan shorts described by the two boys and Fay McCoullough, Hall would later become an important prosecution witness at trial.

Donna Ferguson, interviewed by both Moore and Castagnetti, said that between ten fifteen and ten thirty that morning she also saw a white male wearing a maroon shirt sitting on the electric box on Orion Court but took little notice of him. About ten thirty she saw Dawn Hamilton go into the woods, yelling, "Lisa, Lisa," and at about the same time heard a man's voice say, "Lisa and I are playing hide-and-seek; let's go into the woods and find her." She reported, however, that she did *not* see the man who said this and didn't know if he was the same person she'd seen earlier. Ferguson also would testify for the state at trial. There, before a jury, she'd claim that she did in fact see the man who went into the woods with Dawn Hamilton and would identify him as the defendant on trial.

Mrs. Chris Wagner, of Breslin Court, told Robert Capel on the 27th that she'd seen a man in the Rossridge swimming pool who closely resembled the composite. Detective Capel interviewed the pool lifeguard and learned that the man was Thomas Darling. Darling's employment time card showed that he'd been at work all day on the 25th.

One neighbor claimed to have seen a nude man on the playground the week before.

Harriet Forrest, the manager of the nearby 7-Eleven, viewed the composite and called in saying that a man who matched it had been at the store at 10:30 A.M. on the 25th. A store videotape of the subject was played, revealing a white male appearing to be twenty-five to thirty years old, six feet tall, of medium build, wearing a white T-shirt and tennis shoes, but without a mustache. Since he lacked a mustache, the lead was dropped.

On August 1, Gloria Curtis told an investigator that the composite looked like the resident of 8864 Trimbleway, Garvin L.

Porter. Porter turned out to be only five feet seven inches tall and weighed 170 pounds. He was dismissed as a suspect. Considerable weight was being placed on the descriptions given by the two little boys.

Later, on August 1, Jim Greeley and Robert Fertig of Pennsbury Place reported that their neighbor, Mr. King, looked like the composite. It was determined that Mr. King was driving his tractor-trailer all day on July 25.

The composite sketch, it seemed, favored a lot of people.

That same day, a Mr. Constantine of Pennsbury Place, advised police that the picture of the suspect was similar to a man wanted in the Fells Point area of Baltimore for a series of child rapes. This particular lead was never pursued.

A married couple from Orion Court told police that Clarence Conroy, who lived three doors down, had been previously arrested for child molesting, and except for his height—he was only five feet four inches tall—met the description. Conroy went by the nickname Popeye and always wore a Pittsburgh Pirates hat. Police pulled Conroy's record. They later established that on the day of the crime he'd been mowing grass all morning and into the early afternoon at a distant location.

Detective Milton Duckworth, on July 31, tracked down Arnold Sanders after learning that Sanders had been fired from delivering the *Sun* newspapers because he often delivered them in a bikini bathing suit. Sanders had been taking classes at Essex Community College during the entire morning of July 25. His alibi checked out.

Detectives Capel and Ramsey had to sift through all these leads and see to it that each was adequately followed up. It was their responsibility to separate the wheat from the chaff. This was no easy chore. Interestingly, though, given what was eventually to happen, none of these reports suggested anything about a man with reddish or auburn hair or a man with mutton chop sideburns.

When a telephone tip came in suggesting that a W. F. Johnson of Spangler Way should be investigated, that he met the general description of the assailant and had spent two and a half years at the Clifton Perkins State Mental Hospital after being charged with child molestation, it was Detective Duckworth who was again assigned to track him down. Duckworth interviewed Johnson on July 27. He had already learned that Johnson was known to distribute sweets to the children at the Calvary Baptist Church, where he'd earned the nickname the Candy Man. Johnson came across as a creepy guy. He claimed that on July 25 he'd spent the day looking for work, as he'd been doing since losing his job eight months earlier. He admitted that he'd seen Dawn's picture on TV and knew her from church. He admitted giving candy to kids and said he did it because he loved children. Under no circumstances would he hurt one, he said. Detective Duckworth also interviewed the minister of the church who said Johnson was a constant source of concern as he liked to pick the little girls up and put them on his lap. Several mothers had complained about him touching their children. Detective Duckworth felt uneasy about Johnson. Johnson did not match the composite sketch. He was six feet six inches tall, weighed 215 pounds, and had brown hair. Still, Johnson had no verifiable alibi, and Duckworth believed that he should not be eliminated as a suspect.

Then there was Richard Gray. After Detective Bacon had discovered Dawn's body, and the forensic and homicide detectives had assumed control of the crime scene, Bacon had gone back to investigate the man who had coincidentally come upon Dawn's clothes high in a tree. Bacon was assigned to the Child Abuse Division of Baltimore County and had extensive experience with child abuse cases. He found Gray near where his car was parked. Gray was five feet ten inches tall, of slim build, and had dark hair down to his shoulders. He was dressed in a dirty white T-shirt that gave off a strong odor, camouflage military pants, tennis shoes, and carried a nightstick. Bacon noticed a small red spot on Gray's shirt but couldn't be sure if it was blood. Bacon started asking Gray questions and quickly sensed that Gray was nervous. Gray kept insisting that Dawn's clothes were *placed* in the tree rather than *thrown* in the tree. When Bacon looked into Gray's car, which was locked, Gray became even more agitated. Then he vomited. There appeared to be a pair of child's panties balled up on the front console. Also there were about thirty rolled-up newspapers on the passenger seat. Realizing that Detective Bacon had seen the underpants, Gray quickly explained that he had found them two days before in the woods. Gray then agreed to have his car searched. It was also photographed. Bacon asked Gray to accompany him back to the Youth Services station to give a statement and Gray nodded his assent.

At the station, Bacon read Gray his *Miranda* warnings, then began his questioning. Gray told Bacon he'd been riding in his car delivering papers and listening to his scanner when he heard a child was missing and that police had set up a search. He went to the command center to offer his assistance, as he knew the area well. He decided to ride over to the apartments and look around a bit and while doing this just happened on the clothes hanging from a tree. He said that he then went back to his car when a woman pulled up, described Dawn to him, and asked if he'd seen her. He told the woman to go back to the staging area and send out a police officer. He said he waited twenty minutes and when no one came, he started walking through the woods toward the command center. That's when he met Mr. Hamilton. During his statement, Gray constantly referred to children as "little people." Bacon thought Gray was squirrelly, not telling the truth, and a real suspect. Bacon noticed that Gray's hands were clean and wondered how that could be so if he had been rolling and delivering newspapers. Bacon was also suspicious because Gray somehow knew that Dawn had a purse with her. Gray claimed that the woman had told him this earlier. Gray kept motioning that the purse was on a strap across her chest. Bacon was curious how Gray knew to look exactly where the clothes and body were found when at that time the focus of the police search was far away in an entirely different area of the woods. He didn't think Gray adequately answered his questions.

Bacon ran a check to see if Gray had a record and found that he had a prior conviction for indecent exposure in a situation involving a minor. The car Gray was using was an AMC Eagle station wagon rented from Mark's Rentals. Why a rental car, Bacon wondered. And there was that small red spot on Gray's shirt that continued to bother Bacon. He'd been glancing at it since he first met Gray but couldn't be sure. He wanted the shirt taken and tested. He asked Detective McQuinn of homicide to have this done, as homicide now had control of the investigation and the final say over everything. McQuinn checked with his supervisors concerning taking Gray's shirt. McQuinn was informed that Richard Gray was well known to the officers at the Fullerton Police Station; he often dropped by to chat — a sort of police groupie — and that Gray had actually shown up at the station just as the original call came in that morning reporting the child missing, though this was inconsistent with what Gray had said. McQuinn was instructed not to take Gray's shirt.

Detective Bacon was astonished. He knew of the Chris Shipley and Jackie Poling descriptions, but with extensive experience in child abuse cases, questioned whether it made sense to place so much emphasis on descriptions given by seven- and ten-year-old boys. And no one knew for sure whether the man seen walking with Dawn into the woods was, in fact, her murderer. Bacon believed there was probable cause to arrest Richard Gray. The fact that Gray was at the Fullerton station when the call came in didn't rule him out as suspect. The call, he knew, didn't come in until nearly noon, and the girl may have been killed as early as eleven. Bacon wanted hair samples taken and fingernail scrapings secured from Richard Gray. Bacon wondered why his newspapers were undelivered. Why had there been a pair of child's underpants in Gray's car? Why were his hands clean? Why was there blood on his shirt? Why the agitation, the vomiting? He pressed McQuinn to detain Gray. Again, Detective McQuinn contacted his supervisors and discussed whether to arrest Richard Gray. Again, he was told not to do so. Richard Gray was released. Neither his person nor his automobile was ever subjected to a forensic search.

Detective Bacon left the station that night upset. Afterward, he was ordered back to the Child Abuse Division and told to have nothing more to do with the Dawn Hamilton murder investigation. Within a few months he started staying home from work. He sought counseling, took psychiatric leave, and later retired on medical disability. The murder of Dawn Hamilton had affected him deeply.

Two weeks or so after the crime, Richard Gray was given a lie detector test by Detective Darden of the county police department and failed it. By then, however, Detectives Ramsey and Capel had honed in on another suspect, one who fit the FBI psychological profile to a tee, and they believed they had their man. They were on to their prey, like hounds with the scent of the fox in their nostrils, building their case, closing the net. Richard Gray was forgotten. His file was marked cleared. W. F. Johnson was forgotten as well. The Fells Point rapist lead was dropped. Other leads were abandoned. This new suspect had many characteristics similar to the description given by the two boys and looked very much like the composite sketch. Chris Shipley had picked him out of a photo spread. And he had blood in his very name.

NINE

THE BOOK *OUTLAW GUNNER,* by Harry M. Walsh, tells the story of wildfowl hunters, guides, market shooters, and hunting outlaws from earlier days in and around the Chesapeake region. Kirk Bloodsworth keeps a copy in his home and is proud to display the page depicting a photograph of his great-grandfather, John Bloodsworth, standing on a sunken river blind with a large pump gun resting in the crook of his arm. Kirk has a romantic fancy for the old days. In addition to being some of the earliest settlers of Maryland's Eastern Shore, his ancestors, he believes, have also been sailors, pirates, rum runners, as well as fisherman—for the most part seafaring people who've stayed close to and lived off the water. As his father, Noble Curtis Bloodsworth, would say, "Kirk was born and bred with salt in his veins."

Family history has the Bloodsworths first emigrating from Scotland, Ireland, and England in the mid-1600s. They landed on a small island off the western edge of the Chesapeake Bay, low-lying, marshy, but teeming with life—ducks, geese, oysters, crabs, clams for the scooping. They built houses on stilts and laid claim to what became Bloodsworth Island in Dorchester County, Maryland. As

Kirk remembers from visiting as a boy, "The tide goes up there and you go with it . . . Water comes right up across the road, sometimes four foot high. You could dip up soft crabs and buckrams right there in your own backyard, and have 'em fried up for breakfast."

Kirk's great-aunt Agnes lived to be 110, and he grew up listening to her tell stories of the old days. The extended Bloodsworth family gradually moved off the island in the 1930s to get to electricity, she told him, to find higher ground and a dryer way of life. The U.S. Navy bought the island from the family for fifty cents an acre in 1955 and used it for target practice. After they stopped shelling it, it became an egret sanctuary. Not many people venture onto it because it's supposed to be full of unexploded bombs.

For two hundred years the male descendants of Kirk's family have been watermen—an Eastern Shore term for people who make a living off the waters of the Chesapeake Bay. His grandfather, John Noble Bloodsworth, was an oysterman, fisherman, crab scraper, and trapper. Kirk's father, Curtis, was as well. Folks say Curtis was one of the best hand-tongers ever. He had a knack for finding the fattest oyster beds, and he could rake the shells up from the bottom, filling bushel after bushel, as fast as anyone. When the oysters got scarce, though, Curtis regretfully went into the seafood business, buying a refrigerator truck and driving the local produce up to New Jersey to sell. This happened when Kirk was about ten. But by then Kirk was a waterman in his own right.

Since age five, he'd been hunting with his father in the duck blinds that dot the creeks and cuts around the Choptank River. When he was just six, he started helping his father tong for oysters. Kirk would serve as his father's culler, knocking the spat off the shells. One November, during low tide, after a northeast wind sucked the water right out of the river, his father sailed their boat right up on an oyster bar and Curtis and Kirk just picked up the oysters by hand. They filled a whole flatbed pickup with oyster bushels that day, and the family celebrated by inviting the relatives over for an oyster feast that night—oyster stew, oysters on the half shell, oysters Rockefeller, fried oysters, you name it.

For Christmas, Curtis always gave Kirk muskrat traps. From January to March Kirk would get up every morning at four thirty, ride his bicycle out to the marsh to where he'd laid his traps, harvest his muskrats, reset his traps, and ride home. He used Connabear traps, named for Fred Connabear, the mountain man, and would mark their locations with red flags tied to gum poles cut from the gum thickets. The black pelts sold for ten dollars apiece back in the 1970s, and the browns would fetch seven or eight. Riding home on his bicycle, he looked like a miniature woolly mammoth, the muskrats hanging all over him on strings. Several years running, Kirk won the Dorchester County junior trap-setting contest at the outdoor show. He won the oyster-shucking contest a couple of times, too.

When the weather turned warm, Kirk and his friends would start fishing, crabbing, and frog-gigging. Kirk fished with a gum pole for a rod and half a spark plug for a sinker, and despite his primitive gear, as his father tells it, "He could really smoke 'em." He'd often come home with stringers of perch so long that he wasn't tall enough to lift them off the ground, and they'd drag behind him. His grandma, Miss Vinnie B., was very fond of the perch roe, and when Kirk was fishing there was always plenty of roe for breakfast. Kirk used a four-prong spear on the nights he went bullfrogging in the marsh, and sometimes would fill several gander sacks full with the frogs. Pritchett's General Store bought all the frogs he could catch. It bought his muskrat pelts too. Pritchett's was real country in the country with creaky, old wooden floors, and selling turtle meat and cow's tongue, tripe and marinated duck eggs. After being paid, Kirk liked to sit on the rocker out front, sip a cool lemon freeze, and talk to the customers. He never thought about it much because it was all he knew. But the open country, the wind on the water, the changing landscapes of the marsh—this natural beauty and freedom was stamped inside him and was what he cherished.

The Bloodsworths lived on Atlantic Avenue in the town of Cambridge, Maryland. Kirk was eight when, as he remembers it, Rap Brown and the Black Panthers blew the corner of the courthouse right off its foundation and set half the town on fire. His aunt lived across the street from the courthouse, and the explosion knocked the windows in her house out. The Cambridge riots of '68 put the town on the map for a while, brought to light the injustice of inchoate segregation and the poverty of country existence. Kirk's mother, Jeanette, was one of the few who stood up for their local black friends at the time. She was an angelic woman, a devout Christian, who always had a smile and was ready to play. She ran a clean, scrubbed house, though, and allowed no nonsense when it came to chores, manners, or religion. When things got tight she'd help out at Netty Brown's, the local beauty parlor, but mostly she kept the house and looked after Kirk and his older sister, Vickie. Jeanette insisted that the fire was the work of a few bad apples who'd come to stir up trouble, and that none of the townsfolk she knew could be involved. "It's what a man's heart says," she'd drum in to Kirk. "That's all that counts. It doesn't matter what the color of the skin is. And you must stand up for this in life. Stand up for your principles." Kirk believed what she told him. Later, when he was in prison, these teachings probably saved him.

After middle school, Kirk attended Cambridge High for a while, then transferred to the Open Bible Academy, a small, church-run vocational program. He had a girlfriend named Cathy Wheatley and occasionally they talked about getting married, but Kirk knew he wasn't ready. At around age sixteen he started drinking beer, and he first smoked marijuana when he was seventeen. Kirk's mother hoped the Christian school would keep him on the straight path. But pot was prevalent in Cambridge in the late 1970s, and it seemed that at every party he attended, it was there for the taking. It was at the Open Bible Academy, though, that Kirk first started throwing the discus.

He had always been naturally strong and developed an interest in strength as he grew up. He'd played softball in junior high but was clumsy and not well coordinated. But even as a boy, he'd been muscular. Before his head reached above the tailgate of his father's refrigerator truck, Kirk was heaving hundred-pound crates of seafood and ice up into the truck bed. He enjoyed anything requiring strength and read the biography of Paul Anderson, the world's strongest man. By age fourteen, Kirk could dead-lift five hundred pounds. At the Open Bible Academy he met Richard Drescher, who'd been a Pan American Games discus champion in 1971. Drescher taught him the techniques of throwing the discus, and Kirk couldn't get enough. He practiced in his yard at home, and according to his father, "Kirk busted many a shingle off the house and broke quite a few windows. He'd try to throw from the front driveway to the backyard and sometimes his aim was just off." But the practice paid off. Kirk won the national championship for Christian schools and then won the state championship in Elkridge, Maryland, by more than thirty feet.

Kirk, admittedly, wasn't much of a student. He did manage to graduate, but since the Open Bible Academy wasn't accredited, he didn't receive a diploma. This didn't matter much at the time because by then he'd made plans to join the Marine Corps. Curtis had been a marine, and Kirk got the notion in his head that he could throw the discus for the marines. He graduated from high school in the summer of 1977, signed up for a four-year tour, and headed off to Paris Island for his basic training.

• • •

KIRK FELT RIGHT at home at Paris Island, which sits in the flat marsh country of South Carolina. He was strong and in decent-enough shape. He didn't much care for the screaming and hazing, but the physical conditioning didn't faze him. From Paris Island, he shipped out to Camp Pendleton in California for two months of infantry training. He'd never been at any elevation above sea level and didn't take well to humping the mountains, but he adjusted. He began inquiring about the Marine Corps track team, but none of his superiors seemed to take seriously his aspirations to become a corps discus thrower. To them, he was just one more grunt with unrealistic expectations and looking for an easier ride.

Kirk graduated from infantry school and was assigned to a marine base in Riota, Spain. There he renewed his requests for an opportunity to tryout for the Marine Corps track team, but again his requests were ignored. The marine base there was commanded by a Major Howell, a man insulated from his men, who didn't deign to give Kirk an answer. Even so, Kirk took great pride in being a marine. He particularly excelled at inspections. He practiced perfecting his uniform, made up his bunk with razor-blade creases, polished his dress shoes until they reflected his face like a mirror. He developed his own technique for cleaning his rifle, one he'd learned hunting coon and deer back home. Most of the marines tried using brass or silver polish to make their weapon look clean. Kirk used polish first. But then he finished by using the back side of the foil from a Juicy Fruit chewing gum wrapper to put a silver shine on every part of his rifle—the barrel, breach, trigger, even inside the muzzle. One afternoon during an inspection, a visiting major general walked alongside Major Howell. When the major general got to Kirk, he stopped, impressed with his bearing and uniform. Kirk's shoes were impeccably shined. His buttons sparkled in the sunlight. When the major general looked at his rifle, he did a double-take. He took the burnished steel weapon and examined it everywhere. He showed it to Howell, then to other marines in the inspection line as an example of perfection. He then returned it to Kirk, complimenting him before moving down the line of men. Once inside the bunkhouse, the major general asked to see Kirk's bed. It looked right out of a marine manual, without a wrinkle. The major general began asking Kirk questions about marine SOPs— standard operating procedures. Kirk knew all the answers. The major general gave Kirk three outstanding inspection citations. Each one entitled Kirk to a ninety-six-hour pass. Kirk asked the major general if instead of the passes, he could have something else. He wanted to make an alternative request. He asked if the senior officer would consider it. The major general looked at Major Howell, then said he'd listen.

Kirk told the major general of his dream of trying out for the Marine Corps track team as a discus thrower. At the time, in order to qualify for a tryout, a marine had to beat every man on the base. Kirk told him he could do this. The officer studied Kirk for a moment, surveying him from head to foot. He asked Kirk if really he was any good. Kirk replied that he'd had an Olympic coach in high school who thought he was really good, that there were some people back in his home state who thought he was really good cause he'd beaten them all, and that if the major general didn't believe him and wanted proof, he'd prove it to him. The major general chuckled at this brashness. He then asked Kirk how far he'd have to throw it to qualify. Kirk answered 150 feet. The man said, "Well, can you throw it that far?" Kirk answered, "Sure, I can throw it that far."

The major general turned to Major Howell, winked, then ordered someone to get a discus. He had an orderly mark off 150 feet. He told Kirk to go over to the mark and throw the discus back toward them. When Kirk got there, he shouted over, "Well, I'm sort of in a bad way, sir, 'cause here I got my dress shoes on." The major general shouted back, "You said you can throw it 150 feet. If you can, you can damn well do it in your Sunday finest."

Winding his body in a coil around the discus, Kirk then did a 360-degree rotation and unleashed it. It sailed over the head of the two majors, over the storage shed behind them, and landed maybe 175 feet from where Kirk was standing. The major general laughed out loud, had the discus retrieved, and hollered for Kirk to do it again. Kirk repeated the performance, throwing it even farther. The major general, without even conferring with Major Howell, then said, "Marine, go pack your shit. You're going out on the next transport with me. Tryouts are in Quantico, Virginia, and that's where you're headed."

Kirk not only made the marine track team three years in a row, but became the All-Marine Discus Champion for each of those three years. He'd spend four months stateside each year training and competing, and the rest of the time he'd be back in Spain, with relatively easy duty, often with too much time on his hands. He chased girls and first smoked hashish when in Spain, and drugs became an easy way to relieve the boredom. While on the base, he spent much of his time training and coaching other discus throwers and shot-putters. In the national tournaments in which he competed, though, he never was able to throw his best and his career as a discus thrower faltered. He served for a while as a base security guard. Gradually he grew impatient with the restricted life of the military, the repetitive days, the monotony. He longed to be back on the river, free, working the water. When his tour finally ended, on October 16, 1981, he received an honorable discharge from the marines, made his way back to Baltimore, and boarded a Greyhound bus headed home to Cambridge.

Bill Elliot, a crab-potter off Hudson Point on the Little Choptank River, gave Kirk a job that fall. When crabbing season ended Kirk tried oyster tonging, but the oysters were scarce. Kirk had spent everything he'd made while in the marines, so he needed work. He picked up different odd jobs trying to get by, hoping to save enough money to buy his own workboat. Some months he helped his father loading seafood; others he worked jogging papers for the *Easton Star Democrat*. He also worked for one of the town morticians, Raymond Curran, of Curran's Funeral Home. Kirk had seen another boy fall into a crab scrape once and drown, and when he was pulled up he was all mangled and in terrible shape. At his funeral, though, he looked decent. Kirk developed a respect for mortuary science. When not crab potting or helping his father load the seafood truck, he worked on and off for Curran over the next couple of years, assisting him at the funeral home.

After coming home, Kirk let his hair grow out again. It was fiery red and curly, though with weeks in the sun it tended to bleach to a ginger blond. He grew a mustache and thick mutton-chop sideburns. He stood just under six feet tall and was anything but thin. Burly, barrel-chested, and still very strong, he weighed about 212 pounds. Perhaps as a reaction to the cooped-up life of the military, Kirk went a bit haywire in Cambridge, smoking pot, drinking too much, chasing girls. Raymond Curran, fed up with Kirk's sporadic attendance and sloppy work, eventually let him go.

In early 1984, just after Valentine's Day, Kirk took a road trip to Baltimore with a friend to carouse at a hardhead nightclub called Hammerjacks. From there the two friends ended up at a bar in Essex called Skip's Tavern. It was at Skip's Tavern that Kirk ran into Wanda Gardenier, "rough and ready," as he described her. They danced together, went outside to smoke a joint, danced again, and found they couldn't keep their hands off each other. Kirk spent the night with her and to hear him tell it, he was just a goner, hook, line, and sinker.

Wanda was ten years older than Kirk, more experienced, and their lovemaking was unlike anything he'd ever known. She hung out with a tough crowd—bikers and gang members from the Out-laws. She had hair down to her waist, liked to lounge around in bars and drink, smoke reefer, and party. She had two kids from a previous marriage who stayed with their father in Pennsylvania. Wanda lived in Baltimore, and what she did mostly was play. What magic she had, she worked on Kirk, because he couldn't say no to anything she asked. Kirk's parents disliked her at first and then came to despise her. They begged Kirk to break away. But on April 14, 1984, two months after he met her, they married at the Christian Tabernacle Church in Middle River, Baltimore. Kirk's parents were so upset that neither attended the wedding. Curtis showed up briefly at the reception and gave Kirk $200 as a wedding gift. Kirk and Wanda used the cash for their honeymoon in Ocean City over the weekend, where they mostly stayed drunk. While trying to get a cork out of a champagne bottle, Kirk broke off his front tooth. They laughed at this, as Wanda had a broken front tooth as well. They were alike now. They tried to settle down in Cambridge, living at Miss Libby's Boarding House on Henry Street. But Wanda was neither a small-town girl nor the domestic type. Things quickly turned bad, then went from bad to worse.

As Kirk recalls it, Wanda wouldn't work and wouldn't stay home. She was constantly high and wanting to party. She was never home when he got off work, and he'd have to search the bars to find her. She'd disappear for days at a time. They fought often. Kirk tried to get her to look for a job, but as he remembers her, "Wanda wouldn't work in a pie shop sampling the pies."

In early June, Kirk was working with Bill Elliot, getting the crab pots ready to set, when he got a call from the emergency room at Dorchester Hospital. Wanda, who didn't have a driver's license, had taken his car keys off his dresser, driven out to Big Boys Bar, stoked herself up on about fifteen Jack and Cokes in the middle of the afternoon, and wrecked his car. She'd broken her nose and looked like a raccoon when he saw her. They had no medical insurance and Kirk had no auto insurance. His car was wrecked and he had to borrow money from his father to pay the hospital bill and then hire a lawyer to defend his wife in court. He was fed up.

With the assistance of the lawyer Kirk hired, Wanda got a thirty-day suspended sentence for driving under the influence of alcohol and was put on a year's probation with the requirement that she attend alcohol counseling. A few days later, Kirk got a call from the sheriff's office that she hadn't shown up for her initial meeting with her probation officer. She'd been missing for two days. Kirk borrowed a motorcycle and rode down to Ocean City where he found her in the Purple Moose Saloon, barefoot, drunk, dirty, and crying. He drove her back on the bike. He felt his heart was going to break, but it was obvious she just couldn't stand living in Cambridge. Kirk gave her all the money he had at the time, about twenty dollars, and put her on a bus to go back to her mother's house in Baltimore.

But Kirk couldn't stay away. Despite everything she was and had done, he longed for her and couldn't stop. His insides were all twisted up and his mind confused. He thought of her constantly. The Friday of July 4 weekend he telephoned Wanda's mother, Birdie Plutschak, and found out where Wanda was staying. Then Kirk called Wanda and told her he was coming. He'd find some kind of work in Baltimore. He just wanted to be with her. She said, "Okay," like it was no big deal. He hitchhiked up there with a ten and change in his pocket and just the clothes on his back.

Wanda had moved into a two-bedroom row house at 30 South Randolph Road in Essex with her half sister, Dawn Gerald. Others were living there as well. When Kirk arrived, he found in addition to Wanda and Dawn, Wanda's two brothers, Joey and Kirk Martin; and Tammy Albin, a club dancer up in the city. Dawn and Tammy brought home boyfriends, bikers mostly, and Joey and Kirk Martin were always trying to hustle girls in there. The place was a constant party.

Kirk found a job working for a woman named Donna Hollywood, loading wicker furniture at a nearby outlet called Harbor to Harbor, about a mile away. He worked four days each week and, with no car, walked to and from work. In fact, he walked everywhere. He and Tammy were the only two in the group house that were employed, though Tammy worked nights.

Whenever Kirk was in the house, it seemed like a circus—filled with nonstop hard rock, spilled beer, marijuana smoke, toked-up bikers, wired-up chippies partying all night, fights, sex. Dawn Gerald and her half brother, Joey Martin, slept in the same bed. Kirk and Wanda lived out of cardboard boxes. They were given a pullout couch in the living room to sleep on, but it was seldom quiet enough to sleep and they had no privacy. Everyone was ramped up. Kirk was constantly borrowing money from people in the apartment who were constantly fighting over money. And Wanda acted no differently than she had in Cambridge. If anything, her conduct made Kirk feel even worse, as it took place in front of so many people. She'd disappear with biker friends and binge through the night. Kirk would come home from work having bought groceries for supper, and she wouldn't show up till near dawn. He was sleep deprived, always broke, jealous, and heart-shattered.

When Wanda stayed out late in the beginning of August, they got into a screaming fight. Later, he tried to calm her down, to appease her. He told her he'd bring her dinner that night, her favorite, a taco salad. But as the morning dragged on they continued to snipe at one another. "You need to make more money," Wanda carped. "Work more. You need to give me more room. You're just always jumping in my ass. You're always up my crawl." Something snapped in Kirk. He was done. He left the house that morning without a word.

He walked over to his workplace, told his boss, Donna Holly-wood, he was sick and wanted his paycheck, walked to the Golden Ring Mall where he cashed the check, and started hitchhiking home. But he was sunk in a swamp of confusion and remorse. He stopped along the way and spent the night in a room at the Pilot Motel. What was he going to tell his parents? He was embarrassed and didn't want to face them. He still ached for Wanda and felt guilty for deserting her. He called Birdie, Wanda's mother, just to talk. She was not friendly. Kirk told Birdie that he'd done some-thing bad, that he was supposed to bring Wanda dinner the night before, had promised to pick her up a taco salad, but instead had just gotten mad and left. He'd stayed out all night. Birdie told him Wanda would be angry and that if he left Wanda would take him for everything he had. Kirk hung up. He tried to reach his father, but both Curtis and Jeanette were away. The next day he walked over to Route 50 and hitched a ride all the way to Cambridge. Kirk arrived home on Sunday, August 5. He'd been living in Baltimore for exactly one month. Unbeknown to him, out of anger or spite, Wanda, at Birdie's urging, filed a missing persons report with the local police in Baltimore County the next day, listing Kirk Bloods-worth as mysteriously gone, whereabouts unknown.

TEN

FOR HOMICIDE DETECTIVE Sam Bowerman, a twelve-year veteran of Baltimore County's police force, the Dawn Hamilton murder provided the opportunity to assist his hometown department with a new and specialized law enforcement tool. Bowerman had been selected as the first local police officer in the country to attend the FBI Academy in Quantico, Virginia, to study the art of creating psychological profiles of violent criminals. Thirty-three at the time, Bowerman was in the middle of this fourteen-month fellowship when Dawn Hamilton was murdered.

For years criminal investigators had informally profiled suspects, trying to narrow the range of a search by keying in on the modus operandi or particular methods a given criminal might use. The characteristics of a crime, the unusual clues left behind, often pointed to certain traits of the culprit, even at times to a form of signature. Profiling first became a recognized, formal, investigative technique in the early 1970s when the FBI created its Behavioral Sciences Unit at Quantico. Studies of unsolved murders, coupled with the evaluation of serial killers such as Richard Speck, who killed eight nurses in Chicago; John Wayne Gacy, who killed thirty-three men and boys; and David Berkowitz of New York City, the notorious Son of Sam, led to the development of a more formal system for analyzing violent cases, particularly those with strange or bizarre aspects to them. In 1978 a research project combined FBI agents with behavioral scientists to conduct detailed examinations of some of the nation's most notorious crimes. Several dozen of these notorious criminals themselves were interviewed. The findings and conclusions of this study led the FBI to develop a database and a systematic approach to profiling. FBI agents were trained to be experts in the field, and Detective Bowerman, through his fellowship, had become skilled in these same techniques.

While not all homicides lend themselves to the development of a psychological profile, the FBI felt that the Dawn Hamilton slaying presented the opportunity because the killer was clearly psychopathic. "The public perception is of a monster," Bowerman told a reporter at the time. "But it's not the guy in the dirty trench coat hiding behind a tree. It's the guy who looks to be in the mainstream. Very few insane people commit violent crimes; it's the people with personality disorders."

Bowerman, along with other FBI profilers, and assisted by other Baltimore County detectives, took on the job of developing a psychological profile of the man who murdered Dawn Hamilton. They scoured the photos of the crime scene; studied the autopsy report; scrutinized the physical evidence and the eyewitness reports and descriptions; and closely examined the victim, her family, and social history, attempting to produce a written portrait of the man who took Dawn's life.

The final psychological profile prepared by Detective Bowerman and the FBI was seven and a half pages long and presented a disturbing picture of the crime and perpetrator. It concluded that the crime was one of opportunity, as opposed to one that was planned ahead of time. The killer had probably been dominated by women most of his life and had repressed rage against females bottled up inside him. When the rage boiled over, he struck. The report re-created the sequence of the attack on Dawn as follows:

The victim was initially approached because of her vulnerability, age, and what she represented to the assailant. . . . The victim, when offering resistance, was struck in the face by the assailant's fist. After being rendered semi-conscious from this blow, the victim was probably rammed head first into a nearby tree or into a stationary object on the ground. He then placed his foot on her throat in an attempt to totally silence her. He then rolled her over and stood on the back of her neck, thereby pushing her face to the ground in attempt (again) to silence her, as she was still alive and probably making unintelligible noises. In a moment of frustration and rage, he then kneeled over her and viciously struck her on the back of her head with a large rock at least twice. He then lowered his pants and anally assaulted her. Upon completion, he took a nearby branch and inserted it into her vaginal vault.

The report concluded that there was nothing to suggest the killer and victim knew each other. It suggested that the assailant had more than passing familiarity with the area, though, and resided, attended school, or worked in the immediate vicinity.

Regarding the offender's physical characteristics, the report concluded he was a white male, age eighteen to twenty-six. As to his personality and social situation, it posited a number of interesting theories. The following paragraphs, excerpted from the profile, painted a vivid picture.

We would expect him to be single, or possibly previously married. If he is presently married or living with a female partner, it is likely that there would be some obvious characteristic of the woman which others would notice, she would be much older or younger than he, she may border on retardation . . . or have problems causing others to consider her behavior to be weird or irrational. We would more likely expect him to be residing alone or with another person on whom he is economically or emotionally dependent. . . .

Although he fantasizes a great deal about indulging in sexual relationships with mature, physically developed women within his age group, and has a pornographic-type collection of literature, etc., reflecting same, he is inadequate and lacks confidence in himself and therefore his overt behavior would involve much younger, impressionable females or, perhaps, older women who would be more vulnerable. Developmentally, it is quite probable that he was brought up under the auspices of an overbearing mother or some other significant female figure who caused him great anxiety and dictated proper behavior/conduct to him.

Vocationally, if working, we would expect him to be involved in an employment setting in which he does not have a high degree of contact with the public; interpersonal relationships would be minimal.

In considering numerous other similar cases, we would initially expect the perpetrator to show little regard for his personal appearance. . . .

His need to at least partially fulfill his fantasies would cause him to be involved in nuisance offenses such as window peeping, fetish burglaries, exhibitionism, and obscene telephone calling. . . .

. . . it is likely the killer experienced an especially stressful time (possibly involving or caused by a significant female) . . . which set him off. . . .

Following the murder he would become more withdrawn and preoccupied. Others will definitely notice a change in his behavior as his lifestyle becomes temporarily very structured and

*rigid. . . . If employed he will likely call in sick or feign illness to
isolate himself from others. . . .*

*If the opportunity presents itself he will attempt to temporar-
ily leave the area through legitimate means. . . .*

*We believe that, when he feels safe from detection and his
anxiety levels, sex drive, etc., reach such a point that his usual
fantasizing/masturbation venting and the reliving of this crime
no longer constitute sufficient relief, he will strike again.*

Bowerman and the FBI cautioned that a psychological profile
was not to be considered a substitute for a thorough and well-
planned investigation. It was merely one tool and was based solely
on probabilities. It was best used in narrowing the field of suspects—in eliminating some and in raising additional suspicion as
to others. In fact, typically the FBI wouldn't honor a request for a
profile until the investigation was complete. In the Dawn Hamilton
investigation, these warnings were not well heeded. The psychological profile played a very significant role. The report became the
Rosetta stone for Detectives Capel and Ramsey. It caused them to
single out a suspect who had previously received scant attention
and later helped convince both of them and the state prosecutors
involved that this suspect was truly the murderer. The psychological profile became an important part of the foundation for their
unwavering belief that the man they arrested was guilty of the Dawn
Hamilton slaying.

ON JULY 28 a police telephone operator had received an
anonymous call, logged in as tip number 286 out of an eventual 500
plus, suggesting that a man by the name of Kirk, who worked at
Harbor to Harbor, looked similar to the person in the composite
sketch. This was just one more lead, one more caller who felt the
composite looked like someone they knew. Police were still doggedly

tracking down every possibility. The tip was duly noted, to be followed up in time.

About a week later, a police officer contacted the Harbor to Harbor establishment. An employee reported that a man named Kirk Bloodsworth had recently worked there as a laborer. Bloodsworth had no car, walked to work, and mostly kept to himself, the employee volunteered. After just a month at work, Bloodsworth had apparently become ill, the employee added, and had abruptly left his job on August 3. When asked about Bloodsworth's work schedule, the Harbor to Harbor employee had told the officer that no, Kirk Bloodsworth had not been at work on July 25. Wednesdays were always his day off. The officer ran a records check on Kirk Bloodsworth. Bloodsworth had no criminal history, but the check matched Bloodsworth with the missing persons report Wanda had filed. This information was relayed to Capel and Ramsey.

Nearly two weeks had passed since the murder. With each passing day, the trail of the killer got colder. This new lead, though, sparked the interest of the homicide detectives. What particularly intrigued them about this new suspect was that everything they learned about him suggested that he matched the person described in the psychological profile prepared by Bowerman and the FBI. Bloodsworth was familiar with the area. He lived and worked within a couple of miles of Fontana Village. Clearly he had a problem with his wife, a much older and probably domineering woman. The information suggested that he'd been under considerable stress. He had feigned an illness and suddenly left both his job and Baltimore County. His wife didn't even know where he was. Detectives Capel and Ramsey sensed a breakthrough in the investigation. They decided to track down this Kirk Bloodsworth and pay him a visit.

On August 7 Ramsey located Wanda Bloodsworth, who confirmed that Kirk had left town on August 3 and had complained of being sick for a few days before he disappeared. She suggested Ramsey try looking in Cambridge. Capel and Ramsey sent a colleague to the Cambridge Police Department soliciting its cooperation in locating their suspect. Both detectives were confident he'd soon be found.

ELEVEN

Cambridge, Maryland, has always been a small, mostly blue-collar town, filled with farmers, watermen, truck drivers, and local merchants. It sits on the flat piedmont of the state's Eastern Shore, alongside the mile-wide Choptank River that runs down through Delmarva's poultry country, past the town, and into the broad Chesapeake. West and south of town stretch the Dorchester marshes, miles of low-lying mud bank, silt, and salt lick, covered with an array of grasses dominated by the spiky spartina. The economy of Cambridge has languished since the middle part of the twentieth century when the oyster, fishing, and crabbing industries reached a peak and began to decline. Some people grow corn or soybeans. Others raise chickens or dairy cows. Opportunities for the young and ambitious are not plentiful. The soggy land is flat. The schools are average. Some leave after high school, but most, for one reason or another, end up staying or returning later. It's hard to remain a stranger for long in Cambridge. People tend to know one another or at least know of one another. Kirk knew nearly everyone. It was no different when he came back from Baltimore than it had been before.

When he'd gotten back to town, he'd gone by his parents' house first, but it was locked as they were away for a short holiday. He had a sack full of dirty laundry and not much money, and it was hot, the hottest August he'd ever remembered. He walked over to the house of an old friend, Tommy Tyler, a small-time pot dealer who lived on Henry Street, and told Tommy he needed someone to talk to. The two got high, and Kirk spent the weekend on Tommy's couch. On Monday, August 6, Kirk went down to the pool hall and drank some beer and shot some eight ball to stay cool. When he walked back to Tommy's, Tommy wasn't home. The temperature was in the upper nineties. Tommy's neighbor, Rose Carson, who had known Kirk for years, saw him with his bag of clothes and told him to come into her house to get out of the heat. Rose was thirty years old and lived with her younger sister, Thelma Stultz. Rose was known as a "banger," someone who liked to snort or shoot crank, a street version of methamphetamine—"cranked-up speed." She'd dropped out of high school after eleventh grade, worked on and off as an aide at the nearby nursing home, and occasionally took in boarders to help defray costs.

Rose later told police that she thought Kirk had seemed strung out. He looked liked he was wasted, a total mess. He was constantly smoking weed.

That afternoon Kirk told Rose that he and Wanda were having trouble and that he had done something bad and was afraid it would keep him and Wanda from ever getting back together. Rose figured he was talking about some kind of marital fight and never pressed for details. Kirk asked Rose if he could crash at her place for a few days, and she said sure. He said he planned to get a job at Kool Ice and Seafood and needed to save about $2,000 before he could go back to Baltimore. He told her he'd pay her board.

The next morning, August 7, Kirk told Rose he was going to the state hospital to get some help. Kirk said he hoped they'd admit him for detox, to help him just dry out. When he returned, he told Rose that the doctor told him he only needed consultation, not to be admitted. This was a lie. He'd never made it to the hospital. He was just looking for some sympathy from Rose.

In the afternoon he was sitting out front of Rose Carson's, buzzed on some redbud that he'd gotten from Tommy Tyler earlier that morning, wondering what to do next. Kirk had used the little money he had to buy a quarter ounce of the pot from Tommy. He'd smoked a joint, then stuffed the redbud, rolled up in a small cellophane bag, down into his tennis shoe. Kirk was stretched out in a shady spot, stoned, watching the occasional car go by, trying to stay cool. Detective Mark Cottom of the Cambridge Police Department rode by, recognized Kirk, and pulled his squad car over to the curb. Cottom and Kirk knew one another slightly. Cottom said hello. Cottom thought Kirk seemed jittery, which he was, considering the pot in his shoe. Cottom told Kirk that his wife had filed a missing persons report about him in Baltimore County and that the police there were looking for him. Kirk seemed to relax some after hearing this. "I don't want Wanda knowing where I'm at," he told Cottam. "Least not just yet. I gotta' find some work. Get myself straight first."

Kirk wrote out a short note to Wanda on Cottam's pad and asked Cottam if he'd pass it along. Cottom wanted to know where Kirk would be staying, and Kirk gave him Rose's address, 319 Henry Street. Cottom said good-bye, then immediately reported to the Baltimore homicide detectives that he'd made contact with Bloodsworth and that Bloodsworth had acted nervous. When Capel and Ramsey got word, they arranged to meet Cottom the next day.

WEDNESDAY, AUGUST 8 was another scorcher. The sun rose large and pulsing over the town of Cambridge and quickly baked hot the black macadam asphalt of the streets. There was no breeze, and the flat river simmered in the heat. The air was thick and sultry.

Kirk had hooked back up with Tommy Tyler the previous night, and the two stayed up late smoking pot, drinking beer, and listening to music. He slept till noon and was still groggy when he fixed himself a sandwich in Rose's kitchen. His clothes were disheveled, and he soaked his shirt through with sweat before he finished eating. In the kitchen, he rolled a joint, stuffed the redbud back in his sneaker, got stoned, then went outside for a look around. He was more than surprised when Detective Cottom pulled up again, this time accompanied by a heavyset detective he'd never seen before.

Robert Capel introduced himself. He told Kirk that he wanted to talk to him about a missing persons report his wife had filed. Capel was polite. He seemed nice enough. He then said he also wanted to ask Kirk about the murder of a little girl at Fontana Village, near Baltimore. And he said he'd like to take a Polaroid of Kirk.

Kirk realized for the first time that they might be thinking that he had something to do with that murder in Baltimore. He'd heard about it, as had everybody. He'd also seen the composite and knew it favored him some. But this . . . Shit, he thought to himself. He gulped down some air.

Kirk said to Capel that he'd read about the murder in the *Times* and seen something about it on TV. This didn't seem to help. Capel just nodded, studying him.

Kirk was uncertain what to do. He was also nervous about the reefer in his shoe.

Capel asked him again if he could talk to him and take a picture, down at the Cambridge station. It wouldn't take too long, he promised. Kirk thought about it. He figured why not. He nodded, okay; sure, he'd talk to them and they could take a picture, but he asked if he could change his shirt first. He also wanted Capel to promise that they wouldn't make him go back to his wife in Baltimore. Kirk hoped he could get rid of the pot when he changed his shirt. Capel agreed to what Kirk asked but stayed with him while he went inside to change. There was just no chance to ditch the pot.

Back outside, Capel escorted Kirk to an unmarked police car. Before Kirk really understood what was happening, he was being whisked away. He noticed that other police cars had pulled up and that officers were going into Rose Carson's house and starting to search it. Sitting in the back of the unmarked cruiser, he wondered how he'd gotten tangled in this one. He mostly worried about the pot, though. When the detectives seemed preoccupied, he tried to push the rolled-up plastic bag of redbud further down into his shoe.

Before arriving at the Cambridge Police Station, Ramsey and Capel had stopped off at the local Kmart and purchased a pair of little girl's panties and a pair of dark blue shorts matching those Dawn was wearing on the day she was killed. Ramsey had also picked up a piece of loose concrete from the parking lot. This was their gambit. According to agents at the FBI's Behavioral Science Unit, Dawn Hamilton's killer would have a strong reaction if confronted with these items. An innocent person would have no reaction. Ramsey placed the panties, shorts, and rock on the center of a wooden table inside the police interview room before Kirk arrived. When Kirk was brought into the small room, he displayed no reaction to the items on the table. Ramsey then picked the items up and placed them in a corner, out of Kirk's sight.

Kirk saw the items clearly and immediately assumed that the rock must be the murder weapon. What else could it be? He was curious, though, why they were all taken off the table so quickly and then never mentioned by the detectives. What kind of game were they playing?

Capel began asking him questions. He was courteous, though firm. He asked Kirk where he was on the day of the murder.

"I ain't sure, exactly," Kirk said. "I was probably at home on South Randolph Road, because I think that was my day off." He thought he'd hung around in the morning that day, he told Capel, then gone over to Wayne Palmer's house for the afternoon. Kirk said there were others in the house that day who might remember if he was at home.

Capel flipped a picture of Dawn Hamilton down on the table and asked Kirk if he knew her, and Kirk told him no. Capel asked him if he'd ever met her, and Kirk said absolutely not. He asked Kirk whether he'd been by a pond or seen two boys fishing that day, and Kirk answered, "No sir." He asked if he knew anything about the murder, and Kirk told him only what he'd seen on television and read in the paper.

Standing the entire time at "parade's rest" and staring him down was Detective Ramsey. Ramsey wasn't as tall as Capel but seemed more intense. He wore a short-sleeve white shirt decorated with a plastic pocket protector containing several pens and a nondescript tie. His graying hair was gummed back against his head. His eyes bore into Kirk's, and Kirk recalled later that he had never felt so small as he did in that room. Ramsey asked Kirk what his shoe size was, and Kirk answered size 10½. Ramsey then ordered him to hold up his shoe for them to see. Kirk's brow was slick with sweat. He lifted his shoe—the one without the pot. Ramsey told him to lift it higher so they could see what the underside of the sole looked like. He did. The sole was not in a herringbone pattern. Ramsey then snapped several pictures of Kirk. Capel promised Kirk he'd return the photographs to him once he was cleared. Capel asked Kirk where he'd be staying and Kirk told him. He told Kirk there was nothing to worry about but asked him not to leave town until this was resolved.

Kirk thought that was the end of it, that it would be over. His picture, he figured, would clear him. But still, the interview had upset him. Ramsey had made him feel awful. And to think they really thought he might be involved in the murder of a little girl. It made him sick. And what was with the panties and the rock? Driving through town, he couldn't wait to get out of Capel's car. At that instant, he mostly wanted to get stoned again. He asked Capel to drop him off back on Henry Street. Outside, it was still stifling hot.

When Kirk got to Rose Carson's, she was washing dishes. She was spitting mad. She cursed at him because the cops had found a marijuana roach in one of her ashtrays. Still, she let him in. Rose's sister, Thelma Stultz, was there. Thelma had also known Kirk for a number of years. Both women could see that Kirk was upset, agitated. They'd heard about the murder from the officers who'd searched Rose's house, but they were curious and wanted to hear from Kirk what happened at the station. They peppered him with questions. Kirk began rolling a joint on the kitchen counter. He was still sweating. His hands were unsteady.

"Do you know what they wanted?" he said. "I can't believe this. Jesus. I can't believe it."

"No," Rose answered, "What?"

"I'm a suspect in the rape of a little girl. Freakin' crazy." He licked two of the rolling papers so they would stick together. "And do you know which one?" he went on.

Rose again answered, "No."

"The one that's dead. That got murdered up in Essex. That's the one." His body gave up a shiver. "I'm really freakin' out. I just can't believe this."

Rose had heard enough. She was already mad at Kirk over the pot and anxious over so many police coming around. And now she was scared. She started ranting about how much trouble Kirk was causing. She told Kirk not to smoke any more dope in her house. Then she said he'd just have to leave. Kirk shrugged. He'd finished rolling the joint. Thelma, who was pregnant at the time, said, "Well, you going to get me high too?" Kirk said sure. Something he didn't know was that Thelma was friendly with Detective Cottom. She had promised him, after Kirk had been taken to the police station, that she'd report back anything Kirk said about the little girl. Kirk and Thelma walked outside and started up toward the elementary school. Kirk lit the joint, and the two shared it. According to what Thelma later told Cottom, Kirk couldn't stop talking about what had happened at the station. He rambled, talked excitedly, acted strange. Kirk told her the police had put the girl's shorts and a rock on the table. He told her that by putting the girl's underwear on the table, the cops had gotten him upset, but that he wouldn't ever let them see him cry. He also said he felt guilty about what had happened to the little girl.

Kirk was, in fact, distraught. The whole experience had unnerved him. And too, he felt the need to explain what had occurred so that his friends wouldn't think he'd gotten busted for having weed and agreed to become a snitch. The two walked back toward Rose's house with Kirk still talking about the little girl, ranting some, and muttering to himself.

Near Rose Carson's house, Kirk ran into some guys he knew who needed help lifting a broken motorcycle into the back of a pickup truck. Kirk offered his assistance. There were two girls with them, Tina Christopher and Tina Furbush. Thelma said good-bye and went back into Rose's. With Kirk's help, the guys heaved the bike into the pickup and then took it over to Tina Furbush's garage. Kirk knew Tina Furbush but had never met Tina Christopher. Tina Furbush was nineteen and Tina Christopher was just eighteen. Tina Christopher, it turned out, had dropped out of high school after tenth grade. After the guys left, the two Tinas invited Kirk into the house. He rolled another joint and they all smoked it. They all got seriously ripped. Kirk started talking about a little girl and being accused of killing her. About how it had happened in Baltimore. He mentioned two boys, a pond, and a rock. One of them asked him if the rock was the murder weapon, if it had blood on it. They talked about whether it was a bloody rock. Kirk kept rehashing what the cops had said to him. He seemed obsessed, went on about the clothes, the rock. His words, at least the ones Tina Christopher claimed to hear, would become the darts that would later be hurled against him.

Tina Christopher, when questioned two days later by the cops, was vague about what Kirk had said. But she thought he'd talked about the clothes the little girl wore and a rock that was supposed to have been bloody. He mentioned a pond and two boys, she re-called. And she thought she heard Kirk say that the girl went off into the woods with a guy that Kirk was with. She described it as a lot of rambling nonsense. The police typed up a statement and had her sign it. Over the ensuing months, she would often contradict herself to investigators about exactly what it was she'd heard.

Kirk, after his arrest, said she'd either misheard or misunder-stood him. He admitted that he might have told her that the rock was the murder weapon and he agreed he probably told her what he'd read in the newspaper about the pond and the two boys, but he denied ever saying that the rock was bloody or that he was with the man who went into the woods with the little girl. And he never told anyone, ever, that he was involved with the crime.

Thelma Stultz, back at Rose Carson's, called Detective Cottom and repeated what Kirk had said to her about a rock and about be-ing upset and feeling guilty when he saw the girl's clothes. Cottom thought Bloodsworth's remarks were damning. He filled in Capel and Ramsey on what Kirk was saying. Bloodsworth knows things only the murderer would know, Capel and Ramsey concluded. And by then they had an identification. They had, they believed, found Dawn's killer.

Kirk Bloodsworth, unaware of his increasing jeopardy, went over and visited with his parents, who had returned from the beach. His mother cooked fried chicken and cobbler. His parents were both quiet. It was obvious they were waiting for him to tell them what was going on.

First he told them about leaving Wanda. This was welcome news. Then he mentioned being questioned concerning a little girl's murder. His mother was sitting at the table quietly. When she heard this she began rocking back and forth moaning, "Oh, God . . . Oh my God . . ."

"It's gonna' be all right, Mom," Kirk told her. He put an arm around her.

"You didn't have nothing to do with that?" she moaned with her lips pursed and her eyes shut.

"No, Mom," Kirk answered.

"What the hell've you gone and done?" Curtis wanted to know. He had grown worried, impatient. "People's been calling here . . ."

"Nothing, Dad," Kirk answered. "See, I ain't done nothing. Believe me, they questioned me, and it's over with."

"Well, just don't try and get into something to see if you can get out of it," his mother chimed in. It was a favorite saying of hers.

"Right, Mom."

"Well, if you hadn't married that bitch," Curtis started, "and we begged you not to . . ." And with that they began to fight. Kirk and his father started shouting at each other about Wanda. Kirk lost it, got mad, threw his napkin down, and left. It was the last meal he would ever have with his mother.

Needing a place to sleep he went to the pool hall and from there called his cousin, Cindy Bloodsworth. "Cindy," he said, "I've gone and landed myself in a fine kettle of shit." He then went on to tell her how he'd left Wanda and somehow become a suspect in a murder case. He was innocent, he assured her. "It's just that everything seems to be taken the wrong way." He was sure he'd be cleared, but

he needed somewhere to stay and some time to get himself together. Cindy picked him up and took him over to her place.

Despite having been wasted for most of the day and night, Kirk
had a hard time finding sleep. He lay on the couch at Cindy's for a
long while regretting how he'd cursed at his father. He thought of
how close he'd come to ruining his life. The doping, the drinking,
Wanda—all were wrong turns. Now he was even a suspect in an insane murder. He thought of days past, days more innocent, when
all he'd wanted was a fine morning in which to work the river.
Knowing the tides and the pull of the moon, knowing the weather,
being in synch. Working for himself. No compromises, no excuses.
Enough was enough. He promised himself to make a change. And
if he put a measure of weight on anything in this world, it was on
his own word, on his own commitments, even if only to himself.
His time with Wanda was over. Come the new day he planned to
hunt down Bill Elliott. To start working the water again. And to
save his money and get himself that workboat he'd dreamed of
since being a boy. For the first time in an age, he fell asleep with a
plan, with a sense of a future.

Soon after he dozed off, he heard from somewhere far away a
pounding noise. It became louder. As he came awake, he realized
the pounding was there in front of him, on his cousin Cindy's front
door.

TWELVE

FOR A LAW ENFORCEMENT officer, the objective of any identification procedure should be to ensure a reliable and trustworthy result. Because cops sometimes get carried away, become, perhaps, too eager to make that collar, courts must occasionally wade in and remind them of this purpose. During the late 1960s and early 1970s, in a series of criminal cases raising issues of constitutional due process, the United States Supreme Court addressed the problems inherent in eyewitness identification. The Court ruled that identifications stemming from unnecessarily suggestive police identification procedures were fundamentally unfair and would be inadmissible as evidence. The Court recognized that eyewitness identification, particularly in the criminal context, is by its nature difficult and fraught with possible error. People with similar features can easily be confused one with another. For the typical identification witness, who first sees a perpetrator amid the stress of a criminal encounter, the risk of a mistake increases in any kind of suggestive setting. Showing a witness a single suspect at the scene or in a squad car is suggestive. Showing a witness just one photograph is suggestive. This is because such procedures suggest to the witness that the police think the one person, or the person depicted in the single photograph, is the culprit. Some witnesses tend to want to please the police. Others are easily led or susceptible to being influenced. The victim or witness typically wants to identify the culprit, wants to be of help. Giving the witness only one choice stacks the deck. And once a witness's identification is tainted—that is, the product of an unduly suggestive procedure—all the subsequent identifications that witness makes may be unreliable, mere repetitions of the first.

The Supreme Court was careful to prohibit only *unnecessarily* suggestive identifications. It chose a term that could be interpreted flexibly by the lower courts in order to meet the endless exigencies of law enforcement and the varied factual situations that arise. Sometimes an on-the-scene arrest coupled with a prompt identification of the suspect by the victim is as reliable as an identification can be. Police remained free under the Court's guidelines to solicit identifications in myriad settings. Nonetheless, nonsuggestive identification procedures, as the Supreme Court ruled, were always to be preferred if available.

To be trustworthy and not suggestive, a good photographic spread should contain numerous pictures of individuals who have the same characteristics the perpetrator was known to have, characteristics consistent with the witness descriptions of the person sought. The people depicted in the photo array should be somewhat similar in appearance. If a suspect has already been apprehended and a photo spread isn't necessary, a nonsuggestive lineup should be conducted. The lineup also should include a number of people with characteristics consistent with the description of the perpetrator. Witnesses should never see the suspect in a suggestive situation before viewing the lineup. Child witnesses are particularly prone to error and suggestion. Working with child witnesses requires extraordinary care in the investigative setting.

The same evening they'd interviewed Kirk Bloodsworth, August 8, 1984, Detectives Ramsey and Capel drove back from Cambridge to the police station in Towson and prepared a photo array of six pictures. Included in it was the photograph of Kirk Bloodsworth. Of the five pictures Ramsey and Capel put with Bloodsworth's, one showed a man who was clean-shaven with no mustache and one showed a man with a full beard. Only three photographs depicted men who were similar to the descriptions given by Chris Shipley and Jackie Poling. Later, the detectives testified that several of the photographs in the array were of other potential suspects in the case.

At eight o'clock that evening, Capel and Ramsey showed the array of photographs to seven-year-old Jackie Poling at his home. Jackie sat at his kitchen table. His mother was out, but a babysitter was there with him. Jackie looked at the pictures one by one. He then told the detectives that he did not see a picture of the man who'd been at Bethke's Pond with Dawn Hamilton. None of them was the one. Capel later testified that he thought Jackie was distracted, preoccupied, more interested in getting back to the television than in looking at the photos.

At 9:45 P.M., Ramsey and Capel showed the pictures to ten-year-old Chris Shipley in his home. His mother also was present. Shipley studied the prints, then pointed to photograph number four. "That looks just like him," Chris told them. Then he added something. He told them that the man's hair was a slightly different color. "The man at the pond didn't have as much red in his hair. It seemed lighter," he told them. Still, he was pretty sure the man in picture number four was the guy at the pond. Picture number four was the photograph of Kirk Bloodsworth.

Back at the station, Capel and Ramsey discussed the results of the photo ID procedure. Jackie Poling had never been certain of anything. He was maybe just too young. Chris Shipley, on the other hand, seemed to know what he'd seen. He impressed them as a trustworthy witness. While there, they learned of the statements Kirk Bloodsworth had been making in Cambridge, statements that were obviously incriminating. They marveled again at how closely he fit the psychological profile. It all seemed to fit. The difference in hair color mentioned by Shipley when he selected the photo was somehow overlooked. The fact that Jackie Poling had described the man at the pond as skinny and Chris Shipley had described his build as slim to medium was also forgotten. The height discrepancies were rationalized away. Capel and Ramsey were convinced they had their man.

The detectives prepared an affidavit and obtained a warrant for Kirk Bloodsworth's arrest. They drove back to Cambridge, arriving sometime around midnight. Working with Detective Cottom and others, it took a few hours to trace Kirk's movements to his cousin's house. But they found him.

When Kirk Bloodsworth answered the pounding on Cindy Bloodsworth's door, a dozen police officers stood outside. A spotlight shone in his eyes. Disoriented, he looked over his shoulder behind him, wondering who or what they wanted. He heard one of the cops yelling, then, that he, Kirk Bloodsworth, was under arrest for the rape and first-degree murder of Dawn Hamilton. Police were suddenly everywhere. "You have a right to remain silent," he heard a man shout. "Anything you say can be used against you in a court of law . . ."

Kirk's first reaction was to lose his temper. He began cursing the lot of them. Someone knocked him hard in the small of his back, sending him against the wall where he was pinned and told to shut up. He did. Kirk realized this wasn't just some lurid game. He was up to his ears in it, and he had no idea what to do.

All Kirk was wearing was a pair of blue shorts. They handcuffed him roughly, led him outside barefoot, without a shirt, and pushed his head down and into the back of a police car. The night was hot and he could hear the bullfrogs from the ditches, and the cicadas from the hedgerows. He grew more afraid. Police cars were all over the street with their red and blue lights rotating through the trees and against the row of houses. He stared at the windshield feeling helpless and sick. His life was over, he kept thinking. Over. He could see what looked like movie credits in red lettering scrolling down the car's windshield: *The End*, they read.

He was driven to the Cambridge Police Station, where Ramsey and Capel took him into the same interview room as the day before. Configured the same way, the room was bare except for the table and two chairs in its center. There, the detectives interrogated him for several hours. Ramsey, this time, took the lead. "How come you're telling people the rock had blood on it?" Ramsey demanded to know. "How would you know about a bloody rock?"

"What the hell you talking about?" Kirk answered, denying at first that he'd said anything about a bloody rock.

"We got the witnesses," Ramsey told him. "You've been talking about a bloody rock all over town!"

Kirk backtracked. He told him he never said it had blood on it, but that they'd made him think it was the murder weapon when they put it in front of him.

"Why'd you think the rock was the weapon," Ramsey said. "Whatever gave you that idea?"

Kirk told him again he'd assumed it was the weapon when they put it on the table. They'd tricked him into thinking something he wasn't supposed to know, he said.

Ramsey scoffed at this. "Oh, so you're the detective, now, are you?" He threw Dawn's picture down in front of Kirk. "You kill that little girl?" he asked. "Why'd you kill that little girl?"

"I didn't kill no little girl, sir. No, I did not."

"Why'd you do her, Kirk? Why did you do that to her?"

He asked it over and over.

Each time Kirk denied it.

Ramsey wouldn't quit. He kept coming back to the same question. Then he demanded to know where Kirk was the morning of July 25.

Kirk couldn't think straight, was too afraid. He told them he wasn't sure. He thought he was home. He thought he'd met a friend named Wayne Palmer who sold pot.

"Tell us about the little boys at the pond," Ramsey said. "Before you took Dawn into the woods."

Kirk shut his eyes and shook his head.

Ramsey threw the child's shorts and panties that Kirk had seen the day before on the table. "Look at them," he ordered. "Look at them!"

He pressed Kirk again about killing Dawn Hamilton. "You killed that little girl, didn't you," he said. "You're going to the gas chamber, if you don't tell us." Ramsey repeated the words slowly, enunciating each one, "*The gas chamber . . .*"

Gas chamber. This sunk in. *Christ . . .*

All the while, Capel sat in the corner and never spoke.

Ramsey pointed his finger at Kirk and started in again.

Finally, Kirk went off. He grabbed the girl's panties from off the table, shook them in the face of William Ramsey, and screamed back, "I didn't kill that little girl and I don't know who did neither . . . But it wasn't me! You hear me? You listening?" Kirk threw the panties at the detective. "I wouldn't do a thing like that and if you think I would then you're crazier'n hell!" Kirk started crying. He asked to see a lawyer.

Ramsey rose from the table and walked out of the room in disgust. Capel just shrugged and recuffed him.

When they put him in the police car for the drive to Baltimore County, the tip of the sun was just rising over Leggett's Store.

Through the dawn haze it flashed like a roadside flare, stippling the river's far edge with garish flecks. Riding across the old Fishing Pier Bridge, Kirk wondered whether he'd ever see the old bridge again, ever see the river again. He shut his eyes on the highway. He wished it might all be a bad dream. Minutes later he heard the officer in the front passenger seat say, "How can he sleep? How can someone who's done what he has done ever sleep?" Kirk wanted to answer him but he didn't know how.

THEY TOOK HIM to a holding cell at the police station in Towson. It was the first time he'd ever been in a cage. It smelled of stale urine. Other detectives questioned him again about his whereabouts the morning of July 25. They acted friendly and said it would help him if he could remember. One detective handed him a calendar through the bars and encouraged him to work backward with the dates in order to figure out his whereabouts. Kirk tried and told him that he was home, that July 25 was his day off. Kirk asked the detective to talk to his housemates. He was sure they'd confirm this. He repeated that he was nowhere near where that girl was killed.

But Kirk felt he wasn't explaining himself. His words seemed to fall flat. He didn't know what words would serve to make them understand. He was running out of words. He was running out of strength. It was overwhelming. It seemed like some cosmic nightmare. Some surreal hoax. He tried to explain again to another detective that he was home on the 25th but couldn't find the language to sound convincing, even to himself. At one point he just lost it. "I'm an innocent man!" he screamed through the iron bars. "I'm not guilty! Don't you understand? What are you doing to me? Why are you doing this to me?"

Later that morning Ramsey and Capel showed up. Kirk was allowed to make his first telephone call from the station and was able to reach his father. In broken words and between sobs he tried to tell his dad what was happening. Curtis angrily demanded to talk to Detective Ramsey. Ramsey took the phone.

"Sir," Ramsey said, "we're charging your son with the first-degree murder of Dawn Hamilton."

Curtis cleared his throat. "Man," he answered him loudly, "do you know what the hell you are talking about?"

"We think we do," Ramsey said.

"Wait a minute! Don't be talking this fool stuff. Let me get a lawyer and get up there and talk to you—"

"I'm sorry. We've already charged him."

Curtis couldn't believe what he was hearing. "Do you know what the hell you're saying?" he asked again. "You're devastating a whole family here! A young man's life and his mother and sister and myself!"

Kirk could just hear one side of the conversation—Ramsey's side—but he got the gist. Curtis was going on as though it all were a misunderstanding that could be straightened out over the phone. Ramsey was losing patience. The detective handed the phone back to Kirk. Kirk tried to get his father to understand that it was more than that. He'd need a lawyer, he told Curtis. Right away. A good one.

The detectives told Kirk that they were taking him to a hearing. He hadn't yet seen or talked to anyone except his father. They told him there would be press there, and lots of cameras. They asked Kirk if he wanted a blanket to put over his head. Kirk had been up all night. He was half terrified, half crazed. He answered, hell no, he didn't want no blanket. He hadn't done nothing wrong and didn't care if the whole damn world saw him. A big mistake. Ramsey and Capel just shrugged. The detectives should have known better, should have insisted.

Barefoot, still, and wearing his blue shorts and a dirty terry-cloth shirt one of the police officers had given him, Kirk was taken in handcuffs to the courthouse. Reporters jostled one another to get a look. Cameras flashed. Television crews filmed him being taken out of the police car and walking along the corridor. Bystanders stared at him, and Kirk could see the hate in their faces. Someone yelled that he was a child killer; someone else called him a motherfucker; others cursed him. What was happening had begun to sink in.

Inside the courtroom, the clerk announced the case of *The People v. Kirk Bloodsworth*. District Court Judge Gerald Wittstadt told Kirk he was there to set bond and asked Kirk if he had anything to say.

Kirk answered that yes he had plenty to say.

The judge interrupted him. Wittstatd cautioned him that there were tapes running and that they would record every word he said.

"I don't give a damn what you got," Kirk responded, "I didn't kill that little girl and I don't know who did. You got the wrong man. I was at my home. I didn't do it . . ." Saying that in the courtroom, in public, lifted his spirits a notch.

The prosecutor, a smartly dressed woman in heels named Susan Schilling, just twiddled her pen and seemed preoccupied. Finally she rose and said a few words to the judge, something about it being a capital offense. Judge Wittstadt nodded, then denied bond. It was over before it started. Kirk was hustled out, surrounded by police. Appalled, frightened, alone, this time he hung his head. He felt stained, gnawed down, a bone-bare scarecrow of a human. When he glimpsed up, in every look he saw disgust. He saw the look people give a sick-minded monster. Four officers escorted him to a squad car that was waiting for him outside the courthouse. It would deliver him to what would become his new home, the Towson Detention Center.

That night all of the local television stations prominently displayed his face on their news shows. He was shown being taken from the police car and being escorted to the courthouse, shackled, disheveled, and surrounded by uniformed police. For anyone watching, he couldn't have been exhibited in a more suggestive way.

DETECTIVES RAMSEY AND Capel ordered a lineup to be held the following Monday, August 13. With each new piece of information they became more convinced that Bloodsworth was the killer, but they wanted the other adults who'd seen him around Fontana Village the morning of the murder to pick him out. They expected them to clinch the identification.

Kirk Bloodsworth and five other men would stand in the lineup. Two of the men would be police officers, and three of them would be maintenance workers. All would be dressed identically, in prison jumpsuits and barefoot. Four of them were of equal height, close to six feet tall. Most had mustaches. Bloodsworth would be man number six. Only Bloodsworth had hair that matched in style that of the man in the composite sketch.

The men would stand in a row, behind a one-way Plexiglas screen, facing the witness room. The witnesses, brought into the room one at a time, would be able to see the suspects through the glass shield, but the suspects would not be able to see them.

After watching Kirk's picture being taken by so many media cameras outside the courtroom on the day of his arrest, though, Ramsey and Capel realized they might have a problem. If their potential identification witnesses saw Bloodsworth on TV first, handcuffed, under arrest, and surrounded by cops, the reliability of their lineup identifications might be called into question. Before the local news shows aired the evening of Bloodsworth's arrest, Ramsey and Capel arranged for the witnesses they considered key to be contacted by police.

Nancy Hall was one of these. She was in her early thirties and one of the people who'd reported seeing a strange man with a thin build and dark brown curly hair standing outside of Orion Court the morning of the slaying and later sitting on a green electrical box. Hall was a friend of witness Donna Ferguson. It later came out that both were drug users and had smoked marijuana the morning of the crime. Hall was the one who'd told police to arrest Mickey Manzari. She'd said that Manzari looked just like the man depicted in the composite sketch. Hall, it seems, had known Manzari for years. Manzari was cleared. Having identified the wrong man once, though, didn't stop Nancy Hall from taking a second shot.

On the afternoon of Bloodsworth's arrest, a police detective telephoned Nancy Hall and told her he wanted her to attend a lineup the following Monday. He told her that the police had arrested and charged a suspect named Kirk Bloodsworth and asked her not to watch any television news shows over the weekend. He told her that if she did, it might hurt the case. Nancy Hall couldn't help herself. After all, this terrible crime had happened in her own backyard. She watched all the news shows. She repeatedly saw Kirk Bloodsworth. She saw him in handcuffs, surrounded by police, being taken to the courtroom, being led away. The next Monday, she had no trouble identifying man number six in the lineup, Kirk Bloodsworth, as the stranger she'd seen outside Orion Court. Who else would she possibly pick? Nancy Hall became a key prosecution witness at both of Kirk Bloodsworth's trials.

Donna Ferguson, Hall's neighbor, had also seen the stranger on the electric box, and later heard a man calling "Lisa, Lisa" but hadn't seen whether it was the same man. Donna admitted during her trial testimony that the morning of the crime, at around 10 A.M., she'd smoked a half joint of marijuana. A neighbor, Lorraine Trollinger, told defense investigators that Ferguson and Hall often did drugs together and that both had gotten stoned while sunbathing the morning of the crime. The police officer who called

Donna Ferguson to warn her about watching TV never identified himself. He told Donna the same thing told to Nancy Hall. Again, Kirk Bloodsworth was mentioned by name. Donna Ferguson denied she ever saw Bloodsworth on television but admitted the TV was on most of the weekend. She too picked Bloodsworth out of the lineup and would also testify against him at his trials.

Debbie McNamara also had seen a man on July 25 sitting on the green electrical box. She was also telephoned by police, told that Kirk Bloodsworth had been arrested, and asked to attend a lineup to identify him. McNamara saw Bloodsworth on television before the lineup but thought she only saw the back of him as he was being led to a police car. She identified Bloodsworth out of the lineup but later recanted, claiming that she'd confused him with another man who was the spitting image of Bloodsworth. She'd seen this other man driving a Thunderbird with a white vinyl top, and he'd been cruising the area frequently. Debbie McNamara was never called as a prosecution witness.

James Keller, an elderly black man living in Fontana Village, saw Kirk Bloodsworth on television. He mentioned something about it to his wife, and she then called the police. The man on TV was the same man he thought he'd seen at about 5:45 A.M. the morning of the murder. He reported this to Detective Capel for the first time on August 10, the weekend of Kirk's arrest, and sixteen days after the crime. Keller had been driving, on his way to work. He only saw the man for a second as he passed by him. The man was lounging by the fence next to Bethke's Pond and was wearing light-colored shorts. Even though he had seen Bloodsworth on TV, Keller was asked to attend the lineup that following Monday. He picked out Bloodsworth. Keller testified at both trials that Bloodsworth was the man he'd seen the day Dawn was killed.

Chris Shipley and Jackie Poling both attended the lineup. They were driven there with their mothers, all in the same car, by police officers from the Fullerton district. Bloodsworth was not the only man in the lineup whose picture had also been in the photo array. Ramsey had arranged for one other of the men whose photograph had previously been shown to the two boys also to stand in the lineup. They were the only two, though, in both arrays.

When Jackie Poling attended the lineup, he was visibly frightened. Detectives observed that he was actually shaking. When asked if he wanted the men behind the glass wall to do anything, he said he wanted them to leave. The detectives in the room laughed. Poling pointed to number three, someone other than Bloodsworth. Two weeks passed before Denise Poling, Jackie's mother, contacted police and told them that the night of the lineup, after they had gotten home, Jackie had told her he'd picked out the wrong man. He said he'd recognized number six as the man by the pond but was too scared to say it. He was afraid, his mother related, that the man might hear him. Why she waited two weeks to provide this important piece of information was never made clear.

When Chris Shipley viewed the lineup, he did not choose anyone while in the lineup room, but upon exiting the lineup room told detectives that number six, Bloodsworth, was the man by the pond with Dawn Hamilton.

Fay McCoullough, who'd worked with Detective Capel to try and create an accurate composite sketch, went to the lineup and failed to identify Bloodsworth. The strange man she'd seen in Fontana Village the morning of Dawn's slaying was not in the lineup, she told the detectives. Others came and failed to identify Bloodsworth as well. But with the two boys, Shipley and Poling, and the three adults, Hall, Ferguson, and Keller, the detectives felt they'd already built a convincing case.

RAMSEY AND CAPEL had zeroed in. They were the ones with the responsibility for solving this crime. It was no light burden, no cakewalk. The FBI profile made clear that the killer would strike again. The community was frightened and expectant. The two detectives were in a fishbowl, treading water. With leads pointing everywhere they must have been feeling the pressure. Like the prosecutors who succeeded them, like the jurors who judged the two trials, they wanted to believe they had their man. They weren't overly concerned with the suggestive circumstances surrounding many of these identifications. They bypassed the fact that Chris Shipley had not been completely satisfied with the composite sketch he helped create. They weren't unduly troubled over whether his photo identification, qualified as it was by his statement that the hair color was off, might have resulted from his memory of the composite as opposed to a real recollection of the stranger at the pond. And they apparently never worried that Chris Shipley's lineup identification might have come from his having drafted the composite, from having seen Bloodsworth's picture in the photo spread, from having seen the same image too often—errors compounded by errors, reasons why the boy might be mistaken. The detectives yielded, perhaps, to the all-too-human desire to hastily find and punish this child killer.

PART IV

TRIAL AND ERROR

Until the infallibility of
human judgment shall
have been proved to me, I
shall persist in demanding
the abolition of the death
penalty.

—Marquis de Lafayette

THIRTEEN

KIRK WAS TAKEN from his initial hearing before Judge Wittstadt to the county detention center and handed over to the jail guards there. He was made to strip and take a lice bath. They gave him an orange jumpsuit, a throw blanket, a small rough pillow, and a toothbrush. He was escorted upstairs to lockdown in Section 3E and led into a tiny rectangular cage. Three of the walls were beige cinder block, the floor rough concrete. A steel wall surrounding a door completed the enclosure. Part of the door, a hinged, free-swinging hatch, allowed him to receive food and drink. The cell contained one wrought-iron bunk with a green Naugahyde mattress, a stainless steel sink, and a toilet. A small air vent with slats angling down was built high into the far wall. If he stood on tiptoe and looked down, he could see a sliver of baked ground, little else. With his arms outstretched, he could touch both sidewalls of the small room. Many of the inmates in the detention center had free range of the tiers. Because Bloodsworth was charged with a capital murder, he was on lockdown. He would spend twenty-three hours a day in this cell for most of the next eight months.

That first night Kirk started hearing it. The guy in the cell above him started chanting it. It came through the vent right into Kirk's cell. Quiet at first like a rustle, a whisper, then louder. He was going to do to Kirk what he'd done to that little girl. "I'm going to fuck you in the ass with a mop handle," Kirk heard him say, "like you fucked her, you dirty son of a bitch." Other inmates joined in. Soon it was screamed down the tier. "You're all ours now . . . We gonna rape you like you raped her, boy. You're our boy now . . ."

Sometime in the dark, while he lay awake listening to this, someone knocked open his food hatch and squirted a bottle of piss all over his cell floor. He heard a crazy laugh and footsteps running on the tier. He was too scared to move off his cot. Breathing the stench made him want to vomit. The guards must not care, he thought. He lay quiet, curled in the fetal position, trembling, tears streaming down his face. The chants continued. One inmate would stop and another would start. These chants would go on for months. Inmates sprayed his cell with urine night after night.

Curtis came up the next day for a jail visit, accompanied by his brother, Kirk's uncle Billy. Curtis hadn't been able to eat a thing since Kirk had called. Kirk came out into the interview booth in his orange jumpsuit and chains. Curtis moaned, "Oh Jesus Christ," when he saw him. Billy just shook his head. They had to speak through a phone. Curtis looked his boy right in the teeth and asked him straight up. "Son, you didn't have anything to do with this crime now, did you?"

Kirk looked at his father. He began crying over his father even asking it. "Dad," he said, "you know damn well I couldn't do anything like that."

Curtis could see in his face that he was innocent. Billy too. Billy also started bawling right there. Driving home, Curtis cursed the detectives.

The first lawyer Curtis contacted was John Wheeler Glenn of the firm O'Connor, Preston, Glenn and Smith, P.A. Glenn was recommended to Curtis by a real estate buddy who'd told him that Glenn had represented their state senator, Fred Malkus. Glenn's firm had an office in Baltimore and a satellite office in Cambridge. Glenn came to see Kirk and listened to his story, his claim of innocence. Kirk again broke down. Glenn had his hair all slicked down on one side and reminded Kirk of a dime store manikin. "Either you're a good liar or you're an innocent man," Glenn told Kirk. "You're very convincing."

"The reason for that, sir, is that I didn't do what they're saying I done," Kirk replied. "I didn't kill no little girl . . ."

A few days later Glenn called Curtis on the phone. He told him that he was sorry, but the case was just too controversial. He couldn't take it on. His firm sent Curtis a bill for just under $500.

Curtis started calling around trying to find a lawyer who might take his son's case. He even called F. Lee Bailey. Bailey wanted $100,000 before he'd agree to visit Kirk. Meanwhile, Kirk had heard the name of Russell White in the jail several times. White was supposed to be good, a real hot shot, and his office was in Towson. White, everybody said, knew the court and all the local angles. Kirk asked Curtis to contact White.

Russell White was well aware of the case. Initially he wanted $100,000 to represent Kirk. Eventually, he agreed to do it for $75,000. Curtis didn't have that kind of money. On August 16 Curtis borrowed $15,000 from the National Bank of Cambridge, using as collateral the savings he and Jeanette had accumulated over the years and placed in a certificate of deposit. On August 17 Curtis reluctantly forwarded to White a check for $10,500 and asked him to get started. He figured he'd just have to come up with a way to raise the rest. He planned to go back to the bank and take out a larger loan, using the little remaining equity in his house as collateral, but that would take time.

White began his investigation. As part of it he arranged for a polygraph examiner to privately administer a lie detector test to Kirk at the detention center. Polygraph tests are not admissible in evidence. They are based on heart rate, breathing, and perspiration, internal measures of stress. They are error prone. Courts over the years have considered them insufficiently reliable to be introduced into evidence. Still, they can help in plea negotiations and certainly in bolstering a lawyer's confidence in his client. The results were not encouraging. The polygraph examiner concluded that Kirk lied about all the relevant questions concerning Dawn Hamilton.

White told Curtis Bloodsworth that the lie detector test results were "inconclusive." But that wasn't what Curtis had hoped to hear. Kirk's father had already begun sinking down over Kirk's arrest. He was drinking heavily. The polygraph results just torpedoed him. Having his only son accused of such an atrocity had turned his world inside out. Curtis had always believed in authority. He'd been a decorated marine, loyal to his country, and had worked for Tidewater Fisheries, which served as the local marine police. He trusted law enforcement, trusted figures of authority, believed they knew what was best. He was conflicted now. Torn between this system he'd always believed in and the word of his son. And the financial burden itself was just a back breaker. He began closing up, withdrawing; he wouldn't eat; he couldn't bear to see anyone. Only Kirk's mother, Jeanette, never doubted. When she'd first heard of Kirk's arrest she said to Curtis, "I know he didn't do that crime. I don't even have to ask him." On her first visit to see her son at the detention center she said, "This will all be righted." She spoke like that sometimes, like a fortune-teller might talk. "I knew you'd one day get in trouble, and I know it will all be made right," she said. She told Kirk to hold his head high and to never give up.

Russell White came to visit Kirk at the jail and brought with him a retired homicide detective whom he planned to use as an investigator. Kirk spent two hours telling the two of them his story. He was certain by then that he'd been home the entire morning of July 25. When he went out that afternoon, it was with Wayne Palmer to buy some pot.

White seemed genuine, sincere, and picked up on everything. Sharp as a paper cutter, Kirk felt. White told Kirk that he believed him. That he didn't believe he'd done it. He added that he thought there were too many unanswered questions, too much suspicious circumstantial evidence for Kirk even to have been arrested. He promised Kirk that he'd find the answers. "Immediately," he said, "we'll begin our own investigation."

Curtis continued to try to help Kirk through the people he knew, through his connections. He went to see state senator Fred Malkus, and spoke to a trusted friend, Ira T. Tide, who had money and had always let Curtis hunt on his farm. Ira Tide said, "Look, I've heard all about this. Let me make some calls around town and see what I can find out." Early the next morning Tide called Curtis back. Tide said he'd spoken to a Judge Simpkins from Crisfield, who had been close to the previous governor. Ira said that Simpkins recommended Kirk get a public defender. Public defenders were expert in these types of cases and free. "Otherwise you might just be throwing your money away," Tide told him.

Curtis discussed a larger loan with the folks at the bank. While they didn't turn him down outright, they impressed upon him how much money he was talking about. They seemed less friendly. Curtis felt like a pariah in town. White had told Curtis that for the fee, he would also handle Kirk's appeal, if necessary. Curtis worried why White was already talking about an appeal before he'd even been paid for the trial. Curtis decided to trust the advice of Ira Tide and Judge Simpkins. On September 13, when the next installment was due to White, Curtis called him and ended White's representation. Most of the $10,500 had been spent, but White promised to turn over to Kirk's new lawyers his investigative reports. When Curtis told his son of this, Kirk was crushed. White had seemed like a winner. He had given him a boost.

Up in Towson, the Baltimore County seat, Curtis met with the district public defender there, Thomas Saunders. Saunders was patient but professional. Saunders told Curtis that someone in his office would represent Kirk until Saunders could find two able lawyers to take over the appointment, private lawyers with real trial experience. The case was going to draw a lot of heat. Saunders decided to farm it out to Steven Scheinin and Scheinin's younger partner, David Henninger.

Scheinin had been a prosecutor with the state's attorney's office for ten years. He had prosecuted numerous murder trials. Two years before, convinced that his boss, State's Attorney Sandra A. O'Connor, was about to run for higher political office and that his future as a high level assistant in that office might be in jeopardy, Scheinin had resigned and gone into private practice. While he had never defended a death penalty case before, he was an experienced trial lawyer. He had tried dozens of murder cases for the state, and he knew the detectives and the prosecutors well.

Before Scheinin and Henninger entered their appearances in the case, however, Kirk was indicted. The state's prosecutors, Robert Lazzaro and Ann Brobst, had brought the witnesses they wanted into the grand jury room and had them testify before the grand jurors, a place where defense lawyers are not allowed. The grand jury handed down the indictment on September 12. On September 17 Kirk was taken in his orange jumpsuit before Judge John Raine of the Baltimore County Circuit Court for his arraignment. While there in court the prosecutors filed the state's formal notice to seek the death penalty. Kirk had known it was coming but still hadn't been able to prepare himself for the blow. It sent him into freefall.

FOURTEEN

IT IS EASY TO understand why most young lawyers fresh out of law school who aspire to be criminal litigators would want to be prosecutors. They want to be on the side of right and justice, fighting for a safer world. What is curious is why so many gravitate toward defense work. There's something in a person's makeup—perhaps a wild gene—that makes him or her want to champion the underdog, even when the underdog is usually an outlaw.

Public defenders, particularly, are a strange breed. They have a thankless job. They work to try to free criminal defendants who comprise the poor, the destitute, the most desperate, the most violent. The pay is pitiful. Most people in the community scratch their heads and wonder how anybody could represent such people. Often their clients distrust them, at least at first. After all, it's the state that appoints and pays the public defender—the same state that's trying to convict the client. And you get what you pay for; the clients have learned that much: anything free can't be worth a damn.

Public defenders typically last as such for only a few years. The work is just too grim. The daily contact with grinding poverty and wasted lives has a cumulative effect. It takes a strong stomach, an idealistic outlook, and a youthful courage. Most public defenders are young, with idealistic notions that they can help balance the scales of justice, scales that are always tilted, scales that rarely favor the poor.

It was early October when Steven Scheinin accepted his appointment from the Office of the Public Defender in Towson to represent Kirk Bloodsworth. Scheinin, while not a public defender, would serve as an appointed contract lawyer, working under its guidelines. He would be paid $25 an hour for out-of-court work and $200 a day during trial, with an overall $10,000 cap on attorneys' fees. An investigator, Janet Moss, was assigned to assist him. Because Maryland law required that two defense lawyers be appointed in every capital case, his law partner, David Henninger, was selected to assist him. Scheinin had no qualms about the death penalty. But he relished the challenge of the case. He'd be in all the papers and would get a lot of free publicity. If he could win, it might boost his practice. The cash he'd make wouldn't hurt either.

When Scheinin first visited Kirk, Kirk had already been in the jail for over two months. The state had its case neatly arranged. The trial was scheduled to begin in February, only four months away. Scheinin was way behind the eight ball.

The first meeting between lawyer and client, at least from where Kirk sat, did not go that well. Scheinin was shorter than Kirk, portly, wore glasses, and was dressed in a shabby suit that didn't quite fit. His trousers looked too tight and his jacket sleeves too short. He interviewed Kirk in the jail's visiting room. They were separated by a shatterproof glass window and had to talk through a phone. Scheinin introduced himself, telling Kirk that he'd been chosen by the public defender and appointed by the court to represent him. He explained that his partner, David Henninger, would be joining the team. Scheinin was confident that he could handle things. He began to tell Kirk all about the case and what he'd found out. Scheinin went on for half an hour before he ever asked Kirk a question. He seemed impatient as Kirk went over his story. After Kirk finished, Scheinin began telling Kirk how certain he was that they'd find a way out of this mess. Together, he stressed. He put his palm on the glass for Kirk to match. It seemed like an overly dramatic gesture. "I know my way around the criminal justice system," he assured Kirk. "I know my way around the courtroom, and I know my way around this case. I'll find us a way to get out of this." With that Scheinin picked up his briefcase, said good-bye, and turned and walked right into the cinder-block wall behind him, knocking off his glasses.

After the interview Kirk felt sick. He called Curtis and begged him to find the money to bring Russell White back. Curtis told him that he needed to trust the system. That the system was a good one. Kirk's head throbbed. He felt he was drowning.

TRIALS IN OUR justice system are categorized as either civil or criminal. Criminal cases are brought by the governing authority, either federal or state, against individuals and entities for breaking the law. Civil cases are everything else: contract fights, injury claims, malpractice suits, antitrust, and a host of other noncriminal disputes. In civil trials, the participants are entitled to what is called open, or full, discovery. Each side is entitled to learn from the other all the information in its possession that is pertinent to the case. Written interrogatories posed by one side must be answered by the other under oath. Depositions of the parties and the parties' witnesses may be taken. During these depositions, the lawyers can ask relevant questions and receive answers, again under oath. There aren't supposed to be any surprises at a civil trial. It's meant to be a search for truth.

Criminal discovery is different. It's what is termed limited discovery. There is no right to send interrogatories or take depositions.

Each side's access to what the other knows is curtailed. One reason for this is that prosecutors are not able to force the defendant to divulge any information. The Fifth Amendment to the Constitution—the privilege against self-incrimination—protects every defendant. Since the defendant doesn't have to tell what he knows, the prosecuting authority need not reveal all it knows. The ironic result is that where freedom as opposed to money is on the line, where a person's very life may be on the line, the parties must face a trial without knowing all the facts, without knowing who all the witnesses may be or what they might say, with potential surprises around every curve.

Whereas civil trials usually are fought between parties of equal resources, such is typically not the case in criminal court. The state has an abundance of prosecutors, detectives, police officers, lab technicians, scientists, and money to throw at a case if it chooses to do so. The typical criminal defendant, like Kirk Bloodsworth, can barely scrape together bus fare, and the budgets of public defender offices are usually meager.

Under the limited discovery rule, prosecutors, while not re-quired to divulge the substance of the testimony expected from the witnesses they intend to call, are required to disclose the identities of their eyewitnesses and any identification procedures used. They must produce for the defense any physical evidence they intend to introduce at trial. Statements made by the accused must be turned over. Significantly, prosecutors must also share with the defense any exculpatory evidence that they come across—evidence that might exonerate the defendant, might show that he is not guilty. This rule stems from a 1963 United States Supreme Court case called *Brady v. Maryland*.

The defense has its obligations as well. Alibi witnesses and character witnesses must be disclosed well in advance of trial. And each side must disclose to the other the identity of any expert witnesses it intends to call.

Discovery in a criminal case is conducted through lawyer meetings, letters, and motions. Between November, when he first entered his appearance in the case, and March, when the trial began, Steven Scheinin, with David Henninger's assistance, engaged in an intensive campaign to learn everything he could through the discovery process. He filed motion after motion trying to push for more information, trying to reap some benefit.

Scheinin filed a motion for the production of witness statements and police notes (it was denied), a motion for production of photographic copies of the scene (denied), a motion to suppress the witness identifications as stemming from unnecessarily suggestive procedures (denied), a motion to strike the state's election to seek the death penalty (denied), a motion for additional jury strikes (denied), a motion for early production of the grand jury testimony of witnesses (denied). There were many others. The court did grant a motion requiring the state to produce written statements pertaining to its identification witnesses and also granted a motion requiring the state to preserve all police notes. The court was required to conduct a hearing on the identification procedures used, and the state was required to call its identification witnesses to testify at that hearing. This gave Scheinin the opportunity to see them on the stand and ask them questions. It was clear, though, that the state's witnesses were locked into believing that Bloodsworth was the man.

Kirk's misgivings about his lawyer notwithstanding, Scheinin made a real effort to try to save his client. Kirk had told Scheinin where he was the day of the murder and that his housemates would testify as alibi witnesses. Scheinin and Henninger interviewed them all. They were hardly a tribe of churchgoers, and their recollections were not consistent. Kirk's lawyers had to wonder how they'd come across before a jury. Scheinin believed they were telling the truth, however, and they were all Kirk had.

Wanda Bloodsworth had worked her mind back to July 25 and remembered that she'd had an appointment that day at the Eastern Community Mental Health Center. She was supposed to go for alcohol treatment related to her driving conviction. She and her half sister, Dawn, had also gone by the welfare office to get some money. They needed their welfare checks to keep food on the table. Wanda's mother, Birdie, had come over to the house to wake her up. This was around nine that morning, and Kirk was still asleep. Wanda said the cat jumped up on Kirk and peed on him. This caused Kirk to try to get into the bathroom to clean himself off. Dawn Gerald was taking a shower, and Kirk was frustrated he couldn't get in the bathroom. Wanda and Dawn Gerald didn't leave the house until ten fifteen or ten thirty, and Kirk was still there.

Dawn Gerald also remembered the counseling appointment and going by the welfare office that day. Her recollection was slightly different than Wanda's, as she remembered that they both left around nine. Kirk was still in the house.

Birdie Plutschak, Wanda's mother, remembered going over to Wanda's at a little after eight on July 25. She went to wake her kids because she knew Wanda had a doctor's appointment. She did this often, apparently. She recalled the cat wetting the sheet covering Kirk while he was sleeping and Kirk's getting upset. Birdie stayed at the Randolph Road row house until almost noon. According to Birdie, Kirk was there the entire time. The reason Birdie left the house was to have lunch with her husband, Jerry. After lunch she came back to the house sometime around one thirty. Kirk was out but came back a little while later with Wayne Palmer. They'd been out buying pot.

Tammy Albin also remembered the day because it was the morning her kitten had peed on Kirk. She was asleep at the time but got an earful about it later. She got up around ten thirty, and according to her, Birdie, Wanda, and Dawn were all still there. Kirk was home and stayed in the house until one thirty, she recalled.

Joey Martin remembered waking around ten and seeing Kirk in the house. Kirk stayed inside and didn't leave until after one.

Wayne Palmer was marginally helpful. He had initially given a statement to the police that Kirk wasn't with him the day of the murder. Later, he realized that he'd mixed up two different afternoons. He'd cashed his last paycheck from the pool company on the afternoon of July 25. Kirk had been with him then. Palmer remembered that just afterward the wires in his car caught fire and Kirk helped him put them out. Kirk was with him for a couple of hours from about one to three. Kirk had run out of pot, and they'd gone looking for a guy who sold it. Palmer had contacted the police department and told them of the mistake he'd made in his statement, but no one had ever come out to take a corrected report.

With the help of the investigation performed at the behest of Kirk's prior lawyer, Scheinin tracked down Jeffery Wright. Wright recalled that on July 25 he'd gone with his brother to the South Randolph Road row house to try and sell a rifle. They arrived there in the early afternoon, and Kirk was home. A guy named Wayne was there. Wright also wanted to buy some pot and asked Kirk if he knew where he could get some. Since no one at the Randolph Road address wanted to buy the rifle, Wright had gone to a neighborhood sporting goods store and sold the rifle there. Then he returned, and with the money he made he, Wayne, and Kirk, had gone out and bought the pot. All this happened between about one and two o'clock.

Like Wayne Palmer, all of these alibi witnesses had been interviewed by homicide detectives before Scheinin became involved. Their recollections were already recorded, pinned down. And none had even started trying to remember their respective whereabouts on the day of the crime until August 9, when Kirk was arrested, over two weeks after the murder occurred.

CHARACTER TESTIMONY IS usually not permitted in trials. A criminal defendant, however, is the rare litigant in our justice system who has the right to bring in witnesses to testify to his character—his reputation in the community for traits that would be inconsistent with those of the person who committed the crime. Character testimony can be a powerful defensive weapon. When the famous trial lawyers Edward Bennett Williams and Michael Tigar defended Governor John Connally of Texas in Washington, D.C., they brought in the Reverend Billy Graham to testify as a character witness on behalf of Connally. Asked to introduce himself, Graham, with his hand still on the Bible, said something along the lines of "My name is the Reverend Billy Graham and I preach the Gospel of Jesus Christ from one end of Christendom to the other." When an elderly black woman juror in the front row heard this, she apparently couldn't help herself. She let slip a loud "Amen." Williams and Tigar knew then and there that they had won the case.

Calling a character witness can be extremely dangerous, though. Once a character witness testifies, the prosecutor is free to question that witness about all the dirt that's been dug up on the defendant. This is only fair, to test the knowledge of the witness. The testimony of a character witness opens the door, so to speak. A prosecutor can sometimes ram a cartload of prejudice through that open door.

Bloodsworth was the rare criminal defendant without even an arrest record and without any history of bad acts. Scheinin set about finding character witnesses on behalf of his client—people who might be impressive to a jury. Kirk didn't know anyone with the status of Billy Graham, but Scheinin developed a large list, then pared it down to include Richard Drescher, Kirk's discus coach; Milton Hubbard and Frank Krewen, both of whom had coached and taught Kirk at Cambridge High School; and Frances Bloodsworth, Kirk's aunt. Frances had taught at the Open Bible Academy.

SCHEININ ALSO PURSUED the forensic evidence taken from the crime scene. That's the place where he hoped he'd find proof that would absolutely exclude Kirk as the killer. Items taken from the crime scene or developed during the autopsy for possible testing, all of which potentially could reveal the identity of the killer, included the following:

One pair of child's panties, and one pair of child's shorts
One piece of concrete
One Big Red gum wrapper
Soil samples
One foreign human hair and one red fiber
The stick
Vaginal, rectal, and oral swabs from the victim
Smears from the swabs preserved on glass slides and frozen
Washings from the victim's vagina
Scrapings from the victim's hands
Photos of shoe prints taken from the victim's body
One vial of the victim's blood
Other assorted clothes from the victim
The white sheet the victim was wrapped in when taken to the
    morgue

The medical examiner at autopsy, looking for evidence that might lead to the assailant's blood type, had used cotton swabs to retrieve fluid samples from the victim's mouth, vagina, and rectum, and then by brushing these swabs over glass slides and staining the samples with a preservative, he created smears for microscopic

examination. Under the microscope, he'd visualized some spermatozoa on the vaginal smears and many sperm on the rectal smears.
He'd also obtained a vaginal wash. The swabs, along with the contents of the vaginal wash, were turned over by the medical examiner to Detective Ramsey on July 26 to be transported to the FBI lab
for testing. Along with these items, Ramsey took all of the physical
evidence listed above to the FBI for analysis. The smears on the
glass slides were retained and frozen by the coroner.

When Bloodsworth was arrested, detectives searched all of the
various places he'd stayed. Rose Carson's house was ransacked.
Cindy Bloodsworth's and Tommy Tyler's homes were searched.
Dawn Gerald's place on South Randolph Road was torn apart. All
of the clothes the police believed might be Bloodsworth's, including shirts, socks, tank tops, jeans, and a pair of beige shorts with
red trim, were seized. All of these were submitted to the FBI for
testing.

Fiber analyses were performed. No textile fiber matches were
found linking Bloodsworth to the crime. The FBI was unable to lift
any fingerprints from Dawn Hamilton's clothes. The Big Red gum
wrapper was also tested for prints, as were the stick and the piece of
concrete, but no fingerprints were developed from them. The blood
on Dawn's clothes and in the soil sample was hers. The spot of "possible blood" on the rock was indeed blood but in too small a quantity to be tested.

Several pairs of tennis shoes were also seized by the police and
delivered to the FBI lab. The shoes were all tested for soil samples.
None matched the soil samples taken from the scene. The shoe
prints from the various tennis shoes were compared with the marks
on Dawn Hamilton's body. No conclusive match was found. One
pair of tennis shoes, taken from Dawn Gerald's house, had soles,
according to the FBI, with "limited design similarities" to the
bruises found on the victim. Detective Ramsey told Steve Scheinin

that the shoes were size 10½. Bloodsworth wore size 10½. Scheinin never saw the shoes until the middle of trial. When he did, he saw that the shoes were marked size 8. Ramsey claimed at trial that he'd measured the outside of the shoes with a ruler and that they were 10½ inches from front to back. That's when Scheinin first believed Ramsey had purposely misled him.

Bloodsworth eagerly volunteered to give up a head hair sample and a pubic hair. Anything to clear him. Hair samples from Thomas Hamilton and the rest of those living with Dawn Hamilton on the day of the murder were also submitted. A hair sample from Detective Bacon was submitted, since he found the body and had leaned over it to check for a pulse. The one hair sample found on the scene did not match that of Kirk Bloodsworth. The other hair samples taken and submitted to the FBI, for some unexplainable reason, were never tested for comparison.

From early on, Scheinin had pressed the prosecutor's office to provide him access to the assailant's fluid samples and the physical evidence so that he could have it all examined and tested by his own serologist for a possible blood type—one that might eliminate his client as the perpetrator. He had received misleading reports about where the fluid samples and physical evidence were located. Initially, he was told it was all at the police department. He went there and then was told it was in transit to the FBI. On November 27, 1984, he wrote to the prosecutor requesting that he and his expert be provided access to all of the fluid samples and that he be permitted to view all of the physical evidence. Shortly thereafter, Scheinin received the FBI written report. According to the FBI, no semen was identified on any of Dawn's clothes, including her panties. And despite the fact that the autopsy report indicated that the coroner had seen many spermatozoa on the rectal smear, and occasional sperm on the vaginal smear, no sperm were reported seen by the FBI on the cotton swabs or in the vaginal wash. What had happened to this vitally important forensic evidence—evidence from which a blood type analysis might have been performed—a test that might conceivably have cleared Bloodsworth? Had it been mishandled and destroyed? Scheinin never got an answer. In January 1985 Scheinin sent the FBI report, along with the autopsy report, to his retained expert for review and comment. Scheinin continued to press the prosecutor for information concerning an anal washing supposedly taken from the victim's body during the autopsy procedure. Since the swabs inexplicably turned up negative for sperm, he hoped to use sperm from the anal washing to develop a blood type for the murderer. Washings consist of fluid introduced into the victim's body cavities, then retrieved in a glass tube. Scheinin had first been told that this specimen was with the FBI. Then he was told the sample had been lost or destroyed. Then, on February 11, 1985, Scheinin received a letter from the prosecutor informing him that no anal washings were ever taken from the victim. The letter explained that the only sperm found in sufficient quantity to test was in the anal cavity, but that because of bacterial contamination, such samples were typically never kept by the medical examiner and would be of no use anyway. This absence of fluid evidence was a major setback. Accepting the FBI's conclusions, Scheinin never had his own expert examine the victim's clothing or the smears and swabs. The handling of the physical evidence from the crime scene was, in retrospect, grossly inept. Still, none of it, not one shred, linked Bloodsworth to the crime.

Appreciating what a critically important role the eyewitness identification testimony would play, Scheinin lobbied the public defender's office to approve his hiring a psychologist, an expert in the field of memory, perception, and recollection. The request was approved. Scheinin sought out and hired Robert Buckout from the Brooklyn College of New York. Buckout was the director of the Center for Responsive Psychology at Brooklyn College and had

coauthored books on witness psychology. He had also written frequently on the subject of eyewitness identification, suggestivity, and
the potential fallacies inherent in lineup, photo array, and in-court
identifications. Buckout was sent police reports, copies of the photo
spread, the lineup, the composite sketch, and a description of the
two boys and their respective identifications. Buckout conducted
an analysis and was prepared to offer his expert opinions concerning the unreliability of the eyewitness identifications.

Having learned of Scheinin's intention to use Buckout, the prosecutors filed a motion asking the court to exclude his testimony. His
opinions were not part of mainstream science, the prosecutors
argued, and they would unfairly invade the province of the jury.
Judge William Hinkel, who would preside over the case, reserved
ruling. He would decide the issue only at the time Buckout was
about to be called as a witness. The lawyers were skirmishing, battling over what evidence the jury would be permitted to consider.
Kirk Bloodworth, unaware of the nuances of lawyering, sat locked
up in an eight-by-ten-foot cell, trying to keep from slipping on his
urine-wet floor, mired in a Kafkaesque nightmare and praying for
his life.

IN THE MONTHS leading up to the trial, Kirk learned to
cope—as much as a man can— with life in the detention center.
One of the supervising guards was named Flaherty. He had tattoos
up one arm, and Kirk learned he was a former marine. Kirk said
"Semper fi" to him one day, and from then on Flaherty cut Kirk
some slack. They chatted sometimes about life in the marines.
Flaherty even relocated some of the prisoners who were constantly
threatening or harassing Kirk. He gave Kirk hall duty—running er-
rands, delivering messages—that gave him a break from the sick-
ening claustrophobia of his cell. Flaherty kept a close eye on him,
though. He knew Kirk was a big target.

Curtis would come every week to visit and drop off money for commissary. And Kirk's mother came occasionally. Wanda and Birdie came a few times to visit but not often. Kirk's cousins and some friends from Cambridge came to bolster him, but Kirk was embarrassed. He hated for people to see him there.

Scheinin and Henninger had met with him almost weekly since their representation started. They came less often after the new year. Kirk had trouble reaching them on the phone. He had to trust them, he kept telling himself. They were all he had.

When he visited in February, Scheinin was concerned about the tennis shoe the police had found at Dawn Gerald's—overly concerned, Kirk thought. The shoe belonged to one of her half brothers. It wasn't even his. He told his lawyer this. Scheinin, relying on what Capel had told him, still thought the shoe was Kirk's. To Kirk, Scheinin seemed preoccupied with this shoe business.

At his last visit just before the trial started, Scheinin brought his female investigator with him. They went over the trial strategy. Scheinin planned an aggressive cross-examination of the state's ID witnesses. He hoped to drive home the lack of hard, scientific evidence. He planned to call the alibi witnesses, the character witnesses, and his identification expert, then finish with Kirk telling his story.

They went over the questions he intended to ask Kirk. He told Kirk not to look the witnesses or the jurors in the eye during the trial. Best to avoid eye contact, he suggested, at least until Kirk took the stand to testify. He didn't want any of them thinking Kirk was trying to intimidate them. He instructed Kirk to avoid getting emotional. Toward the end of the meeting, he began pressing Kirk to tell him more of the truth. "Are you telling me everything?" Scheinin said. "It's of vital importance that you've told me the whole story. That you haven't left anything out."

Kirk took this the wrong way. He lost it, flipped out, started shouting at his lawyer, called him a fucking idiot. "All this damn time, and now the day before we're going to court, and here you're telling me you don't believe me?" He was mystified, upset, and becoming only more lost in this crazy maze that seemed to offer no way out.

FIFTEEN

THE POLICE INVESTIGATE the crime, narrow the suspects, gather the evidence, and arrest the assailant. Typically, in a capital case their work and conclusions are reviewed by the prosecuting authority, in this case the Office of the State's Attorney for Baltimore County. The prosecutors then take over, interviewing witnesses, preparing the evidence for trial, planning the strategies necessary to win before a jury. Sandra A. O'Connor—not to be confused with Sandra Day O'Connor, the Supreme Court justice—was the state's attorney for Baltimore County. A Republican, O'Connor was first elected to the position in 1974. Prior to that, she'd worked as a prosecutor in Baltimore City for eight years. O'Connor's policy was to seek the death penalty in every first-degree homicide case that qualified under state law. She'd make an exception only when the victim's family opposed it or when the only evidence of guilt was the testimony of a co-defendant. Prosecutors in other jurisdictions in Maryland took a different view. In neighboring Balitmore City, for instance, the lead prosecutor used more discretion. The death penalty there was rarely invoked. O'Connor preferred the consistency resulting from her approach. She removed any randomness from the decision process.

No one could accuse her of racially biased prosecutions where the death penalty was concerned. Every defendant meeting the criteria faced a death sentence. She was a tough prosecutor.

O'Connor had assigned one of her most capable trial assistants to convict Bloodsworth, Robert Lazzaro, and Lazzaro had hand-picked his trial assistant, Ann Brobst. Lazzaro was impressive, a man with a presence in the courtroom. He had graduated first in his class in the evening division of Baltimore University Law School and had been hired by O'Connor, rising quickly in the ranks and earning the reputation of a superb trial lawyer. He'd already tried two death penalty cases and not only won them both but obtained death sentences in both. He was two for two.

He'd also had some experience with FBI profiles. Lazzaro had attended a seminar at the FBI training center at Quantico conducted by two experienced profilers, who taught by going over past cases in which skillful profiles had led to the solving of some horrendous crimes. Lazzaro had been very impressed. He'd become a believer in psychological profiles.

Tall, handsome, dark haired, and sporting a trim mustache, Lazzaro seemed to own the courtroom. His suits were dark, conservative, and impeccably tailored. His shirts were starched, his shoes shined. He was always dressed to the nines, in glaring contrast to Scheinin. Lazzaro's delivery was always articulate, self-assured, smooth as ice. He was likable, the classic icon of authority. The jury took to him immediately.

Brobst, the junior of the two, was a short, thin woman, blond, stern, and formal, with blue eyes that to Kirk were cast-iron cold. She wore stiff dress suits to court. She was all business. Throughout the trial and often during recess, she bore her eyes into Kirk with a ferocity that shook him. She'd stare at him with malice in her eyes, like he was some beast, like she wanted to burn a hole right through him, until he had to look away.

Sandra O'Connor had sent a strong team. She did not like to lose. Her office had no intention of losing this one.

The trial of the case was assigned to veteran Judge William Hinkel of the Baltimore County Circuit Court. Judge Hinkel was a tall and imposing man. Standing at six feet two inches and weighing two hundred pounds, in his dark robes he reminded Kirk of an imperious and frightening version of Ichabod Crane. His head was mostly bald, and he wore a well-trimmed Van Dyke beard. Hinkel was known as a trial machine. He moved things fast and rarely recessed. Only reluctantly would he take a bathroom break. It quickly became evident that he was tough as an old farmer. Kirk had heard he was hard on criminal defendants, and Hinkel did nothing to dispel this notion. The way Kirk saw it, he ruled consistently for the state. Often during the trial, he'd put his hands behind his head and turn his chair away from the proceedings toward the wall, as though he'd already heard enough, as though he'd already made up his mind.

On February 25, 1985, Kirk was brought from the county detention center to the county courthouse to begin a trial that might lead to his execution. He was scared and felt totally outgunned. He tried to think of God, of his mother and her faith. He was caught in a strong tide, he knew, and could only pray that the truth would be seen, that the jurors would discern who he really was, that the system would work for him.

Baltimore County's courthouse is an imposing rectangular structure built from blocks of gray granite. Out front, a large circular fountain shoots up a constant spray of water. Speckled cobblestones surround the fountain. To the side of the building, a large stone memorial honors members of the Baltimore County Police Department killed in action. Shackled with handcuffs, leg irons, and a waist chain, Kirk was brought in through a private entrance on the side opposite the memorial, prodded along by the sheriffs who guarded him. Once inside, he was led through a tunnel to a bull pen in the back of the sheriff's department. There he changed into a set of street clothes his father had brought for him. When Judge Hinkel was ready for him, he was escorted upstairs to the holding cell behind Hinkel's courtroom.

Each time Kirk was brought into that courtroom over the next two weeks, he felt disoriented. He felt he was coming in through the wrong door. The courtroom, like the building around it, was rectangular. The walls were wooden, with rows of wooden benches for spectators. They were filled every day. On the floor, a cranberry-colored carpet ran the length of the room back to a set of double oak doors. The jury box was off to the side of the witness chair. The judge's bench was polished teak and elevated above everything else. Behind the judge's bench, hanging on the wall in large display, was the circular Great Seal of Maryland.

On February 25, the first day of trial, Judge Hinkel disposed of most of the pretrial motions. There was no jury. The lawyers kept arguing. Kirk had no idea what was happening. Hinkel finally adjourned, having scheduled voir dire—jury selection—to begin on March 1. Kirk was led back into the holding cell. He felt left out, in the dark, bewildered by most of what was happening.

IN MARYLAND, WHEN the state is seeking the death penalty, it is entitled to what is known as a death-qualified jury. During the jury selection process, in addition to being asked the standard questions—whether they know about the crime, know any of the participants, have worked as police officers, have ever been arrested—prospective jurors are asked whether any hold strong opinions about the death penalty. Jurors who respond that they don't believe in the death penalty or would not impose it are stricken. Only those willing to impose the death penalty, if justified by the facts, are left on the prospective panel.

Defense lawyers have contended that those who are opposed to the death penalty are also those who are most likely to have an open mind, to accept the presumption of innocence, to give a criminal defendant a fair shake, to actually apply the reasonable doubt standard. Removing such people from a prospective panel unfairly favors a hangman's jury, they've argued. The courts have disagreed.

Regarding jury selection, Scheinin had filed a motion asking for individual voir dire of each juror on all questions. He also had filed a motion asking for additional peremptory challenges or strikes. Under the law, he had no absolute right to either. Judge Hinkel had the discretion to grant these requests, but he denied both motions. Many of the prospective panel members had heard about the crime, but it took Judge Hinkel little time to cull out those who'd already formed opinions. Once that was done, Hinkel was quick to select a death-qualified jury of eight women and four men. He went through the entire voir dire and picked a jury before the luncheon recess. Opening statements were scheduled to begin that afternoon.

Curtis had visited his son the night before. He promised Kirk that he would be there every day. He was in a panic mode now for his boy. He believed in his innocence, he told him. He wouldn't give up on him. Not ever. Father and son sat, separated by the Plexiglass screen, unable to touch, and wept together.

Following the lunch recess, when he was led into the courtroom, Kirk couldn't believe the crowd. There was standing room only. Sheriffs, reporters, sketch artists, the family and friends of the victim, and people from Fontana Village had all packed their way in. Kirk craned his neck to find his parents and saw them in the back. Jeanette seemed small and frail. She waved meekly and Curtis nodded. Kirk saw two of his cousins. There weren't any other friendly faces.

After some brief remarks to the jury, Judge Hinkel called for opening statements. Bob Lazzaro slowly rose and then paused. He knew how to create a dramatic effect. He first thanked the jurors for their service and then he began. His opening told a story: the story of what happened at Fontana Village on July 25. He spoke of Dawn Hamilton, who she was, how she'd gone missing, and the frantic efforts of Elinor Helmick to find her. He described how Chris Shipley and Jackie Poling had been fishing and caught a turtle, and how they'd waved over a stranger to proudly show him what they'd caught. Lazzaro described how the two boys had spoken to the stranger at length and seen him clearly before he took Dawn into the woods. He somberly told of the police search and of their gruesome discovery: the death and mutilation of this little girl. Lazzaro went through the identification procedures and stressed how certain these boys were that Bloodsworth was the man they'd seen. He mentioned the state's other identification witnesses. He hinted at Bloodsworth's bizarre behavior following July 25, how he'd feigned an illness and abruptly fled the area. He softly recounted the incriminating statements Bloodsworth made in Cambridge. Lazzaro deftly handled the circumstantial nature of the evidence. Trial evidence was like a puzzle, he said. The jury would have to put the pieces together. The picture, once complete, would convincingly show that Kirk Bloodsworth was Dawn Hamilton's killer.

The prosecutors were trained in the art of conjuring up images for the jury. Bob Lazzaro understood the importance of detail—of selecting the right word, of gesture, intonation, understatement, a pause—and how these can weave an indelible tapestry in the mind's eye. His opening statement bespoke authority. He was natural, sincere, his manner genuine. The facts were terrible but fascinating. He held the jury in his sway.

Steven Scheinin tried a contrasting approach. His opening was short and abrupt. His spoke in a loud nasally voice. He ranted about how dozens of police had haphazardly trampled through the woods that day destroying evidence, polluting the crime scene. The physical evidence would clear Bloodsworth, he told the jury, and mentioned the single head hair and a fingerprint. The print, the jury would later learn, had been found on an old church flyer, yellowed with age, which had been picked up off of one of the dirt trails a long way from where Dawn's body had been discovered. Scheinin never mentioned the alibi witnesses or where Kirk was during the crime. He never explained why Kirk knew the rock was the murder weapon, why Kirk had left the Baltimore area abruptly, or what he'd meant by his statement to Rose Carson that he'd done a bad thing. He never mentioned that Kirk would testify and deny the crime. To Kirk, Scheinin looked unprepared and overmatched. His opening statement resembled a carnie act. Watching his lawyer, Kirk was scared to death. He sat there feeling the suspicion already emanating from the judge, from the jury. He was terrified that the die was already cast.

A trial is a game. A contest. A re-creation that may or may not bear any semblance to what it purports to mimic. The lawyer's job is to win this contest. To convince the jury of what the lawyer advocates. Good lawyers can make a difference in a case, irrespective of the truth. Lazzaro and Brobst knew their job well. The next day they began by calling Elinor Helmick to the stand, who quietly replayed for the jury how on July 25, 1984, she'd gone searching for Dawn and then called the police for help. Elinor was followed by Thomas Hamilton, who in a grieving voice related how he'd found his little daughter's shorts and underpants in a tree. The story the jury had already heard from Lazzaro began to unfold.

Detective James Roeder was called to identify and describe the items taken from the crime scene. Dawn's clothes, the stick, and the rock were all entered into evidence. Through him the prosecutors also sought to introduce color photographs of the scene and more importantly, of Dawn Hamilton's body. Scheinin objected. He'd previously filed a motion seeking to exclude these pictures. They were too prejudicial, he argued. Would evoke too much of an emotional response from the jurors. They weren't necessary to the state's proof. The prosecution countered that they were the best available evidence proving the location and state of the body, the nature of the wounds, the amount of blood, the various aspects of the crime scene. Judge Hinkel had to weigh whether the probative value of the photographs was outweighed by their prejudicial impact. He ruled that the pictures could come in. They were introduced—handed one by one to the jury to study and circulate. Color photographs of the little girl with her head bashed in, blood covering her face and eye. Close-ups. Her body, half nude, on the ground. Photographs of the killer's footprints on her neck. Photographs of the broken tree branch stuck up her vagina. The jurors were horrified. Kirk could see some of them physically recoil, could feel their visceral revulsion.

Lazzaro called the medical examiner, Dr. Dennis Smyth, to testify as to the cause of death. Smyth explained how Dawn Hamilton had died from a combination of strangulation and blunt trauma to her brain. He also described how at autopsy he'd used an instrument similar to a Q-Tip to take swabs from the mouth, rectum, and vaginal cavity of the victim; smeared a small portion of the fluid from these cotton swabs on glass slides; and stained them for preservation. Smyth had visualized some sperm on the vaginal smears and a larger amount of sperm on the rectal smears. Thinking that the semen might yield a blood type, he'd given the original cotton swabs, containing the bulk of the fluid samples, to Detective Ramsey to take to the FBI lab for testing.

Detective Ramsey followed Dr. Smyth on the stand. He first related for the jury his experience as a crime fighter: five years with the Baltimore City Police Department, followed by ten years with Baltimore County, four of those as a homicide detective. Ramsey then described the crime scene, the location and state of the body, and how he and his detectives had canvassed the area for clues. Ramsey explained how he had attended the autopsy and then transported the crime scene evidence—Dawn's clothes, the cotton swabs, the rock, the gum wrapper, the stick, and the sheet Dawn's body was wrapped in—to the FBI laboratory for testing. He told the jury that in October he'd picked up the vaginal washing from the medical examiner and taken it to the FBI as well. He volunteered that a piece of yellowed paper, an old flyer from the Calvary Baptist Church, had been picked up by Thomas Hamilton on one of the trails in the woods. Scheinin got him to acknowledge that it contained a fingerprint that wasn't Bloodsworth's. So what? Ramsey testified he'd suspected that the pair of tennis shoes recovered from Dawn Gerald's Randolph Road row house were Bloodsworth's and that he'd measured them with a ruler to be 10½ inches from toe to heel, similar to the size Bloodsworth wore. This testimony surprised Sheinin. Apparently, it surprised Lazzaro and Brobst as well. All the lawyers had assumed the shoes were actually size 10½. Sheinin, having finally seen the shoes in the courtroom, and realizing that they were in fact size 8, later recalled Ramsey and examined him relentlessly on this deception.

Lazzaro next called William Heilman of the FBI and asked him about the shoe print. Heilman claimed to have expertise as a shoe print examiner, though he had never before been qualified in a court of law as an expert in this field. He had attended a seminar on the subject, he testified, and read several books on shoe print comparisons. Scheinin objected to his testimony and argued that he was not sufficiently qualified to give opinions as an expert. Judge Hinkel overruled the objection and allowed him to testify.

Heilman told the jury that he had compared the herringbone marks on Dawn Hamilton's neck with the soles of the sneakers taken from Dawn Gerald's house. He'd even prepared a blowup chart for the jury with side-by-side photographs of the neck marks and the shoe print. He opined that while there wasn't enough of a body mark to compare it with an entire shoe sole, the portions of the body mark that were visible did correspond with portions of the shoe soles. On cross-examination, he couldn't say whether the body markings were from a right shoe or left shoe. He couldn't even say whether the impressions on the body were made by the shoes in question. He agreed with Scheinin that hundreds of thousands of the type of tennis shoe seized from Dawn Gerald's house were sold every year. The gist of his testimony was that he couldn't conclusively link the marks to the shoe. He could only say that the marks *might have* been made by the shoe.

A fingerprint expert from the FBI testified that he'd tried both the chemical ninhydrin and a laser technique in an effort to lift prints from the stick, the gum wrapper, and the rock. He'd been unsuccessful.

Jack Quill, an FBI fiber analyst, testified that the one head hair retrieved from the scene was intertwined with the red fiber. The fiber was probably from a carpet. Could the head hair have gotten to the scene because Dawn Hamilton had been playing on a carpet and picked up the loose hair before she'd gone outside, the prosecutor suggested? Quill thought it was a reasonable theory. He'd never been asked to compare the hair with those of the victim or anyone other than Bloodsworth. While it wasn't the defendant's hair, it could have been anyone's.

William B. McInnis was called as the FBI serology expert. McInnis had obtained a Bachelor of Science degree in zoology from Louisiana Tech University, undergone fifteen hours of postgraduate training in forensic science, spent a year as a crime scene trainee, and had several years' experience as a crime scene analyst. He'd previously qualified as an expert in court over a hundred times. McInnis testified he had examined both Dawn Hamilton's shorts and underpants and had made black markings on the panties. He testified that he'd not been able to identify any semen on either piece of clothing. The cotton swabs had no identifiable semen on them either. He found some traces of blood on the rock but of an insufficient quantity to test.

With each of these witnesses, Scheinin made his points on cross-examination. He got Jack Quill to reiterate that the one human hair recovered could have been from the killer and definitely was not Bloodsworth's. He had Ramsey acknowledge that none of the physical evidence linked the defendant to the crime. He asked McInnis why there was no semen on the FBI swabs when sperm had been found on the smears taken from those same swabs by the medical examiner, Dr. Smyth. He got McInnis to admit that semen, if found, might have yielded a blood type that potentially could exclude a suspect. Where were the sperm cells? Where was the scientific evidence, which might have revealed the killer's blood type and exonerated his client? But after seeing the bloody photos of Dawn Hamilton, was the jury even listening?

Lazzaro and Brobst then began with their identification witnesses. Nancy Hall was first. She told the jury that the man seated at the defense table was the same man she'd seen on Orion Court outside her Fontana Village apartment the morning Dawn was killed. Hall said she'd seen the man twice in the area in the week before the crime. Scheinin made some headway with her. He had her explain how she'd believed that the composite resembled her friend Mickey Manzari and that she'd even told police where to find Manzari to arrest him. But Scheinin never brought out that Hall had seen Kirk on television before going to the lineup.

James Keller was called next. A small, gentle black man, he took his time walking from the double oak doors to the witness stand. He couldn't hear too well and put his hand to his ear. Keller told of seeing a stranger on the way to work the day of the crime. He recalled for the jury going to a lineup and picking Bloodsworth out.

He identified Bloodsworth in court as the man he saw. He maintained that he was certain of his identification. Scheinin never brought out how Keller came to the attention of the police, that the first time he claimed to have recognized Kirk and contacted them was the weekend of Kirk's arrest, over two weeks after the crime. And Scheinin never questioned Keller as to whether he'd seen Bloodsworth on television before attending the lineup.

Chris Shipley took the stand. It was clear that he was frightened, that he didn't want to be there. Lazzaro asked him what the stranger by the pond looked like. "Curly hair, a bushy mustache, and muscular," he said. Lazzaro walked him through the creation of the composite, his photo ID, the lineup. And when asked if he saw the man standing by the pond on that terrible day anywhere in the courtroom, Chris didn't hesitate. He raised his arm and pointed to Kirk Bloodsworth. Scheinin couldn't go too hard with Chris or it might look like he was bullying a child. But he might have done more. He asked Shipley how tall the stranger was, and Chris answered that he was about six feet tall. Scheinin never confronted Chris with his original height description, that he first told detectives that the man was six foot five. Scheinin did, however, enter into evidence the statement Chris had given detectives on the afternoon of the crime, which contained the height description. He also had Chris admit that the stranger by the pond did not have red hair. It was honey yellow, Chris agreed. For the most part, though, Chris's trial testimony was believable and compelling.

Little Jackie Poling was called and failed to identify Kirk in the courtroom. But he was followed by his mother who told the jurors how Jackie had come to her after the lineup and told her that number six, Kirk Bloodsworth, was the man at the pond. Scheinin did little with her.

Donna Ferguson testified after Jackie and also pointed to Bloodsworth as the strange man in Fontana Village the day of the slaying.

She claimed she'd seen him walking with Dawn, that he told Dawn that he was playing hide-and-seek with Lisa, and that he invited Dawn to help him go find Lisa. Ferguson said she was just six feet away from Dawn and the stranger. "I got a good look at his face," she said. Scheinin did better with Ferguson. He brought out her prior inconsistent statements, that she'd originally told the police that she never saw the face of the man with Dawn. And he got her to admit she'd smoked a joint the morning of the crime. But she was the fifth one to identify Kirk. Five different identification witnesses. Hard to overcome.

Lazzaro and Brobst weren't finished. They called Detective Capel to fill in the blanks, wrap up the story, reiterate how the composite was created and how the photo and lineup identifications came about. Capel mentioned the missing persons report filed by Wanda Bloodsworth and described the gambit played on Kirk, suggesting that the detectives didn't think Bloodsworth even saw the rock on the table. Capel repeated what he considered to be the incriminating statements Bloodsworth had made afterward about the rock. He also volunteered that Bloodsworth had said that he'd been out buying drugs on the afternoon of the murder. Cross-examining Capel, Scheinin brought out that Chris Shipley had first described the strange man as being six feet five inches tall. Scheinin got Capel to agree that Bloodsworth must have seen the rock on the table, given what he said afterward. The two fenced, back and forth. Scheinin asked Capel about the man who'd found Dawn Hamilton's clothes, Richard Gray, and elicited that a pair of panties had been discovered in Gray's car. During the redirect examination, though, Capel told the jurors that Gray had been eliminated as a suspect through interviews.

Donna Hollywood, from Harbor to Harbor, then testified, providing information about Kirk's strange behavior after July 25, his claim of illness, his abrupt departure. The prosecutors finished by calling Rose Carson and then Tina Christopher. Rose told the jury that Kirk, after he came back to Cambridge, told her that he'd done "a very bad thing, and also that he'd gone to the state hospital for help." Tina Christopher said that she couldn't remember back to August "too good." She was asked if she saw Kirk Bloodsworth in the courtroom, and she answered no. When prodded by Ann Brobst, she remembered that back in August, Bloodsworth had helped some friends move a motorcycle and then had talked to her of a murder. He went on about a little girl, a bloody rock, and some guy that was with him who was supposed to have done it, she said. She testified that about three times he told her that there was a guy with him who took the little girl off. Because she seemed to be having trouble remembering, Brobst showed her a written statement police had taken from her and asked Judge Hinkel to admit the written statement into evidence. Scheinin objected, but the judge allowed it. During cross-examination, Scheinin brought out that Tina was smoking marijuana when she supposedly heard Kirk talking about the murder.

The state's case had gone in well, gone in with hardly a glitch.

SIXTEEN

STEVEN SCHEININ THEN had his turn. He began the defense case by calling several police officers who'd taken statements from Nancy Hall and Donna Ferguson the day of Dawn's death. These officers testified as to the early descriptions these women had given and what they'd said that day, statements different from what they told the jury. He brought in Officer Charles Moore, who'd taken the statement from Donna Ferguson that she didn't see the man calling for Lisa and didn't know if he was the same man that she'd previously seen sitting on the electric box. Lazzaro, cross-examining him, pointed out how little experience he had in felony investigations compared with the homicide detectives handling the case.

Scheinin tried to call other officers to make the point that dozens of police had gone around Fontana Village broadcasting the description given by the two boys and showing the composite sketch, suggesting to everyone the characteristics of the assailant. Judge Hinkel wouldn't allow any of it. He sustained the prosecutors' objection to this whole line of questioning as irrelevant.

When it came time in the trial for Scheinin to put on his alibi witnesses, it was nearly noon. Scheinin asked Judge Hinkel for a luncheon recess, one that would have allowed him time to talk to them before they testified, to perhaps do some last-minute preparation. Hinkel wasn't ready for a recess and denied the request. Scheinin had no choice but to call them. One by one, they took the stand. They did not seem well prepared.

Joey Martin went first, followed by Tammy Albin. Wanda Bloodsworth went next. Birdie Plutschak and Dawn Gerald testified as well. All swore that Kirk was home at the South Randolph Road address the morning of July 25. But the prosecutors knew how to make these witnesses look confused, uncertain, like their stories were contrived. It wasn't hard. Ann Brobst cross-examined Wanda Bloodsworth. "When did you first try to remember back to what happened that day?" Brobst asked her.

"When Detective Capel had told me he suspected Kirk of murder," Wanda answered.

"And do you remember when that was?"

"I don't remember exactly what day it was."

"Well, surely that was very upsetting to you?"

"Yeah," Wanda answered.

"You can remember that day, I imagine, vividly, isn't that correct?" Brobst's tone was facetious.

"Yes."

"But can you tell us what day of the week that was that Detective Capel talked to you?"

Wanda started to fidget. She looked around the courtroom, as if for help. "No," she said. "Because he was there more than once," she added.

Brobst asked some other questions, then worked her way back to this same point—Wanda's inability to accurately remember dates. "Now, would you please tell the members of jury what time you got up on July18 the preceding week?" she asked.

Wanda was baffled. She again looked toward Scheinin, as though he could answer for her. "I don't know," she finally said.

"You don't remember that?"

"No."

"Do you remember what you did that day?"

"No."

"Do you remember what you were wearing that day?"

"No."

"Do you remember what you had for dinner?"

"No."

Brobst kept her off balance. "Now, you said that it was the day that Kirk was arrested, that you first realized you would have to think back to the 25th and that you believe that was about August 7?"

"Yes."

"So it was about two weeks later?"

"Yes."

"What were you doing two weeks ago today?"

"Two weeks ago today?"

"Hmm, hmm." Brobst was patient now.

"February, I was here I think it was—oh, no." Wanda put her hand over her face. "I don't know what I was doing," she said.

Others fared worse. Ann Brobst sensed that Joey Martin was repeating a canned story. "When did you first realize that you would have to come in and tell the members of the jury what happened on the date that Mr. Scheinin directed your attention to?" she asked.

"Last night."

"And was that the first time that you tried to remember what happened back on this date?"

"No. I remember a lot of it, but the date, the day and the date itself, I'm not too sure of." Joey was easily confused.

"Okay," Brobst pressed. "Now, do you remember what you were doing July 18, 1984?"

"Is that the day?"

"I'm asking *you*, if *you* remember."

"I don't remember. If that's . . . I don't know . . . Dates I'm not good with."

Scheinin called Wayne Palmer and Jeffrey Wright to complete the alibi. They held up no better on cross-examination than the others. Of them all, Birdie Plutschak was the most composed. Brobst did little to dent her testimony.

While Birdie was on the stand, Scheinin asked her whether Kirk had called her the night he left Baltimore. She answered that yes, he had. Scheinin asked her whether Kirk had told her then that he had done something bad. She said yes again. Scheinin asked her to tell the jury what that something was. The prosecutors objected. The question called for hearsay, they argued. Judge Hinkel sustained the objection and told her that she wasn't permitted to answer the question. She couldn't repeat what Kirk had told her the bad thing was. She did manage to blurt out that it didn't have anything to do with Dawn's murder, but the jurors never heard her confirm that he'd mentioned a taco salad.

But Scheinin had reason to hope. At least he'd put on the stand more alibi witnesses than the state had put on ID witnesses. He also offered some confirmation that the alibi witnesses were correctly remembering the date. Wanda had brought to court a copy of the mental health clinic record from July 25. It confirmed that she was at least remembering the right day. A receipt from the sporting goods store confirmed that Jeffrey Wright sold his rifle there on July 25. Details that might make a difference.

Scheinin also thought his next witness might win over some jurors. In the middle of trial, after seeing for the first time the tennis shoe that Capel had measured and noticing that inside it was marked size 8, Scheinin had contacted Richard Rudolph, the proprietor of Towson Bootery, and asked if he would testify as a shoe expert for the defense. Rudolph was known as the Mayor of Towson. His shoe store, located in the heart of town, had been a local fixture, a hangout for gossip and political talk for decades. Rudolph had fit many generations with shoes. If you needed a pair, your children needed a pair. And if you needed a favor, something done, a good word with the town council, say, or some Orioles tickets, Rudolph was the man to see. Large, engaging, and robust, he was a local legend. When Scheinin called him to the witness stand, Rudolph brought with him his own specially designed foot and shoe measure. There, before the jury, Scheinin had Rudolph measure the tennis shoes that had been seized, the ones Ramsey had measured with a ruler and about which the FBI expert testified. They measured size 8. Rudolph then measured one of Kirk's feet. It was size 10½. Scheinin had Rudolph try to put the tennis shoes on Kirk. Rudolph should have been on vaudeville. He went through great pains to try and jam them onto Kirk's feet. Maybe he tried too hard. He forced them on him, but only after Kirk's toes curled up.

Lazzaro and Brobst that night regretted the shoe debacle. "Sometimes you have to take an arrow and not wince," Lazzaro told Brobst. "We'll have to deal with it somehow in our closing . . ."

Following Rudolph, it was finally time for the defendant. Scheinin called Kirk Bloodsworth to testify. Kirk rose, turned briefly to face the silent crowd, then walked to the witness stand. He steeled himself. He knew it all came down to this moment. Kirk's best chance lay with himself. This was it. No dress rehearsal. No coming back. What he wanted to do was to jump out of the witness box, take each juror there by the collar, and shake hard until each understood that he was innocent. But all he could do was answer the questions posed to him by the lawyers. He was at the mercy of the lawyers.

Kirk raised his right hand and swore to tell the truth, as all the witnesses had done. Scheinin asked him questions about his general background, his time in the marines, his relationship with

Wanda, and he answered carefully, deliberately. His voice was steady. He looked at the jury without trying to stare. He tried to stay calm, to concentrate on the questions, not to be emotional, though he felt like this wasn't who he really was. He described how he'd worked at Harbor to Harbor and been off on July 25. He recounted that he'd been home at the Randolph Road address most of that morning and then gone out with Wayne Palmer to look for some marijuana to buy. He was never anywhere near Fontana Village. He didn't kill anybody.

Scheinin asked Kirk about leaving the Baltimore area, and he explained why he decided to leave. The bad thing he told everyone he'd done referred to his earlier promise that he'd buy his wife a nice dinner, her favorite, a taco salad. Instead of doing this, he'd left his job and left her without even saying good-bye. Kirk replayed his first interview with Ramsey and Capel in Cambridge and denied that he was later talking about blood on a rock, though he admitted talking about the rock and panties they'd shown him. Kirk told the jury the tennis shoes in question weren't even his. Scheinin indicated then that he had no further questions.

Lazzaro stood to cross-examine Kirk. For a moment, he just eyed the defendant, as though sizing up his target, as though adjusting his crosshairs. With his first few words, he threw Kirk off guard. He asked about his mother, whether she was strict, whether she was domineering. The psychological profile was his blueprint. He asked questions about the other women in Kirk's life, whether they were domineering or violent. "Isn't it true, Mr. Bloodsworth, that all of the women in your life scolded you and dominated you? Isn't it true that you were frustrated by that? That this frustration built up over the years? That you finally vented your frustration on this little girl?"

Lazzaro had Kirk recount the stressful living conditions at South Randolph Road, the fights with Wanda. Lazzaro paced back and forth in front of Kirk. He asked him about the statements he made to Rose Carson that he had done a very bad thing. He scoffed at the taco salad excuse. Had Kirk repeat it. Lazzaro's expression showed his incredulity. The jurors, from their reactions, seemed to agree. To all Lazzaro's questions Kirk answered with short, clipped, responses. That's all Lazzaro gave him the opportunity to do. Lazzaro asked about him working in a funeral home with dead bodies. He brought up the comments Kirk had supposedly made to Tina Christopher in Cambridge about a bloody rock, and underscored those for the jury. "Isn't it true that you knew about the bloody rock because you were the one that used it to bash Dawn Hamilton's head in?" He asked Kirk about his strength and muscular condition. If a few of the questions seemed a bit random, they weren't. The prosecution would return to all of these subjects later. They were all grist for the closing argument Brobst would give and the rebuttal argument with which Lazzaro would conclude the trial.

Kirk was on the stand for slightly more than an hour. And then it was over. He was told by Judge Hinkel to step down. He wasn't ready to step down. He felt like he'd never really gotten a chance to explain himself, to let these people on the jury get to know him, to learn and see who he really was. He thought his time on the stand was too short.

Following Kirk, Scheinin called the four character witnesses, one after another. Each told of what a gentle and peaceful man Kirk Bloodsworth was. Each was only on the stand briefly.

His last witness, Scheinin told the judge, would be his eyewitness identification expert, Robert Buckout. The prosecutors asked to approach the bench where they could speak out of the jury's hearing. There they renewed their objection to Buckout's testifying. Judge Hinkel decided to excuse the jury for the day in order to hear argument on this point. He then listened to the reasons given by the prosecution as to why Buckout should not be permitted to testify.

His testimony was unscientific, they argued, unreliable. It improperly invaded the function of the jury.

Scheinin made a proffer to the court summarizing Buckout's credentials and experience and the gist of his expected testimony. Buckout's opinions would criticize the way the composite drawing was made, because it unfairly led the child witness. There were limited foils to choose from. The child had to pick one of these predetermined drawings. Buckout would criticize the other identifications too. He had scientific data showing the significant likelihood of error in such testimony. Buckout took the witness stand out of the presence of the jury so that Judge Hinkel could better assess his testimony. It seemed rambling, confusing. Hinkel asked him to clarify exactly, what he intended to say. Again, Buckout was less than clear:

My belief and sort of underlying theory is that eyewitnesses are really confronted with a difficult situation, and when the circumstances add up to a very difficult challenge to the memory system, these are the things that can happen to various parts of their testimony and various parts of their identification, and testing methods, of course is one of the areas that I have done most of my work on, and the testing method again I see as simply a tool, and the checklist is simply to provide to the jury, or elements of the checklist are provided to the jury, so that they can essentially assess what, at least, the filter of the scientist would say about a given test.

Judge Hinkel heard it all patiently, then ruled out Buckout's expert testimony, concluding that it not only invaded the province of the jurors but was of little value and would tend to confuse and mislead them. Closing arguments would begin the next morning, March 8.

Scheinin was disappointed that the ruling excluded Buckout. Still, all in all, he thought the evidence had gone in well. He was confident that the state's case fell short of proving guilt beyond a reasonable doubt. Scheinin, over the course of his representation, had come to believe that Kirk really was innocent. And after hearing all the evidence, he was certain he was going to win. That night he told all this to his client.

Lazzaro and Brobst conferred upstairs at the state's attorney's office on the fifth floor of the courthouse. They both, in fact, were worried. The evidence was close, they felt, too close. They wondered whether their trial strategy would work. Neither wanted this man they believed was a child killer to go free.

SEVENTEEN

BLOODSWORTH'S TRIAL MADE good copy, and the local papers ran stories each day describing the contest. MURDER-RAPE TRIAL STARTS WITH GRUESOME EVIDENCE, headlined a story by Scott Shane in the *Sun*. DAWN HAMILTON'S COMPANIONS TESTIFY IN MURDER TRIAL was the banner headline for the March 6 edition of the *News American*. FOOTPRINT TENTATIVELY LINKS DEFENDANT TO SLAIN GIRL, 9, headlined another *News American* story written by Cynthia Skove. 5 PLACE MAN WITH SLAIN GIRL, 5 SAY HE WAS HOME, topped another for the *Sun*. BLOODSWORTH ON STAND, DENIES MURDERING CHILD, ran another. Some of the reports suggested that the tennis shoe had connected him with the murder, while some claimed it had not. Some stories emphasized the lack of any scientific proof that he was the killer. Some dwelled more on the identifications. Speculation was rampant as to the outcome.

Thomas Hamilton, after testifying early on in the trial, had then sat and watched the entire drama unfold. He'd previously become convinced by Chris Shipley's certainty, that Bloodsworth was the man who killed his daughter. He wanted to see him convicted, see him get the death sentence. But after watching the witnesses, he feared that the evidence wasn't strong enough. Like Steven Scheinin, he expected an acquittal.

Hamilton and the lawyers may all have underestimated the enormous unspoken pressures that exist in a case of this type. The jurors, simple citizens from the community, were asked to judge a man their own police department, after an enormous investigation, believed was guilty of a heinous crime. These jurors had been handed the responsibility for deciding whether this man went free. It was obvious that the prosecutors also believed he was guilty. Totally and completely guilty. The jurors fully realized that if they found him not guilty and he was in fact the murderer, other innocent children might be raped, tortured, killed. They'd seen the horrible and frightening photographs of what was done to Dawn Hamilton. Photographs that showed flies crawling over this little girl's bloodied body. Yes, the judge gave them an instruction that they had to find proof beyond a reasonable doubt. But psychologically, emotionally, they must have wanted to believe that the state had the right man, that they had the chance to put an end to this sordid tragedy. If the evidence was even close, how in good conscience would they acquit?

On the morning of March 8, the institutional floodlights of the Baltimore County Detention Center came on at 7 A.M. as they did every morning in the jail that had become Kirk Bloodsworth's world. With the lights, the murky images of sleep vanished, replaced, as his mind woke, with the dread of the nightmare that had become his life—the dread of consciousness, of the place he inhabited, of what they were saying about him, and of what he would have to face that day.

He lay unmoving for several minutes, trying to fight off the nausea in his gut, the sickness and fear in his mind, trying to find the will to move, to get off the mattress, to just stand up. Pushing aside the blanket and stepping onto the concrete floor, he walked slowly to the one slatted vent in his cell and squinted trying to see to the outside. There were spits of snow on the ground, and the air coming through was bitter cold. He kept looking out the window grate, trying to spy some grass or a bird, then had to grab the grate for support because his body started to shake and his legs to buckle. If he had the power, he thought, he would rip the grate out and jump to freedom. In a futile gesture he gave it a tug. Everything he tried seemed futile. He took a breath. He heard the rattle of food and coffee being pushed through the compartment in his cell door, but he felt sick and wouldn't eat anything that morning. He thought of the eight women and four men on his jury, of the elderly white-haired foreman who had partly slept through the testimony and who would never look in his direction. They just can't find me guilty, he thought. Scheinin knows what they're going to do. They must be able to see the truth.

After he'd washed in the stainless-steel sink in the corner of his cell, his name was called by the guard in the control booth. Officer Flaherty came to escort him to the holding pen where inmates on their way to court were assembled. Flaherty unlocked Kirk's cell door, opened it, and gave Kirk a nod of support. The two men, Kirk dressed in his orange prison jumpsuit, and Flaherty in his prison guard uniform, walked down the hallway side by side like they were on military parade, like Flaherty was his sergeant.

Once inside the bull pen, Flaherty gave Kirk the clothes he wore each day in court: black slacks, a white shirt, blue sweater, socks, and loafers. Scheinin had arranged for these to be at the detention center rather than the courthouse. Flaherty watched as Kirk changed into these clothes. Then Flaherty put the leg-iron shackles on Kirk's ankles and the chain around his waist. As he placed the handcuffs on Kirk's wrists, he could see and feel them shaking. Flaherty squeezed his hand and looked him in the eyes. "Good luck," Flaherty said to Kirk. "You're a former marine. Remember that. You can handle it . . ."

On the bus, during the ten-minute ride from the detention center to the Baltimore County Circuit Court, Kirk prayed to God for deliverance. Every day before the trial he had prayed for this. He prayed with his head bowed and his eyes shut tight.

At the courthouse, Kirk was led to the general cell block where he was logged in. From there he was taken up the private stairway to the small holding cell behind Judge Hinkel's courtroom. Only then were his restraints removed.

He sat in his cell alone for forty minutes. At 9:20 A.M. he was led into a courtroom packed with spectators, media, witnesses, police—all there to hear the closing arguments of the lawyers. Kirk frantically scanned the crowd looking for and then seeing his father, Curtis, and next to him his mother, who sniffled into a white handkerchief and fearfully waved. He waved back as his two guards sat him down next to his lawyers. The courtroom quieted down and then everyone rose as Judge Hinkel took the bench. The case was called by the courtroom clerk. Judge Hinkel asked for the jury and the twelve jurors and several alternates filed in and took their seats. At the direction of the judge, the closing arguments began.

Ann Brobst rose to present the initial argument for the state. She again thanked the jurors for their service to the community. She was direct and businesslike as she went over the testimony, witness by witness. The forensic evidence was all "neutral," she said. It neither proved he was guilty, nor proved he was innocent. It simply meant nothing, was no help. But the many eyewitness identifications were more than sufficient to prove the defendant's guilt. The identifications, the fact that Bloodsworth was off that day, his fleeing the city, his statements in Cambridge—all these taken together were too much to be coincidental. She argued that the alibi was too consistent, was rehearsed, contrived. She carefully chose her words as she downplayed the importance of the shoe size and the one finger-print found on the church flyer. The shoes may not have been the defendant's and consequently were not significant. The print could have come from anyone. There was litter all over the area. Both pieces of evidence, like the red carpet fiber, the human hair, the lack of other fingerprints, the absence of semen, were all "red herrings." Kirk Bloodsworth's own words, though—his admission that he'd done something bad, that he needed to check into a mental hospital, his lame story about a taco salad, his statements about a bloody rock—when coupled with the many eyewitness identifications were more than enough to prove guilt beyond a reasonable doubt. She somberly asked the jurors for a conviction.

Steven Sheinin rose to counter. He was emotional, theatrical. This time he went on and on in a rambling though passionate plea. His alibi witnesses were not perfect, but they were the people Kirk was with, he told the jury. And they were truthful. But this was not an alibi defense, he argued. "This is a case of the defense saying that the state has not met its burden of proof." The fact that there were no fingerprints, no blood or semen matching his client's, no hard proof, should be enough in and of itself to create a reasonable doubt. The police botched their handling of the crime scene, he argued, and failed to competently preserve the sperm and run the appropriate tests, tests that might have yielded a blood type, tests that might have matched the hair with other suspects. He questioned whether the rock was even the murder weapon, pointing out that it was crumbly, yet no rock fragments had been found in Dawn Hamilton's wounds. The killer was somebody else, he suggested. The hair that was found next to Dawn's body belonged to the real murderer. He tried to underscore the inconsistencies and flaws in the testimony of the eyewitnesses. He argued hard the concept of reasonable doubt. He held up a tennis shoe, mocking the shoe evidence, calling it "appalling," and argued that Detective Ramsey, in claiming the shoes were size 10½, had "tried to perpetrate a fraud from the witness stand." Scheinin surprised Kirk when he contemptuously threw one of the shoes toward the floor where it bounced and loudly struck the wooden panel in front of the jury box. The jurors didn't seem to like that. It was a gesture that seemed wrong, misplaced.

Robert Lazzaro, once again elegantly dressed in a dark blue suit, red silk tie, and gold cufflinks, rose to give the coup de grâce, the state's rebuttal. He spoke with his usual deep, authoritative voice. His presentation, just like his opening statement, was to the point, crisp in its delivery, organized, articulate. He warned the jury not to be misled by Scheinin. "He knows all the ploys," Lazzaro said. He shrugged off the fact that unfortunately there was no sperm, no physical evidence pointing to either guilt or innocence. He admitted that Detective Ramsey made a mistake regarding the shoe size, a simple error, hardly an effort to defraud the court. He reminded the jury that the other suspects mentioned by Scheinin—Manzari and Gray—had been cleared. He reviewed the evidence of guilt, arguing how unlikely it would be that five independent people would identify the same man if he were not the killer. He lingered over the lame explanation of what Kirk Bloodsworth claimed he meant when he admitted to his friends in Cambridge that he'd done something terrible that day and needed to go to a mental hospital. A taco salad? And were all the witnesses in Cambridge lying too? he asked rhetorically. Then Lazzaro pounded home a new trial theme, one the psychological profile suggested. He asked the jurors to look beneath the surface of Kirk Bloodsworth and to see him for what he really was, to see the "monster inside the mind." It was this monster that finally broke free, took control, and killed Dawn Hamilton. Lazzaro cautioned the jurors again about being misled by the contrived alibi of the defense. The alibi was too perfect, he told them, too consistent. He asked the jurors to use the gift of common sense that God had given them. With his words he drove home the horror of the crime and demanded a conviction. "Convict the monster inside the mind," the jurors heard, "the monster within . . ."

After the closing arguments were completed, Judge Hinkel instructed the jury on the law. The elements of first-degree murder and first-degree rape were each explained. Proof beyond a reasonable doubt was required. The verdict had to be unanimous. The jury was told to retire to a back room and to begin deliberations.

Kirk was led back into the small holding cell adjacent to the courtroom. He didn't think the closing arguments had gone well, but he still believed that the truth would win out. He couldn't allow himself to think otherwise.

WHILE THE JURY deliberated, Thomas Hamilton paced the hallway outside the courtroom, wondering what the verdict would be. He held a crucifix in his hand.

When Kirk had been taken back to the holding cell, another prisoner was sitting there, a black man with a yellow scarf wrapped over his head. He was muscular with tattoos going up each arm and showed a gold tooth when he opened his mouth. There were scars on his cheek and neck. The man had a brown paper lunch bag and sat eating a sandwich and an orange. When he finished he crumpled up the bag and left it in a corner. They sat in silence for over two hours. Finally the man spoke. "I've heard about your case from the guards," he said. He spoke slowly, deliberately, and stared at Kirk strangely, like he had foreknowledge, like he was a soothsayer. "Don't worry," he went on. "I know you are going to be all right." He smiled and his gold tooth flashed. "Don't worry, man," he said. "I'm telling you . . ."

It was at that moment that the guards came to retrieve Kirk. The jury had reached a verdict, they told him. After only two and a half hours. Kirk turned his head to look back at the man as the guards took him out.

The courtroom, as Kirk entered it through a side door, was even more crowded than before. Every seat was taken and people stood lining the walls on either side of the benches. Kirk couldn't spot his father or mother. He didn't know that Jeanette couldn't bear any more. After the rebuttal argument of Lazzaro, with tears streaming down her face, she'd said to Curtis, "Can you take me home, now? Can I please go home now?" Kirk was totally alone.

Judge Hinkel was already on the bench. He called for the jury. The jurors entered in single file, heads down, somber, and not one looked at Kirk as they took their assigned seats. Kirk knew then what was about to happen. The white-haired foreman stood up. Judge Hinkel asked him if the jury had reached a unanimous verdict and the foreman nodded his head indicating that they had. "Will the defendant please stand," Hinkel said, but Kirk was already standing. "Take the verdict," Hinkel ordered to his clerk.

"How do you find as to the charge against Kirk Bloodsworth for the first-degree murder of Dawn Hamilton?" the clerk asked.

The foreman did not hesitate. "Guilty as to the charge of first-degree murder! Guilty!" he repeated, though his words were nearly drowned out. The crowd in the courtroom erupted with cheering and screaming. People were yelling, "Thank God, thank God!" One man in the back hollered, "Give him the gas!" Judge Hinkel banged his wooden gavel trying to restore order. He slammed it down again and again and then the gavel broke. Kirk's vision began to tunnel in on itself. He saw the gavel handle land on the floor but then saw mostly darkness. He felt like he was looking through the wrong end of a telescope. He could hardly breathe. He held on to the rail for support. He heard the word "guilty" to the charge of rape. The cheering went on. Another call for the gas chamber. He fell to his knees. He was an innocent man, an innocent man . . . and they were cheering.

Kirk felt a tug and realized he was being helped up and then pulled out by the guards. He was dizzy and nearly fell. The guards had him by his elbows and led him back towards the holding cell. Everything was a blur. He heard only confused shouting. The door to the courtroom closed behind him and the noise muted. The guards opened the door to the holding cell and he went inside. Kirk looked for the black man. No one was there. The cell was empty. The lunch bag was gone. Sick as he felt, Kirk turned and asked the guard where the other prisoner was. "What other prisoner?" the guard said to him, looking hard at Kirk. "You crazy, man? There's been no one in here all day except you."

Later Kirk became convinced that he'd been visited by an angel. Whether he'd conjured him up, a hallucination, a figment of his tormented mind, or whether the man was real, he could never say. But he believed that at his lowest moment, paralyzed with fear and dread, he'd been visited. More than an apparition. There were forces still on his side, he was sure. Reasons to fight on.

EIGHTEEN

UNDER MARYLAND'S DEATH penalty law, as it existed in 1985, a defendant convicted of a capital offense had the right to choose whether to be sentenced by the jury or by the judge. For an innocent man, a real Hobson's choice.

Kirk had put his faith in the jury and they had crushed it. He'd detected no pity in the eyes of any of them when the verdict was announced. Whether Judge Hinkel would be merciful, he didn't know. He hoped Hinkel, with his years of experience, might have seen more clearly what the jurors had not. Kirk thought it might be harder for one person to sentence him to death than for a group of twelve to do so. But Judge Hinkel was pure hardtack. Kirk agonized over which way to go. He listened to the pros and cons of each choice, as laid out by his lawyer. But he had lost faith in his lawyer. Thinking about the decision made Kirk sick. He decided to put his life in the hands of the judge. The sentencing was set for March 22.

After Kirk made his selection and the jury was dismissed from further service, Anthony Pipitone, a reporter for the *Evening Sun,* interviewed six of the jurors, and wrote a story headlined BLOODS-WORTH JURY CONVINCED OF GUILT FROM THE START. According to what they told the reporter, when the deliberations started, only one of the twelve jurors had any doubts about Kirk's guilt. After a relatively quick review of the state's identification witnesses, the one holdout came around and they reached a unanimous decision.

The jurors uniformly found the state's identification witnesses to be credible. They also thought the testimony of the alibi witnesses seemed rehearsed. The similarities between the shoes recovered from Dawn Gerald's row house and the herringbone-patterned marks on Dawn Hamilton's neck and back also convinced them. A bailiff had brought into the jury room the exhibits admitted into evidence. These included the color photographs of Dawn, the tennis shoes, and the exhibit of side-by-side pictures prepared by the FBI shoe expert. The jurors thought that the markings on Dawn's body matched the pattern of the shoe soles. One juror, who wore a 10½ size shoe, tried on the sneakers. His big toe protruded from a hole in the canvas, but he could wear them without much problem. The jurors also found incriminating the statements made by Bloodsworth in Cambridge. One juror termed Bloodsworth's taco salad explanation to be "ridiculous." When these were added to the rest of the state's evidence, it all made for an overwhelming case.

The jury had chosen as their foreman an eighty-seven-year-old man. While exclaiming to the reporter how convincing the evidence was, in the same breath he expressed relief that the jury wouldn't have to decide Bloodsworth's sentence. "I'm glad we don't have to make that decision," he said. "One decision was enough for me." He then made a curious and seemingly contradictory admission. "The whole thing was based on very weak evidence," he said. "That's one reason I'm glad the judge took it out of our hands." At least one other juror also indicated that she probably would not have voted for death.

Kirk's fate, though, was no longer in the hands of the jury. It rested with Judge William Hinkel.

Curtis Bloodsworth, meanwhile, had contacted Ronald Raubaugh, one of the investigators used by Kirk's first lawyer, Russell White. Raubaugh was an experienced ex-detective. Curtis used the little money left from his loan to rehire Raubaugh. He wanted him to find a reason for a new trial, he told him. Curtis was racked with hurt and guilt.

As required by Maryland law, a presentence report had to be prepared, evaluating all of the criteria to be taken into consideration by the court before sentencing. These criteria included a description of the offense, the prior record of the defendant, his family and marital history, his educational background and employment history, a list of his financial assets, and a statement by the defendant. The report concluded with a final evaluation. The quality or strength of the evidence against the person convicted was not one of the criteria to be considered. A verdict of guilty is like a positive test for pregnancy. Under the eyes of the law, you either are or you aren't.

The presentence investigation was conducted by Nancy Huber, a senior investigator with the state's department of parole and probation. Her report was sent to the lawyers and the judge. Regarding the section titled "Statement of Defendant," she wrote as follows:

The defendant states he did not commit the above offense. He claims he was not in the area at the time the offense allegedly took place. He advises he was home at the time. He feels he was "railroaded" and feels the state did not prove their [sic] case beyond a reasonable doubt. He relates the state's case was based on emotion and publicity. He stresses that two wrongs do not make a right and that the senseless murder of Dawn Hamilton was bad enough and now an innocent man's life is in jeopardy which doesn't help the victim in the least. He calls his guilty finding "a great miscarriage of justice." He claims what bothers him most is that the person who actually committed the offense is still out there. He indicates he will not rest until justice is done and he is vindicated. He emphasizes he has no criminal record and is incapable of hurting anyone, especially a child. He feels this case has been a great defamation of character to him and his family.

Kirk's assets in the report were listed as "None."

In her final evaluation, Ms. Huber ended with the following conclusion:

The defendant is charged with the most heinous of all crimes, the rape and murder of a child. He expressed no remorse or responsibility for that offense. There was nothing concrete found in his background to explain his participation in such an offense and one can only speculate as to what led the defendant to commit such a crime.

The prosecutors, as they were required to do, notified Scheinin that they intended to bring to the sentencing one of the FBI profilers who prepared the psychological portrait of Dawn Hamilton's killer. They wanted the judge to hear about the profile, particularly that the FBI concluded that this killer would strike again. Scheinin, through an intermediary, had the report sent to John R. Lion, a clinical professor of psychiatry at the University of Maryland, for review. Dr. Lion wrote a letter criticizing the profile. He called it a "descriptive work" that "resembles the typical mentation of a detective trying to solve a crime." He called the report "dangerous guesswork." He wrote that "there is no scientific literature showing this profile, or anything like it, to have any predictive utility in the determination of clinical or forensic dangerousness." He wrote that because the report had come from the FBI, it had been "endowed with a false sense of prestige."

While Sheinin prepared for the sentencing, Ronald Raubaugh

was out running down possible new leads. Sifting through old police reports, he came across references about Richard Gray, written by Detective Mark Bacon. Through a source in the police department, he got hold of a confidential report written by Bacon. While Sheinin knew that Richard Gray had found Dawn's clothes, and knew that he'd had some panties in his car, the report contained a great deal of additional information suggesting that Bacon thought Gray might have committed the murder. Scheinin, when he learned of it, was furious that this information had been withheld from him. He believed he'd been entitled to it under the *Brady* rule. If he had been able to show the jury that there was another suspect and that the police had failed to fully investigate this suspect, he might have created a reasonable doubt in the minds of the jurors. Scheinin filed a motion for a new trial, arguing that the prosecutors committed misconduct in failing to disclose this exculpatory information. The state filed an opposition. Judge Hinkel set a hearing date on the motion for March 18, a week before the scheduled sentencing.

Scheinin had sent three subpoenas to the Baltimore County Police Department for Detective Bacon, but they all went unserved. Scheinin was told only that Bacon was out on sick leave. The police would not even provide a forwarding address. Raubaugh, though, tracked Bacon down. Bacon was awaiting final confirmation of his award of state retirement benefits. He was reluctant to testify in a way that undercut the state's case until his benefits were finalized. Raubaugh served him with a subpoena anyway, requiring him to attend the hearing.

In court Bacon, who had been out on sick leave since the prior October, had no choice but to testify. Under questioning from Scheinin, he described his investigation into Gray and his suspicions. He reviewed the information he'd accumulated: what he believed was a blood spot on Gray's shirt, how Gray had been nervous and vomited, Gray's clean hands when supposedly he'd been rolling newspapers, the fact of finding a pair of child's panties in his car, panties that Gray claimed he'd found in the woods. His superiors had quashed his investigation, Detective Bacon told Judge Hinkel. They'd given him no adequate explanation. Scheinin argued vociferously that he'd never been informed of this information and that it was clearly exculpatory.

Robert Lazzaro responded that first of all, the report had not even been provided to him. His office had turned over boxes of police reports to the defense. They'd turned over everything they had, he said. If it had been retained by the police department, he hadn't been aware of it. Moreover, it was all inconsequential, a nonissue. Gray did not resemble the composite. He had passed important portions of a polygraph test, Lazzaro reported, information contrary to what Bacon had heard and incomplete at best. Lazarro also explained that homicide detectives had ruled out Richard Gray as a suspect because he'd been at the Fullerton police station when the missing child report came in.

Judge Hinkel denied the motion for a new trial. None of the information, he ruled, tended to either clear Bloodsworth or sufficiently implicate Richard Gray.

ON MARCH 22, 1985, Kirk was brought from the detention center to Judge Hinkel's courtroom to be sentenced. He had never been so scared. Once again, the courtroom was filled. Curtis had come, but Kirk's mother couldn't bear to watch. She had stayed home. Wanda and Birdie were there. Thomas Hamilton and many of the state's witnesses had come. Robert Lazzaro, relying heavily on the psychological profile, told Judge Hinkel that the killing was an act of opportunity, the result of frustration and bottled-up rage that finally boiled over. Bloodsworth had been dominated by women all his life, Lazzaro argued, by his mother, his wife, and his mother-in-law, and he had repressed his anger until the day he lured Dawn into the woods and killed her—a symbol of all females. He then blocked this terrible act from his mind. "If he started out with this crime, where will he go from here?" Lazzaro said. "There is no worse offense that can be imagined. Dawn Hamilton never had a prayer." The state, Lazzaro concluded, demanded the most extreme of all punishments. The state demanded that Kirk Bloodsworth be executed.

Scheinin argued that the death penalty was not the appropriate sentence. Bloodsworth had an unblemished record, he pointed out. He had no history of violence. He had served his country honorably in the Marine Corps. He was a loving son and husband and didn't deserve to die. With a client who continued to protest his innocence, there wasn't much else to say.

Kirk Bloodsworth, standing beside Steven Scheinin, had the opportunity to speak last. He rose and tried to hold his head high. His legs trembled. He told Judge Hinkel once again that he did not commit the crime. He tried to speak loudly, for the whole courtroom to hear, but his voice cracked. "This has been a tragedy of misjustice all the way around," he said. "I'm supposed to come up here and tell you why you shouldn't sentence me to death. These circumstances are not fair because I, Kirk Noble Bloodsworth, did not commit the crime!"

Judge Hinkel took a recess to consider his decision. He had the discretion to go either way. He recalled later, after Bloodsworth had been cleared, that it was perhaps the most difficult decision he'd ever made as a judge.

William Hinkel was a graduate of both the University of Baltimore and the University of Baltimore Law School. He'd worked as an insurance claims adjuster for a while, gone into private practice, and then become involved in local politics. In 1966 he was elected to the Maryland House of Delegates where he served one term.

During his tenure, the legislature was debating a bill concerning the death penalty. Hinkel's colleague, Thomas Hunter Lowe, who later became a Maryland appellate judge, was initially a proponent of a death penalty statute. Hinkel was undecided, torn. Hinkel had amassed a large amount of literature on the death penalty: studies on whether it was a deterrent, whether it was beneficial to the community, statistics on economic considerations. He shared all of this with his friend, Lowe. Ironically, Lowe did an about-face. He voted against the death penalty law. Hinkel voted in favor of it.

Governor Marvin Mandel appointed Bill Hinkel to be a district court judge in 1971. Governor Harry Hughes elevated him to the circuit court in 1981. In Baltimore County, judges with sufficient experience received capital cases on a rotation basis. It was the luck of the draw that he got Bloodsworth. And vice versa.

After the verdict, Judge Hinkel reviewed the evidence. He thought the boys' identifications were credible. He thought the statements of Donna Hollywood, Bloodsworth's employer from Harbor to Harbor, that Kirk had claimed he was sick and needed his paycheck, and had then left town abruptly a week after the murder, were incriminating. The things Bloodsworth said in Cambridge disturbed him. The explanation that Bloodsworth gave as to why he told people he'd done a bad thing, the taco salad bit, he found hollow. It didn't ring true. The alibi witnesses as a group were unimpressive. Taken in total, he agreed with the jury that the evidence proved Bloodsworth was guilty beyond a reasonable doubt.

A judge comes to a case knowing little more about it than the jury. Judge Hinkel was not privy to all that was uncovered during the massive police investigation that went on, the many leads, the various witnesses offering diverse descriptions of the suspect. He had no way of knowing much about Bloodsworth the man. He only knew what was brought out during the trial.

Back in his chambers, he wrestled over his decision. Even though he'd voted in the legislature for the death penalty, he'd never before been in a position to impose it. He was surprised Bloodsworth had chosen the judge rather than the jury to pass sentence. Hinkel actually had come to believe over time that the death penalty should be eliminated. Not so much because he felt sorry for defendants. More that he'd come to believe that as a result of the postconviction delays always associated with a death sentence, it created a prolonged and unnecessary period of uncertainty and sometimes agony for the family members of the victim. While he did not relish having to sentence anyone to death, he couldn't ignore the terrible details of this crime. The legislature had seen fit to pass a death penalty law. If a death sentence was not required for the rape, mutilation, and murder of a nine-year-old girl, it shouldn't be imposed on anyone. Judge Hinkel wasn't one to flinch from what he considered to be his judicial duty. He went over the various criteria required to be considered before passing sentence in a capital case. Then he returned to the bench. "Will the defendant please rise," he said.

Kirk and Steven Scheinin both stood. Kirk Bloodsworth would not flinch this time either. He assumed a military bearing, his head held high. This time I won't buckle, he promised himself.

"This case involves probably the most terrible of all crimes— murder, rape, and sodomy," Hinkel began. "And it was committed upon the most helpless of all citizens, a trusting little girl. The torture she endured and the horror that was visited upon her is beyond my words to describe." He paused, looking at the defendant. "Therefore, I sentence you to death."

This time there was no outburst in the courtroom. Not a word was spoken. The mood was somber. In the hallway outside, Curtis Bloodsworth wept and fumbled through pictures of Kirk's growing up. Through his sobs he said to reporters, "I can feel for the parents of the lost child . . . But to be taking another innocent life . . . This is two crimes . . ."

A warrant of execution was signed by Judge Hinkel on March 28, 1985. Since Kirk was entitled to an automatic appeal to Maryland's highest court, the sentence was stayed pending its outcome.

PART V
THE DEATH HOUSE

Capital punishment is
the most premeditated of
murders, to which no
criminal's deed, however
calculated, can be
compared.

—ALBERT CAMUS

NINETEEN

THE DAY AFTER HIS sentencing, Kirk Bloodsworth was transported from the county jail to the Department of Corrections Orientation Center in downtown Baltimore. There was a protocol to be followed for inmates heading for death row. Death row inmates were special. Particularly in preparing for the long road to execution, the state had its rituals.

At orientation, Kirk received a physical exam, a venereal disease check, had his teeth looked at, and was placed in solitary confinement on suicide watch. For five days he sat in a dark cell, alone, with nothing to do but dwell on his own agony, on his future as a hated man, a man marked for killing.

After the state was satisfied that he had been sufficiently disinfected, a large bus pulled up in front of the building. Kirk was escorted onto it for the trip across the street. He was going into the notorious and ancient Maryland Penitentiary, the one place in the state known as death row. Kirk was the only convict on the bus. As it pulled into the entranceway to the prison, he could see the inmates streaming from the yard up to the perimeter fence. They'd been expecting him.

It was the detention center revisited, but worse. "We got your ass now, Kirk," he heard one say. "Here he is, here he is," he heard. "Child fucker!" was screamed across the yard. Dozens of men in prison clothes began shouting epithets at him. Some made obscene gestures. Some were laughing. "We got us some fresh meat," somebody cried out. "Fresh meat," he heard again. He kept his eyes fixed on the bus driver. He swallowed hard. Kirk wondered how he'd ever survive in such a place.

Guards escorted him out of the bus. For the first time, he got a close-up view of the prison. A castle, a dungeon from another world: walls of pitted black stone, watch towers, turrets, guards with automatic weapons. Prison officials surrounded him as they walked him along the causeway bordered on both sides by a fence topped with razor-cut wire. Inmates pressed against it making threats, sticking their tongues out, hooting at him. He was terrified.

In the receiving area he was given a mattress of cotton wadding and blankets. Still in chains, he was led down several tier hallways, up some stairs, and through a series of locking doors. As each one clanged behind him, he winced. On the third level up, in an area called the South Wing, guards pushed him into a cell. "This is your new home," one of them said. "Welcome to death row."

Roaches crawled over studded cinder-block walls peeling shreds of faded yellow paint. Tiny shadows moved over the bunk and seatless toilet, and scampered into holes in the crumbling concrete. Graffiti was scratched everywhere. The place had the stench of an outhouse. Bars ran across the front. The guards slammed shut the iron door. The lock bolt clicked and echoed in his ears. They walked away. Kirk stood there alone in the foul dimness of his cell and cried.

That evening for dinner a Styrofoam cup was shoved through the slat in the door. It was supposed to be spaghetti. Kirk looked down and saw one large overcooked tomato in the cup. That was it.

He also got a plastic bottle of Kool-Aid—"bug juice" to the inmates. He swallowed the tomato, trying not to taste it. Wrapping the blankets around him, he tried to sleep.

Once the lights were out, more roaches began dropping from the ceiling, landing on the floor, landing on him. In the darkness the roaches came down like snow. They made a constant crackling noise. He tried to seal the blanket around himself but could feel the roaches landing on him and crawling everywhere. It took him most of a week before he could even fall asleep in that hole.

IN THE BEGINNING they kept him on administrative segregation. He remained in his cell twenty-three hours a day, with an hour for a short walk, a phone call, and a shower. He had to be escorted everywhere. It was too dangerous to allow him out into the general population of inmates. Those awaiting execution had to be protected.

The South Wing of the Maryland Penitentiary, at least among cons and ex-cons, was an infamous place. Those on the street who'd survived the South Wing were given a wide berth. When Kirk got there all the guards wore knife vests. A month or so before, a guard had been killed. Word on the tier was that an inmate named Nathaniel Appleby had used a prison-made shank to disembowel the man over a perceived insult. The brutality of the place was palpable. Kirk could smell it, could feel it in the air. The pain and anger were like electric currents pulsing along the floors and walls.

Kirk learned quickly how the inmates communicated after lockdown. Elaborate systems were set up using the most primitive materials. Dental floss was essential. The cons used it to create pulley lines down the length of the hall. Somebody would tie a bar of soap to fifty yards of dental floss and then slide the soap down the tier floor. Some got so could they could sling it from one end to the other. A receiving inmate would grab it through his bars with a jigged-up hook, a bent paper clip on the end of a pencil. The inmate would take what was on the string, tie a pack of cigarettes to it, and send it back or pass it along. The men used pieces of cracked mirrors, which they held outside their cells. Looking in the glass shards, they could see down the tier and know if any guards were around. When the hall was clear, the inmates let their commerce fly. Sandwiches, weed, drugs, "jump steady"—homemade wine from tomato puree—and mash beer all were passed along, bartered for cigarettes, cash, or services. Plastic bottles would go swinging down the tier.

Curtis brought Kirk a small television. Kirk quickly realized he'd need an antenna in order to get reception. Another inmate named Half, a black man with a muscle builder's torso but stubby legs, showed him what to do. He gave Kirk a piece of wire from a broken up radio and had him mash it into a bar of soap with a formaldehyde base. By hanging the soap out the levered window slat, and attaching the loose end of the wire to the TV, Kirk got some programs. Half became Kirk's first friend in the joint. He had a silver-starred front tooth, and liked to lift his lip in a snarl that showed it off. His left bicep was tattooed with an angel of death. He liked to play chess. Sometimes he talked street philosophy. Early on he offered Kirk advice. "Stay away from the gambling," he told Kirk. "Stay away from the queers, stay away from drugs, don't borrow nothing, and you'll be fine . . ."

Around dinnertime every day, the South Wing went crazy. Pandemonium ruled on the tier. The guards rarely ventured in then. Everyone except those on lockdown milled about. It was noisy, chaotic. Springsteen, Prince and the Revolution, or Aerosmith would blare from competing radios. Kirk's first week there, one inmate supposedly committed suicide. He was found hanged in the laundry. Another guy got napalmed. Inmates squirted him and his cell with naphtha, a flammable cleaning solvent used in the machine shop, then threw in a match. Kirk heard the man's screams. He heard them afterward in his dreams.

Kirk saw cons walk by his cell carrying toothbrushes honed into shanks, full soda cans in a pillow case, soap bars in socks—all weapons that could put the hurt on a man. From time to time someone would walk near Kirk's bars and show him a weapon or mumble some guttural threat.

"I'll be there shortly," Kirk would reply. "I'll be there. You won't have to wait much longer . . ."

It was the guys who didn't say a word, though, that frightened him the most. The ones who needed someone new to hate. The silent ones who seethed. They were the ones who'd attack without warning. Here he was, a convicted child killer, the perfect target.

AFTER TWO MONTHS on lockdown, thinking too often about the gas chamber, Kirk badly needed a change. He was sick, bored, claustrophobic, mired in self-pity and depression. It was late spring. He wanted to walk in the yard, to feel the outdoor air. He wanted to go to the weight room, to get a job, have contact visits, to have some kind of life. He needed to use the library. He was ready to risk whatever awaited him. He petitioned the assistant warden to be removed from administrative segregation and put into general population. That's when he first met Sergeant Cooley Hall, the security guard from Trinidad, and first told him that he was holding hostage an innocent man. It was Hall who recommended that Bloodsworth be given a temporary pass to general population. On a trial basis. To see how he did.

Initially Kirk just got tested. Men would watch him, circle him, see if he'd give them something. They'd ask him for things. He knew if he showed any weakness they'd be on him like jackals on a crippled calf. He decided his only chance was to act like a tough former marine, to adopt that "take no prisoners" attitude. He tried to exude the image that the marines had wanted to instill in him: that he was a force to be reckoned with. He was determined never to show fear.

There were tribes within the prison, groups who hung together, protected one another, fought against other tribes. The Muslims fought the bikers. The Aryans fought the blacks. The D.C. guys hung together and avoided those from Baltimore, the B-mores— for "be more careful." There were only a handful of cons from the Eastern Shore. One was named Richard Stillman, who'd killed his girlfriend's parents with a shotgun while they were sleeping. This happened in Cambridge when Kirk was twelve. Stillman, according to the press accounts, had then had sex with the daughter in the same room with her murdered parents. It had been in all the papers. In the prison, Stillman wore bib overalls and a straw hat. He never shaved. With a very long scraggily beard and hooded eyes, he claimed to worship the devil. He kept an altar in his cell. Stillman was called a nighttimer, or a shorteyes, as word in the prison was that the stronger inmates raped him at will. He also was supposed to be a snitch. Half advised Kirk to stay far away from Stillman. Kirk did. Kirk realized, though, that he needed friends. Unexpectedly, he gained a few. Friends like Half, like Big Nick—a very large and fierce-looking ex-Pagan who spotted weights in the gym.

It didn't take long. After a few weeks of being out in general population, Half approached him. "Word is, Blood, that they're trying to hit you," he told Kirk. "Word is there's a fifty-pack contract out on your ass." Kirk had been in the weight room every day his first weeks out. He'd met a couple other lifters. One was Bozo; another was Big Tony. He was getting physically strong again. He knew he'd have no life at all if he stayed locked down in protective custody. "Let 'em come," he said.

It happened, though, when he least expected it, when his guard was down. He was coming out of the weight room in the early afternoon in late May. He wanted to get in a shower before all the scud balls got in there. His mother had sent him a robe, and he went to his cell and changed into it. He wore the robe and a pair of tennis shoes into the shower. Kirk had learned to wash with his back to the wall, always alert. He thought he was alone and started shampooing his hair. He ducked his head under the water to rinse out the suds. Three guys suddenly were there, in front of him, all black men. They must have been waiting for him. One threw a soapy rag in his face, trying to blind him. The idea was to blind you, incapacitate you, flip you around, and then take turns raping you. The idea was to turn you into a punk. As the rag hit Kirk in the face, one of them swung a sock stuffed with batteries, a prison-made bola, and struck Kirk hard in the back of the head. Batteries flew everywhere as Kirk went to his knees.

He flailed back at them with everything he had. They were all slipping on the soapy floor. One tried to get a choke hold around Kirk's neck. Kirk was hurt and woozy, but still strong. He tried to bite the man's arm. He got punched hard and thought he was going to black out, that he was done. That's when Half showed up. Half could act like he was certifiably crazy. He had no fear. The men saw Half run in and they scattered. Half dragged Kirk out of the shower.

"Why did you help me?" Kirk asked him. He was bleeding badly from his head. Blood covered his face, making it difficult to see.

Half shrugged. "'Cause I felt like it." He smiled the snarl that showed off his starred tooth. "'Cause I like your name, maybe. Not so much the Kirk but the Noble and the Blood . . ."

Half had picked up a battery. He showed it to Kirk. "You were lucky, man. If that sock hadn't broke, they'd a whacked you over and over."

Kirk nodded. On the tiled island lay his towel. He used it to try and staunch the bleeding.

"You know, Blood," Half went on, "you're gonna' have to do something about this. I don't care how you get them, but you have to. If you don't, there ain't nothing I can do to help you."

"What?" Kirk said. "What you want me to do?"

"Think of something," Half answered. "'Cause whether you lose or not, you got to retaliate. See, the only way these people will stop messing with you, is if they know they got to fight you every time."

Kirk's head was badly split open. He needed medical care. Much as he hated to, he had to post at the infirmary. The warden got wind of his injury and gave Kirk ten days lockdown in solitary for fighting. The guards never found out who it was he fought with.

Two days after Kirk got back into general population, he saw the man who'd thrown the soapy rag in his face. For ten days Kirk had been thinking about what Half said. He'd never done a violent thing in his life, but he believed Half that they'd never let him alone if he let this go. The man was talking on the phone and hadn't seen Kirk. Kirk backed up around the corner. A skinhead was mopping the floor, using a bucket with a metal mop wringer. Kirk picked up the metal mop wringer by the handle. It weighed at least fifteen pounds. Just as he had riding in that police car the night of his arrest, Kirk felt that he was in some kind of bizarre movie. The man on the phone still had his back to Kirk. Kirk approached. His last few steps were silent. He knew how to track. When he was close enough, when he could hear the man whispering on the phone, Kirk whistled. The man turned, and as he did Kirk gave him all he had with the mop wringer. He hit him square across the temple and knocked the man up into the air and across the hall into the far wall. The man lay on the tier floor twitching. He remained in a coma for three days. No one ever said a word about it. No one saw anything. That was the way of the South Wing.

Half and Bozo came by to see Kirk that night. "See," Half said, "now you'll get some respect around here."

"I didn't like it," Kirk said. But there was an aspect to it that had made him feel better. He'd fought back and finally won a battle.

"You got to get 'em all," Half told him.

Kirk did. He caught another of the men alone, stoned, smoking a joint in a spot blind to the guards. Kirk's first punch caught him in the ear. Kirk pummeled him as hard and as fast as he could until he ran out of strength. The man lay in the fetal position, crying for Kirk to stop. "You leave me the fuck alone, you hear?" Kirk yelled into the ear he had torn and inflamed.

The third man didn't even resist. When Kirk caught him, he just went limp. Kirk shoved his face into a cell door several times. Kirk was learning to fit in.

TWENTY

UNDER THE LAW, when a person is charged with a crime but not yet convicted, that person is cloaked with the presumption of innocence. The burden is on the state to produce evidence to prove guilt beyond a reasonable doubt. Once a defendant is convicted in court, however, that presumption is reversed. A convicted felon is presumed to be guilty. To succeed on appeal, he has the burden of convincing a higher court that the trial judge committed a serious error or deprived him of a constitutional right. He must also show that the error or deprivation prejudiced his case and was not merely what is termed harmless error. Alternatively, if he can find what is referred to as newly discovered evidence—evidence unknown at trial that is sufficient to show his probable innocence, he may get a new trial that way.

Following Kirk's sentencing, Steven Scheinin and David Henninger withdrew as his lawyers. Neither were appellate specialists. Gary Christopher, head of the state public defender's death penalty unit, thought it best to have new, fresh minds review the case. Also, a claim of ineffective assistance of counsel, a potential basis for a new trial, is always a possibility on appeal. With Kirk facing a death sentence, every angle needed to be explored. Scheinin did not object. He offered to help in any way he could. Kirk welcomed the change.

In Maryland each county has its own district public defender in charge of that county's office. The district public defenders are under the supervision of the state public defender. The state public defender had set up a special unit dedicated to countering death penalty prosecutions. Gary Christopher, a University of North Carolina Law School graduate, who had clerked for Judge Marvin Smith on the Maryland Court of Appeals, had been chosen to direct this unit.

Typically, after a conviction, the public defender's office concentrates only on preparing the direct appeal. Julia Bernhardt and George Burns, two lawyers from the state public defender's appellate office, had been assigned this task. They would research and write the appellate briefs. But Curtis Bloodsworth had gone to Baltimore, met with Gary Christopher, and convinced him that there was other information out there that pointed to his son's innocence—information that had not surfaced at the trial. Gary Christopher met with Kirk. He was impressed with this twenty-five-year-old's zeal and his passionate protests that he was not the killer. Even while the appellate process was running its course, Christopher agreed to direct a parallel attack on the conviction.

While Bernhardt and Burns prepared the appeal, Christopher organized another investigation into the crime. Joanne Suder, an assistant trial lawyer, agreed to begin reinvestigating Dawn Hamilton's death, interviewing additional witnesses, looking for new evidence. Joanne worked with an investigator from her office, Doug Cook, a retired state trooper. Christopher also enlisted the help of the district public defender from nearby Montgomery County, Ted Weisman, who had a particular interest in death penalty cases. Weisman was willing to add his support to the effort. He agreed to work with Joanne and offered to lend two of his more experienced investigators, Sam Wallace and Randy Edwards, to help work the case. Together they coordinated the process of finding and trying to interview witnesses, not just the ones called by the state to testify at the trial but all potential witnesses, whether from Fontana Village, Randolph Road, or from Cambridge. They planned to go after anyone who might be able to shed light on the crime. It was an ambitious undertaking.

One way to clear Kirk would be to find the real killer of Dawn Hamilton. That's what Kirk wanted, what he kept insisting on. His new legal team set about trying to track down other suspects. Suder, Weisman, Cook, Wallace, Edwards, and others from their offices began investigating the crime from scratch, as though they were new detectives on an unsolved case. They were committed to changing Kirk's fate. They didn't know how much time they had before the appeal would be resolved, before the postconviction remedies might be exhausted, before the countdown to execution began. Their work took on a new urgency. Over the next year, Ted Weisman would personally devote thirty to forty hours a week trying to save Kirk Bloodsworth while continuing to supervise an office of fifty people.

Experienced investigators never know where the key to the puzzle may lie. They pursue every lead. They chase down the clues. They wring out every rag. When Joanne Suder met with Kirk following his sentencing, she promised him that her office would not rest until they found some way to aid him. Joanne came across to Kirk as someone who believed in his innocence, someone who sincerely cared about his plight. She told him not to worry too much, to keep up the faith. Once again, his hope flared.

Richard Gray was an obvious candidate for further study. Doug Cook interviewed ex-Detective Mark Bacon at his home and Bacon was cooperative, forthcoming. Much of what he offered, though, was suspicion rather than fact. Investigators questioned the residents of Fontana Village about Gray, but they learned little that was new. Detective Darden, the polygraph operator from the county police department, gave a short interview to Randy Edwards. Darden was the detective who had administered the lie detector test to Richard Gray two weeks after the murder. Darden admitted that Gray had failed the polygraph. But he was suspicious and cryptic during the interview. He wouldn't disclose the precise questions that were asked Gray or which ones he supposedly lied about. Darden said he'd talk more freely only if Ann Brobst would give him permission.

Edwards tracked down Richard Gray and cajoled him into talking. Gray told him that he wore size 8½ shoes. Edwards pressed him about some of the questions that had bothered Detective Bacon. Gray explained that he had eaten his lunch just prior to hearing over his police scanner the report about the missing girl. Before eating he had washed his hands at a gas station, which is why they were clean. He told Edwards that the reason he had picked up the underwear that was found in his car was that he always grabbed used rags when he could. He used them for cleaning his cars and shining his boots. Gray denied that he had a spot of blood on his shirt. It was red paint, he explained. He had been painting a gutter for someone the week before.

Gray seemed to have an explanation for everything. The investigators continued to probe.

They went to the *News American* offices where Gray had been employed and began asking around for any information about Gray, about Kirk Bloodsworth, looking for any clue. It was October 1985 when Doug Cook ran into a woman working at the *News American* who told him she was disturbed about the Bloodsworth conviction. She felt uneasy not so much about Richard Gray but about another colleague there, John Michael Anderson.

Anderson looked like the composite, she said. He was over six feet tall and wore a cowboy hat and cowboy boots most of the time. Her fifteen-year-old daughter had ridden with him once delivering papers and had returned home spooked. She'd told her mother she would never get in his car again. He had trash, razor blades, and dirty magazines all over the back and had acted weird and frightening.

Doug Cook found another *News American* employee who told him that after the Bloodsworth conviction, he'd overheard a colleague mention how closely Anderson resembled the composite sketch. A lightbulb flickered. This man had called the Fullerton Police Station and asked them whether Anderson had been investigated. He told them about Anderson's resemblance to the composite. The detective he spoke with told him that no, Anderson had not been investigated. Nor did they have any interest in Anderson. The man thought the detective had been rude.

Cook discussed this information with the lawyers. Maybe in Anderson they'd found their "Cowboy Bob," the suspect who kept appearing on the earlier police reports, the one mentioned repeatedly by the residents of Fontana Village the day of the crime.

Cook learned that Anderson often rented cars from Betz Auto Leasing in Rosedale. Randy Edwards and Sam Wallace visited there. On July 25, 1984, Anderson had rented a 1975 Pontiac LeMans in the morning, then returned it that afternoon and exchanged it without explanation for a different car. The Pontiac had a red interior and the carpet inside was a burgundy color. The carpet was made up of red fibers. A Betz employee who rented the car that day, recalled having seen child pornography in the car when Anderson returned it. It also had boxes of sweets, candy, and gum in it. She believed at the time that the sweets were to lure little girls into the car and advised her boss to call the police. There was also a large stain on the carpet in the trunk. Another Betz employee told the investigators that she remembered a car Anderson returned on a different day, in early August 1984, an Oldsmobile with a trunk full of trash. She'd been the one who had to clean it out. There was a half pint of whiskey, she recalled, a half joint, some gay magazines, a box of child pornography—pictures of children and adults having sex, and some chewing gum wrappers. Big Red gum wrappers, she specifically recalled. It also had empty candy boxes in it.

The Pontiac had been sold some months before. Wallace and Edwards tried to track it down so that the stain in the trunk could be analyzed. They followed it through three different owners, but the trail disappeared. Whoever bought it last had left town. There was no trace of where it went.

Sam Wallace learned that Anderson had a criminal arrest record and had been treated for mental problems. Eventually, he discovered that Anderson had a court appearance coming up in nearby Montgomery County. Anderson had been charged with assault. Wallace was waiting for him.

In the courthouse corridor, Wallace told him he was looking for help in the Kirk Bloodsworth case. He told Anderson he was looking for information about Richard Gray. Anderson had his lawyer with him and agreed to be interviewed. The lawyer left to do other things. Anderson was talkative, friendly. He did resemble the composite sketch. He knew Richard Gray's wife, he said, and liked her, but he thought Gray was dirty, unkempt. He confirmed he often wore a cowboy hat and boots but sometimes wore tennis shoes when he had to deliver papers himself. He told Wallace that he had a mustache back in July and owned some Ocean Pacific shirts. He admitted to using cocaine and pot sometimes and described himself as a binger. As far as July 25, he was out doing his job, he said. He recalled Gray's wife mentioning something about her husband's finding the little girl's clothes, but Anderson couldn't remember where that conversation occurred. July was a while back. He was a bit fuzzy.

The investigative team wasn't about to narrow the scope of its inquiries to one possibility. It also set out to learn more about the suspect known as the Candy Man. W. F. Johnson, the man who passed out lollipops to little girls at the Calvary Baptist Church was the one Detective Milton Duckworth had suspected of committing the murder. Wallace and Edwards interviewed him in February of 1986. They thought he rambled, contradicted himself, had trouble maintaining his focus on one subject. He offered little useful information and said nothing incriminating. They obtained his psychiatric records from the Clifton Perkins State Mental Hospital. The records were voluminous. He'd been treated for pedophilia and discharged in 1975 on a five-year conditional release. Interesting, but not much help.

During this time, Wallace and Edwards continued to pursue interviews of the trial witnesses. Thelma Stultz was questioned in March. She remembered, for the first time, that Kirk had specifically denied committing the crime and had told her that the person who did it was sick. Wallace and Edwards visited James Keller in May. They showed Keller a photographic array that Wallace had put together containing Kirk's picture. Keller identified someone other than Kirk as the stranger he'd seen at Fontana Village on the day of the murder. Throughout the interview, Keller kept pointing to the picture of this other man, referring to him as the one he'd seen.

Donna Ferguson and Nancy Hall were interviewed. While admitting that she was high on marijuana the morning of the murder, Ferguson said, "I don't think I was *completely delirious* when I saw the man." Nancy Hall told Wallace that she'd kicked her drug problem, that she was clean. During their meeting, her eyes were bloodshot, her pupils dilated. They remained so even in the bright sunlight. And she slurred her words. Wallace and Edwards both thought she was stoned.

Gary Christopher met with Kirk numerous times. He went out

to the crime scene and walked it. He didn't believe that anyone not intimately familiar with those woods could have killed Dawn Hamilton and then found a way out through the back paths. The woods were dense with thorny underbrush and covered with poison ivy. Kirk Bloodsworth had not been infected with a rash when arrested. Christopher became convinced that Kirk was innocent of the crime. The question was what to do with all of this information. How to use it to get Kirk a new trial. Gary Christopher and the other lawyers began researching a way to turn it all into a pleading they could file, a way to bring the case back before the court.

TWENTY-ONE

ON THE TIER above the cell where Kirk was imprisoned, almost directly overhead, was the room that contained Maryland's gas chamber. A few of the guards had a nasty habit. They liked reminding Kirk that it was there waiting for him; they got their kicks by talking in his presence about just how the process worked.

In the center of the room, like some large deep-sea diving bell, stood the chamber, a hexagonal structure, eight feet high, made of steel and surrounded by reinforced glass windows. It had been constructed in 1956. Bolted to the floor was what everyone referred to as the captain's chair. It was made of steel with interlocking cuffs for wrists and ankles. It had thick leather straps attached to it that would restrain the body during the convulsions caused by gas poisoning. The glass panels existed so that the select witnesses could watch the final death throes of the person being executed.

Inside the chamber and underneath the chair was a stainless steel vat. Sulfuric acid would be poured into the vat. Cyanide tablets, wrapped in gauze, would then slowly be lowered through a mechanized lever into the acid. As the tablets dissolved, they filled the room with the sharp, acrid, and lethal hydrocyanic gas that burned the eyes, nose, throat, and lungs. It wasn't supposed to take too long, maybe ten minutes or so. Sometimes longer if you were a big person like Kirk. The gas caused gagging, foaming at the mouth, writhing, and convulsions.

Every time Kirk walked into the prison yard, every day, he could see to the roof above the chamber where the state executed its prisoners, where the state was planning to take him. There were ventilation pipes running up through the concrete. These pipes were unique to the prison. They let the gas escape.

Kirk didn't know why he was compelled to look every day. He had a fixation. He couldn't help himself. His neck would just turn, his eyes move to those pipes. He had to see if they were still there.

Once some guards told him they needed him on a painting detail. They escorted him up to the level above his cell. They took him to the room where the gas chamber stood open, handed him a can of paint and a brush, and pushed him inside. They wanted him to see the vat and the captain's chair. "You'll be the captain, soon," one of them said. "We want to get it ready, for you." The man grinned. "Take a good look, Captain Kirk . . . Paint it up. Make it nice and prime for your bad ass . . ."

Kirk began to dream of suffocation. He'd wake up unable to breathe, choking, gasping for breath, as though a kerosene-soaked rag had been stuffed down his throat. He couldn't shake it. He'd wake gagging, run to the toilet, and throw up. This happened over and over.

In Maryland, the highest appellate court, the supreme court for the state, is called the Maryland Court of Appeals. There is also the Maryland Court of Special Appeals. Under the state's judicial structure, the court of special appeals usually hears and decides cases first. Because of his death sentence, Kirk was entitled to appeal directly to the state's highest court.

An appeal of a case is a true exercise in legal scholarship. There are no live witnesses; there is no testimony. Court reporters transcribe all of the proceedings that took place in the lower court. Every word of every witness who appeared at trial is set down. Arguments of the lawyers, objections, and rulings of the judge all are recorded in a transcript that can easily run thousands of pages. Appellate lawyers are given the responsibility of reviewing these written transcripts, looking for judicial error, looking for things that the prosecutors or the judge did that were legally improper and that caused prejudice to the defendant.

A good appellate lawyer must know the law well in order to identify possible issues as the volumes of transcripts are read. Then, once the transcript has been reviewed and digested, the legal research begins. The lawyer must develop the arguments around the issues identified and find the legal cases, whether recent or ancient, that support those arguments. Finally, the appellate brief must be written. If done well, it concisely and convincingly sets forth the facts, the issues, the arguments that mandate a reversal, and the legal authorities that support those arguments.

While the defense team continued its intensive efforts to turn up new evidence, Kirk's appellate lawyers spent months preparing his appellate brief. When they finally filed it, the pleading ran to ninety-two pages. In it his lawyers raised sixteen different questions for the court to consider. Of these, six would be the main focus of oral argument, any of which could possibly win the day. Was the evidence sufficient to sustain the conviction? Was the shoe evidence admissible? Did Judge Hinkel err in refusing to strike a prospective juror who had counseled the mother of the victim? Did the suppression by the state of the Richard Gray material violate the defendant's right to a fair trial? Was Birdie Plutschak wrongly prevented from relating what the defendant had said to her? Did the trial judge abuse his discretion in excluding the testimony of the eyewitness identification expert? As is standard procedure, the lawyers were allotted one hour for oral argument, a half hour per side.

The night before the appellate argument, Julia Bernhardt and George Burns worked late preparing. They kicked the issues back and forth, tried to anticipate the questions the judges might ask, rehearsed what they planned to say.

While in law school, Julia Bernhardt had worked as a law clerk in the public defender's office. Upon graduation, she'd served as a clerk for Judge Joseph Kaplan of the Baltimore City Circuit Court. In 1982 she accepted a job in the appellate division of the public defender and had worked there since. It was agreed that she would prepare and present the main argument. After the attorney representing the state finished arguing, Burns would handle the rebuttal.

The next day, March 4, 1986, Kirk's brigade of public defenders traveled to Annapolis. They came to watch, to hope, and to assist Bernhardt and Burns as they argued their points before the seven judges of the Maryland Court of Appeals.

The court of appeals has an imposing and stately interior. It reeks of old English, of the pomp and circumstance of colonial times. Walking into the courtroom is like walking into a theater. The lights are dimmed. Instead of a stage, a raised dais of polished mahogany four feet or so above the floor spans the front of the room. There are seven high-backed burgundy leather chairs behind the long bench. Behind the chairs, on each side of the platform, are large mahogany doors. When the court is called to order, the seven judges, all dressed in scarlet robes with white dickeys, simultaneously step out through the doors, three judges from one side, four from the other, and take their seats at the raised bench.

When the Bloodsworth case was announced, Julia Bernhardt rose to speak. She took her place behind a wooden podium, inset with a digital timer and a microphone. The timer would tick off her thirty minutes. A red light would flash when her allotted time was up.

Bernhardt began her presentation by arguing that the evidence put forward by the state was weak, of poor quality, insufficient to support a conviction. She liked to begin with an attack on the quality of the evidence, because even if the argument failed, she believed that first thrust tended to soften up the judges, make them more amenable to her other points. She went on to hammer home her complaint about the government's failure to turn over Detective Bacon's report on Richard Gray. This was classic *Brady* material, she argued. It was exculpatory. The defense had a right to know about it. She moved to the exclusion of Dr. Buckout's testimony. While there were a number of issues to address, the judges, from their questions, seemed interested in returning to the sufficiency of the evidence issue and also the *Brady* question. Why hadn't Detective Bacon's report been turned over? And if it had been, might it have changed the outcome?

Valerie Cloutier argued on behalf of the state. Cloutier was no stranger to the court of appeals. She had been a teacher and had also worked for the federal government in military intelligence before going to law school. Like Bernhardt, she too had clerked for a circuit court judge, Judge Eugene Lerner of Anne Arundel County. Following her clerkship, she'd gone to work for the Criminal Appeals Division of Maryland's Office of the Attorney General. By the time of the Bloodsworth argument, she'd been promoted to deputy of that division and had argued dozens of cases in the court of appeals.

Cloutier had seen the photographs of Dawn Hamilton. The photographs were so vivid that they had upset even a seasoned attorney like herself. She assumed they also must also have shaken the jurors. Cloutier appreciated the fact that the evidence against Bloodsworth, since it was mostly circumstantial, might give the court pause. She rose to parry the thrusts made by Bernhardt.

Cloutier was hit with a wave of questions from the bench. Judge Marvin Smith, who ended up authoring the court's opinion, asked in his gravelly voice whether the state really wanted to send someone to death based on circumstantial evidence. His brow was wrinkled. He looked troubled. Judges John Eldridge and Harry Cole pummeled her with similar questions. They asked about the Detective Bacon statement, about why the trial judge hadn't let Birdie Plutschak respond to what the "bad thing" was that Kirk had told her, after the state had placed such importance on Bloodsworth's words. Cloutier could hardly keep up with the barrage of questions. Afterward she felt like she'd been in a prize fight. She felt bruised. She told her husband later that night that the court was going to find some reason to overturn the conviction.

All the lawyers that day were impressive. They addressed each judge by name when answering their queries. Bernhardt and Burns knew that several of the seven were bothered by the issues. They'd need a majority to overturn the conviction. They thought they had a real chance.

On July 29, 1986, almost two years after Kirk Bloodsworth's arrest, the court of appeals handed down its opinion. In its ruling it first concluded that there was enough evidence, viewed in the light most favorable to the prosecution, for a rational fact finder to conclude that Bloodsworth was guilty beyond a reasonable doubt. Bloodsworth lost that one. The court also ruled, after an extensive analysis, that the trial judge did not abuse his discretion in excluding the testimony of the eyewitness expert, Dr. Robert Buckout. Under Maryland law, trial judges are vested with wide discretion in ruling on the admissibility of expert witness testimony. The court concluded that Judge Hinkel had a reasonable basis for excluding Buckout. The court of appeals went on, however, to find that the prosecutors' failure to turn over the Mark Bacon report on Richard Gray was a violation of the state's duty under *Brady v. Maryland* to

provide the defense with all exculpatory evidence. The court concluded that this oversight was "sufficient to undermine confidence
in the outcome of the trial." It also suggested that the FBI "shoe expert" evidence should be left out of any subsequent prosecution.
The court found that Judge Hinkel also committed error in refusing to let Birdie Plutschak testify about what Bloodsworth told her
was the "bad thing" that he had done. Since her testimony would
have offered a contemporaneous explanation of Bloodsworth's
alleged admission to Rose Carson, made before he ever knew he
was a suspect, it should have been allowed. Of critical importance,
though, was that the court of appeals reversed the conviction. The
case would be remanded back to the Baltimore County Circuit
Court. Kirk Bloodsworth was once again presumed innocent. He
would be transferred off of death row and sent back to the county
detention center. He would have the opportunity to try once again
to save his life and clear his name.

PART VI

BROKEN JUSTICE

The quality of mercy . . .
It is enthroned in the
   hearts of kings,
It is an attribute to God
   himself,
And earthly power doth
   then show likest God's
When mercy seasons
   justice.

—WILLIAM SHAKESPEARE

TWENTY-TWO

THE DAY THAT Judge Hinkel signed the warrant of execution for Kirk Bloodsworth, March 28, 1985, he'd received a strange phone call from a man who identified himself as Dr. Gene F. Ostrom. Dr. Ostrom was the director of the Eastern Regional Mental Health Center located near where Dawn Hamilton was killed. Ostrom told Judge Hinkel that he was torn over having to make the call. It was a breach of patient confidentiality, he said. But weighed against the possibility of an innocent man being put to death, he'd concluded it was necessary.

"Yes?" Judge Hinkel said, trying to move things along. He had a busy court docket to handle.

Ostrom told him that on the afternoon that Dawn was murdered, a patient of the clinic had unexpectedly appeared asking to see a counselor to talk about a relationship with a young girl. The patient's name was David Rehill. He bore an uncanny resemblance to the portrait of the killer in the composite sketch.

Hinkel was irritated. "Why wait until now to come forward?" he asked. "After the trial has been completed and the defendant sentenced?"

Dr. Ostrom explained that he'd hoped Bloodsworth might not be convicted. That he had struggled over what to do because of his obligation to his patient.

Judge Hinkel thanked him for the information. He then picked up the phone and contacted Bob Lazzaro at the state's attorney's office. He told Lazzaro what Ostrom had said. "You need to investigate this," he told Lazzaro. "And pass it on to Bloodsworth's lawyers."

Lazzaro discussed this new information with his supervisors. The concensus was that the police should investigate this new information before anything else was done with it. Lazzaro passed the information on to Detectives Ramsey and Capel. He left the state's attorney's office a few months later to enter private practice. Lazzaro never informed Steven Scheinin or any of Bloodsworth's attorneys about the Ostrom phone call, and Hinkel never gave it another thought.

Once Kirk was transferred back to the detention center, he met with Katy O'Donnell and Donna Shearer, both trial lawyers with the public defender service. Joanne Suder was leaving the office, and they'd been assigned as his new attorneys. Both felt that given the nature of the crime, a team of women lawyers might provide Kirk with his best chance in front of a jury. O'Donnell would be lead counsel. She was smart and optimistic that they could win, particularly given all the material her office had uncovered in its investigation. Kirk liked her. But he didn't want to make any mistakes this time. He'd gone with the advice of the public defender in the first trial. A real money lawyer, he thought, a high-dollar guy, somebody who knows the judges, somebody who wins cases, was what he wanted.

Curtis and Jeanette were as ecstatic as Kirk about the reversal and the new trial. This time Curtis promised to do whatever he could, to spare nothing to save his son.

While in the chow line one afternoon, another inmate began telling Kirk about a lawyer named Leslie Stein. Stein was the slickest of slick, he told Kirk. He represented a number of the big-time drug boosters—the ones with money. Stein had gotten a lot of them off. The next day Kirk heard about Stein from a different inmate down in the laundry. He asked around. Everyone said Stein was the man. Even Kirk's marine friend, Officer Flaherty, confirmed that Stein had a good reputation.

Kirk asked Curtis to see if Leslie Stein would visit him. Stein met with Kirk in early October. Kirk saw why people thought the man was smooth. A fast talker, dark haired with streaks of gray, and well dressed, Stein wore a pin-stripe suit, a black silk tie, and a gold Rolex watch. He'd be a good match for Lazzaro. Stein told Kirk right up front, "A lot of things are going to be different this time. We're going to win this thing." He exuded confidence. He picked up on details. "When it's over," Stein said smiling, "I'm buying you a steak dinner at a fine restaurant out on the street." *Out on the street . . .* Those were the words Kirk needed to hear.

Kirk believed him. He needed desperately to believe him. While Kirk liked Katy O'Donnell and the other lawyers from the public defender's office and felt a twinge of guilt about dismissing them after all the work they'd done, this was his life at stake. He needed the very best professional he could afford.

Kirk asked Curtis and Jeanette to meet with Leslie Stein. Kirk knew it would be a stretch for them, but if they were equally impressed he hoped his father would figure out a way to raise the money. He'd pay his father back, he promised. He'd pay him back every nickel.

Stein wanted $25,000 to represent Kirk. He agreed to accept $15,000 up front, with the other $10,000 due April 17. Curtis had spent the little money he had remaining from the 1984 loan. Every week he tried to give Kirk cash for commissary, $30, $40 at a clip.

It added up. Ronald Raubaugh, the investigator he'd rehired, had not come cheap. Now this. But this time he didn't hesitate. He went back to the National Bank of Cambridge and, together with Jeanette, convinced them to lend him another $25,000. In mid-October, he signed a retainer agreement with Leslie Stein, paying him the first installment.

Kirk's spirits were rising. He geared himself up for another fight. He tried to ignore the anger that now constantly welled up. He needed to have a clear mind, to ready himself for war, to prepare better for his testimony this time around. He intended to show the jury who he really was.

But Leslie Stein had other ideas. After reading the transcript from the first trial and meeting with Kirk's alibi witnesses, Stein concluded that the alibi was a loser. It hadn't worked in front of one jury, and there was no reason to believe it would work in front of another. The witnesses were not impressive, and they didn't seem particularly interested in cooperating anymore. He also had doubts as to whether Kirk should testify. He didn't think Kirk had helped himself much by taking the stand. Kirk was already locked into this excuse about a taco salad and Stein thought it was a major liability. He didn't want this next jury to hear what sounded like such a lame and contrived explanation for statements that seemed so incriminating. The state's case was weak, and Stein believed he could discredit the state's key witnesses and create sufficient doubt surrounding the other evidence of guilt: Kirk's leaving town and the statements he made in Cambridge. Stein was good at cross-examination. He relished taking a witness down. He also liked the idea of blaming the murder on someone else—Richard Gray being the prime candidate. Kirk kept bugging him about finding the real killer. If Stein could undercut the state's case and give the jury another suspect to blame for this terrible crime, he thought he could walk Kirk Bloodsworth.

Stein developed some additional strategies. Why were the police so certain that Dawn had been killed where she had been found? And was the rock, the so-called bloody rock, even the murder weapon? There had been only one small spot of coloration on the rock, what one detective surmised *might have been* blood. And though the rock apparently had been tested, there was no evidence that Dawn Hamilton's blood was on it. Stein saw firsthand that the rock was porous, crumbly. Lining the bottom of the plastic evidence bag in which the rock was stored were fragments and particles of the porous material. It had crumbled right there in the evidence room. Yet there had been no rock fragments found in Dawn's skull or scalp, in her matted hair, or in her blood. If she'd been struck by this crumbly rock, why weren't there fragments embedded in her tissues? Moreover there was evidence in the coroner's report suggesting that the injuries to Dawn's brain were *contrecoup* injuries — damage caused not by a hard object striking the brain but by the brain being violently forced against a hard object. Perhaps her head had been slammed into a tree or an asphalt road. If the rock were not the real murder weapon, the fact that Kirk had been talking about a bloody rock actually showed he was innocent — that he had only been duped by Ramsey and Capel's misguided gambit, tricked into believing that a rock had killed Dawn Hamilton when it hadn't. Stein hired a brain specialist to review the autopsy report. The doctor agreed with Stein's theory.

Stein was an experienced and talented trial lawyer. He'd spent seven years as a Baltimore City prosecutor and found an even better outlet for his skills as a defense attorney. He believed his client was innocent. What concerned him most, though, was the fact that this was a second trial. The jurors couldn't help but learn that Kirk had been tried before. Transcripts from the first trial would be used to impeach witnesses. Stein expected the newspapers to run front-page stories of the case every day. He knew of no way to prevent the jurors from learning that Kirk had been previously convicted for this terrible murder. This undoubtedly would make it harder for them to find him not guilty. Stein considered asking for a sequestration of the jury. He knew the prosecution would fight it, and the jurors always ended up angry at the defense for requesting it. After hearing portions of the transcripts read, the jurors would figure out that Kirk had been found guilty anyway. Stein decided to forgo the request. He'd just have to overcome this impediment.

The trial was set for late March 1987, and Kirk had drawn a new judge, James T. Smith. This was a possible break. Smith had worked his way through the University of Maryland Law School at night, earning a living as a law clerk during the day. Once he passed the bar, he began taking appointments defending indigents. From 1973 to 1977 he'd served in a part-time position as the county's deputy public defender. He'd been appointed to the circuit court in 1985 by Governor Harry Hughes. Smith had a reputation for being fair-minded, a middle-of-the-road kind of judge.

Still, as the trial approached, Kirk grew more nervous. He began to second-guess Stein about the alibi. He was truly, in fact, at the row house on South Randolph Road that day, he told Stein. Shouldn't Stein at least call one or two of the witnesses?

A week before the trial, Stein visited Kirk at the detention center and explained again why, in his view, the alibi had backfired in the first case. They discussed again whether Kirk should testify. Stein was sure of himself, cocky. Kirk felt like Stein was trying to sell him a car. Stein told Kirk again that his taking the stand before had only hurt him. He was too easy a target on cross. Stein promised Kirk once more that he'd soon be buying him a steak dinner. Kirk agreed that the alibi witnesses wouldn't be called and that he'd stay off the witness stand.

Since Robert Lazzaro had left the office of the state's attorney for private practice, Ann Brobst was assigned to lead the prosecution team. A new lawyer, Michael Pulver, would assist her. From the first moment in court, it was clear that Brobst would run the show. It was clear too that she hadn't lost her animosity toward Kirk Bloodsworth. Just seeing her caused the fear to coagulate in his chest. He felt it there, heavy, like a palpable knot of phlegm. The woman just made him sick.

Eleven days before trial, the state's attorney's office notified Leslie Stein for the first time about the information provided to Judge Hinkel by Dr. Ostrom—the appearance at his mental health clinic the afternoon of Dawn Hamilton's murder of a man resembling the composite and needing to speak with a counselor. For two years, since March of 1985 and even after the court of appeals had reversed Bloodsworth's conviction for the state's failure to turn over exculpatory information, the state had withheld Ostrom's revelations from the defense. Stein sent an investigator out to Ostrom's clinic, but no one there that day seemed to remember much. With just over a week to go before jury selection and much to do to prepare, Stein felt he didn't have the time to further pursue this new lead. He decided not to ask for a continuance. He made the judgment to forge ahead, to attack the state's evidence, to make Richard Gray the scapegoat, to ignore both David Rehill and John Michael Anderson.

The trial commenced on March 23, 1987. Stein requested that he be allowed to adopt all previous motions. He also argued that because of all the pretrial publicity and because it was a death case, Judge Smith should question each prospective juror individually before selecting a panel. Smith agreed to do this. Again the jury would be death qualified. The questioning of jurors began on the morning of March 24 and ran through March 26.

To Kirk, Judge Smith seemed very different from Judge Hinkel. Smith took his time, went out of his way to be solicitous. He brought Kirk back into his chambers during the jury selection process so that Kirk could watch. He reminded Kirk of Mr. Rogers on children's television. Smith was patient, polite. He seemed to listen with an open mind before he ruled.

The next morning Michael Pulver opened for the state. The state's strategy, like before, was to emphasize the terrible nature of the crime.

> *While murder, rape and sodomy are the technical names we give to these charges, they by no means begin to describe for you the enormity of the crime that was committed or the horribleness of her death. The facts in this case go beyond really my limited ability to express. They go beyond comprehension of any decent person. They are best, I suppose, compared to a nightmare. A nightmare that ended for young Dawn Hamilton when she finally died, after having been crushed with a rock, strangled and sexually assaulted. . . .*

Pulver backed and filled.

> *The defendant then lured Dawn into the woods, deep into the woods, far from the town homes, and then once, as I said, far away from everybody else, far from any potential passers-by, he turned and viciously attacked her with a rock, smashed her in the face and in the skull with a rock, crushing her skull, and he strangled her by standing on her throat for so long and with such force that when he finally lifted his foot, embedded in the soft skin of her neck, was the imprint of his shoe. And as if destroying this little girl were not horrible enough, if that were not enough, he raped her, and sodomized her, and then in one last act of perversion, and I hesitate to even mention it to you, but it is a fact in this case, took a stick and stuck it into her vagina, approximately five and a half inches. . . .*

The worse the crime, the more horrible the facts, the more the jury could be made to despise the perpetrator, the harder it would be for them to acquit. Pulver described the facts in graphic detail. He outlined as well the evidence the state expected to prove. He put the state's spin on the rock-and-panties gambit Ramsey and Capel had used on Bloodsworth:

> *Before talking with him, they went to a local five and dime and they bought a pair of shorts and a pair of underwear that matched those worn by Dawn the day that she was murdered. And from off the parking lot at police headquarters they picked up a large rock. They took all these items and put them in the interview room. It was their hope that if the person that had done this to Dawn saw these items they might react in some unusual manner. . . . Upon entering the interview room, the defendant took no apparent notice of the rock and panties and they were immediately taken off the table, out of view. . . .*

Pulver turned this against Kirk by relating the statements Kirk made afterward in Cambridge about a bloody rock. Pulver insinuated that Kirk had never even seen the rock in the police interrogation room and only knew of it because he'd used it to murder Dawn Hamilton. Pulver described the identifications of the state's witnesses and how they came about. He told the jury to use its collective life experience, its common sense. He asked them to return a verdict of guilty.

Michael Pulver was good, but Leslie Stein was also ready. He first tried to tell Kirk's story from Kirk's point of view: A twenty-three-year-old kid never before arrested who found himself in a strange town and enmeshed in an intolerable marriage. So he left, went home, only to be arrested for the worst of crimes, thrown into his own unimaginable nightmare. Stein then suggested that this case, from the investigative standpoint, was backward. Rather than find clues leading to Kirk Bloodsworth, the police, for the skimpiest of reasons, had zeroed in on Kirk Bloodsworth and then gone out and searched for clues to incriminate him. The police were in a fishbowl,

Stein said. The media coverage was relentless, demanding that the murderer be caught, and the police made assumptions, wrong assumptions, about the murder weapon and the murderer, and everything flowed from there. The eyewitness identifications, Stein promised, would be shown to be unreliable. The witnesses who went into the lineup already knew who they would pick out. Each one of them, he said, had already seen Bloodsworth on television, or somewhere else. The lineup was a travesty. Stein promised the jury a hotly contested trial. He set out to deliver on his promise.

That night, back at the jail, Kirk was excited. His lawyer had been compelling. There was a sense of urgency about Stein's presentation. Kirk felt he'd been effective. Stein had countered Pulver well. For the first time Kirk thought his lawyer might really save him.

TWENTY-THREE

THE STATE DIDN'T deviate much in its presentation of evidence from what had worked as a winning trial strategy before, though this time no forensic witnesses from the FBI would be called. The scientific evidence, the state contended, was simply neutral, not probative of anything. Leslie Stein, though, went off on new tacks. In cross-examining Elinor Helmick and Thomas Hamilton, Stein asked questions about Richard Gray. Early on, he began developing his argument that Gray was more likely than Kirk Bloodsworth to be the murderer.

Again Ann Brobst sought to introduce the grisly photographs of Dawn, and again, over objection, the judge permitted them to be shown. As before, the jurors couldn't help but be viscerally shaken by the pictures.

When Brobst called Detective Roeder, the crime lab technician, Stein began to chip away at the assumption that the rock killed Dawn Hamilton. It was porous and crumbly, admitted Roeder, who'd retrieved the rock from the scene. Stein questioned him as to whether any debris matching the rock fragments had been found in any of Dawn's wounds or hair or anywhere on her skin or clothes.

Roeder's answer was no. If she was struck by a porous, crumbling rock, Stein asked rhetorically, why weren't there fragments in her scalp?

Dr. Dennis Smyth, the medical examiner, testified again. Stein questioned Smyth extensively about the swabs he had taken from the vagina and rectum of the victim at autopsy, samples from which, when smeared on glass slides, the doctor had found semen. Why had the FBI been unable to find any sperm on the swabs? Smyth had no answer. Regarding the cause of death, Smyth admitted the victim's brain had *contrecoup* injuries, which could have been caused by having her head slammed against a hard surface. Smyth also admitted that no one had ever shown him the rock or asked him to test it.

Chris Shipley was the first of the ID witnesses. Now thirteen years old, he told the jury that the height of the man by the pond was "six something." Stein gently took him over the various descriptions he had given since the crime. *Six something?* Stein repeated. Wasn't your first description of the man's height, back on the day of the murder, six feet five inches? And at the first trial, didn't you change it to six feet? And now you're saying six something? "And why does his height change? Why is it six feet five in July of '84; why is it six feet tall in March of '85; and why it is six feet something in March of '86?" Chris had no answer. Stein got Chris to remember that when he'd picked out the photo of Bloodsworth, he told the detective that the man at the pond had hair that wasn't as red. Chris also acknowledged that the man at the pond did not have sideburns. Stein's implication was clear: someone was trying to fit a square peg into a round hole.

Jackie Poling testified, as did his mother, Denise. Ann Brobst didn't even ask Jackie to identify Bloodsworth in court this time, but had both him and his mother explain how he'd recognized Bloodsworth in the lineup but been too scared to tell the detectives.

Denise said her son told her what happened right after the lineup. Stein's tone and manner conveyed his disdain for Denise and for her testimony. Why in the world, given the urgency of a major murder investigation involving the killing of a child, had she waited several weeks before notifying police about what her son had told her? She had no explanation. He asked her then about the reward: "How much money did your son receive or did you receive in connection with his assistance in solving this case?"

"Christian and Jackie each received a check," she answered.

"For how much?"

"Around $230," she said.

"That's a lot of money to you, isn't it?"

"Yes, it is," she answered.

The other eyewitnesses followed the boys. Neither Hall nor Ferguson held up particularly well. Stein made them both look bad. Hall admitted she'd seen Kirk on television the night before the lineup. Who else were you going to pick out, Stein queried, when you saw the man on television the night before? Ferguson admitted she'd been doped up the morning of the crime and had made inconsistent statements to the police. James Keller went last. His testimony exemplified the problems inherent in a trial held almost three years after an event. Keller claimed he was dead-on certain Kirk was the one. Yet on cross-examination, he couldn't recall whether the strange man he'd seen had a beard or not. Stein also had him admit that he'd picked a different man out of the photo array shown to him by defense investigators. All Ann Brobst could do was have Keller reiterate his lineup ID and his certitude that Bloodsworth was the stranger he'd seen while driving out of the Fontana Village complex.

That night, as Kirk obsessed over the evidence, he felt upbeat. He liked the way Stein was going after the witnesses. He thought most of them looked stupid.

Stein had been readying himself to confront Robert Capel. A botched investigation, the improper assumptions made by the detectives, overly suggestive identification procedures—these were at the core of Stein's defense. Stein knew Capel was a pro in court. He'd been testifying for years. Capel took his time on the stand, made eye contact with the jurors, explained things carefully. He'd be tough to crack. Right up front, though, Stein had him on his heels.

"Detective Capel, how long were you at the scene at Fontana Village," Stein asked.

"Twenty minutes," Capel answered.

"And why did you take that rock?"

"The rock was a piece of evidence taken at the scene."

"A piece of evidence of what?"

"We believed that was the murder weapon."

"You made that decision in twenty minutes?"

"No, sir. I wasn't in charge of the crime scene or the evidence."

Stein began to find his rhythm. "So your partner, Detective Ramsey, *assumed* that was the murder weapon?"

"Detective Ramsey took the rock as evidence, yes, sir."

"Did you ever show that rock to the medical examiner?"

"I don't know, Counselor. I believe that was shown to the medical examiner, but I don't know."

"Do you have a report of that?"

"No, sir, I don't believe I do."

"In any of the ten pounds of paperwork was there any report that this rock was ever shown to the medical examiner?"

"Not to my knowledge, sir."

"What then, did you base the assumption on that this was the murder weapon?"

"I didn't assume anything."

"When you first questioned Mr. Bloodsworth in Cambridge, why did you go get a rock—you and Ramsey—go get a rock off the lot and get a pair of panties and put them on the table, if you didn't *assume* anything?"

Capel had no good answer. Stein's insinuation gained credence. The rock had never been tested. There was no evidence in the case, other than the assumptions made by the detectives that it was even involved in Dawn's death.

Stein also tried to raise doubts about Capel's truthfulness. He insinuated that Capel's story of having brought in another detective, shorter than six feet five inches, for Chris Shipley to look at, was made up: "You testified that he described the man as six feet five inches?" Stein asked Capel. "Where in your report does it say that after you took that statement you brought a police officer in there, confronted Mr. Shipley with the height, and Mr. Shipley changed it and said that the man he saw was shorter than the police officer?"

Capel got red in the face. He strained for an answer.

"Concerning all the reports you have written, show me a written report that describes the scenario that you just told us about," Stein demanded.

"There is nothing written," Capel admitted.

"What is the name of the police officer you brought in?" Stein demanded to know.

Capel's confidence was draining away. "I don't know," he said.

Stein kept at him. He had Capel identify again the photograph of Bloodsworth that he and Ramsey had taken the day before Bloodsworth's arrest, in which Bloodsworth had long mutton-chop sideburns. "Let me ask you something," Stein then said. "Did you ever ask Mr. Shipley, who was giving you this composite, did you ever ask Mr. Shipley whether or not the suspect had sideburns?"

"No, sir, I never do that."

"You never did?"

"No, I don't do that."

"And when Mr. Shipley, when you talked to him and he gave a description did he ever say anything to you about sideburns?"

"No, he didn't."

Stein moved on to mine the misguided gambit played out by Capel and Ramsey—the rock and the panties that they placed on the interrogation table before Bloodsworth was first questioned, expecting a reaction if he was the killer.

"I want to make sure I understand your testimony," Stein said. "This little test, the passing grade was no reaction. The failing grade was some sort of reaction, like a violent reaction?"

"Some reaction, yes, sir," Capel answered.

"And did Mr. Bloodsworth have a reaction?"

"Yes, very definite."

Stein was surprised at this. "And what was his reaction?" he queried.

"It was not an immediate reaction, but it was a long-term reaction." Capel tried to explain. "He remembered everything we put on that table although we removed it."

"Wait a minute, detective," Stein pressed. "When Mr. Bloodsworth walked into that room, did he have a reaction?"

"No," Capel answered, reversing himself. "When he walked in the room, I wasn't even sure he saw the items. He glanced around—"

"Did Mr. Bloodsworth, yes or no, have a reaction when he walked into that room?"

"No. He showed no visible reaction."

"And now you're telling us that a possible reason why he had no visible reaction is because you don't even know if he saw the items?"

"I do know now. I didn't know then."

"Then what was the purpose of the test? If the whole purpose of the test was to have somebody look at the items, why did you then take the items off the table?"

Capel answered that he was only doing what the FBI behavioral science unit had recommended. Stein wouldn't let him off that easily.

"Detective," he went on, "when you arrested Mr. Bloodsworth at three o'clock in the morning, you talked to him from approximately three o'clock in the morning to six o'clock in the morning, did you not?"

"Yes."

"In all that time did you ever ask Bloodsworth if he saw the items in the room?"

"Never."

"Because you didn't want to know the answer, isn't that correct? You didn't want to know the answer to *that* question, Detective."

Stein moved to the lineup. "And before you put him in a lineup you called all of your witnesses, didn't you, and told them not to watch television because Mr. Bloodsworth was going to be on television?"

"It is a procedure we use, yes."

"But it was done in this case, wasn't it, sir?"

"Yes, it was done in this case . . ."

Stein closed the loop. "Let me ask you, Detective: you were there at the lineup, were you not?"

"Yes, I was."

"Show me a written report of any witness you ever asked did they see anybody on television."

"I didn't ask it . . ."

Stein elicited from Detective Capel that the head hair found on the scene did not belong to Bloodsworth and that no other physical evidence found on the scene linked Bloodsworth to the crime. By the time he finished his cross-examination, he had pretty well bloodied up Detective Capel.

But Brobst and Pulver weren't finished. They called the witnesses again from Cambridge—Rose Carson, Thelma Stultz, and Tina Christopher. Christopher was the one witness, the only witness, who'd claimed that Kirk had said something suggesting that he was with the man who went into the woods with the little girl. Again, just like at the first trial, she had a hard time remembering, and Michael Pulver had to try to refresh her recollection by having her read over the statement the police had typed for her shortly after Kirk's arrest. When Stein rose to cross-examine her, he took a patient but firm approach.

"At the age of eighteen, in August 1984, you had a bad alcohol and drug problem, didn't you?"

"No, not a drug problem."

"You had an alcohol problem, didn't you?"

"Yeah."

"And this person known as Kirk, had you ever met this person before?"

"No, I have not." Christopher had trouble with her grammar.

"Did you know of any reason in the world why this person would talk to you about these things?"

"No, I do not."

"How long were you in the house with this person?"

"I don't know."

"Well, you were paying so little attention to this person you wouldn't even be able to recognize him today, would you?"

"No."

Stein tried to impress on the jury through his questions the intimidating situation Christopher had found herself in when surrounded by questioning police.

"Before you went to the police station, the police came to your house, didn't they?"

"Yes, they did."

"And there were about ten of them, weren't there?"

"I guess. Seven, eight."

"Ma'am, you have to understand something. This is very important. You just can't guess."

"Well, I can't remember too much."

"You can't remember how many; you can't remember much at all, can you?"

"No, I don't."

"And you really can't remember all the bits and pieces of the conversations that you had, can you?"

"No, I cannot . . ."

Stein kept at her. "And now, you don't remember anything about any bloody rock, do you?"

"Not today, I don't."

"And did you remember it then, or don't you even know what you remember?"

"Well, I must have remembered something because I gave them the statement then."

Stein then directed his questions to that statement—the one typed by the police that they had had her sign, insinuating that the police had put their words down, not hers.

"And you don't really remember even reading it, do you?" he asked.

"Not today, I don't remember," she answered.

"And let me ask you this. Did you ever say to the police, wait a minute, I can write, why won't you let me write out my own statement?"

"No."

Stein then asked Tina Christopher if she recalled that an investigator from the public defender service had interviewed her two months before, in January 1987. She did. She acknowledged that she'd told the investigator that her head was finally clear from drugs and alcohol and that she had no recollection of Kirk's ever saying anything about a bloody rock or about another man he knew who was with the little girl. Christopher had even given a taped statement to the investigator, and Stein played it for the jury. With a clear head she had claimed she had no recollection of Kirk Bloodsworth's making any incriminating statements.

To BEGIN THE defense, Stein started off with two witnesses from Cambridge. He first called Tom Collins, a man in the seafood business who had employed Kirk. Collins was called solely to establish that Kirk had worked for him in June of 1984, then just failed to show up one day. Stein called Billy Elliott, the crab-potter. Elliott too testified that Kirk had a way of quitting by just not returning to work. Stein was hoping to show the jury that Kirk's abrupt departure from Harbor to Harbor was not unusual for him, was typical of his past behavior, and was not necessarily because he'd committed a murder.

Stein called Fay McCoullough, the adult who had worked with Detective Capel to create the second composite sketch, the one he had thrown away. She told the jury how Capel had tried to use the foil transparencies with her to create a likeness of the strange man she'd seen. She described how he'd gotten frustrated and given up, and how he then told her he'd decided to go with the description given by the two boys. She testified that she'd attended the lineup in which Kirk Bloodsworth stood but that the man she'd seen at Fontana Village the day of the murder wasn't in it.

Douglas Orr testified that he had talked to Kirk in August of 1984, after Kirk had left Baltimore. Kirk told him he'd done a terrible thing. He'd left his wife and quit his job. That was the terrible thing he'd done. On cross-examination, Ann Brobst asked Orr whether Kirk had told her he'd forgotten to buy his wife a taco salad, whether, in fact, *that* was the terrible thing he'd done. Later Brobst introduced portions of the transcript of Kirk's testimony from the first trial, where he said his failure to buy his wife a taco salad was the bad thing he'd done. Kirk had followed Stein's advice not to testify in order to keep the taco salad testimony from coming in. Here it showed up anyway.

Stein called Dr. Richard Lindenberg, a specialist in neuropathology. Lindenberg explained the mechanism by which medical examiners can tell from brain injury whether the injury was caused by the head being struck by an object, on the one hand, or the head being slammed into an object, on the other. A *contrecoup* injury, he explained, is brain damage occurring inside of the brain opposite to where the wound is made and suggests that the brain was slammed into an object. If a rock were used to smash Dawn Hamilton's brain, he said, the injury inside the skull would be to that part of the brain closest to the impact. That wasn't the case here. Her brain was damaged in an area away from and opposite to where her skull was impacted. She was not struck with the weapon, he concluded. Rather, her head was slammed down onto a hard surface. She was not murdered, he concluded, by the rock.

But Lindenberg slipped up on cross-examination. He made a mistake, trying to be too glib, perhaps, too much the knowledgeable expert.

"Doctor, now we are talking about a significant force, isn't that true?" Michael Pulver asked him. "We are not talking about a little girl falling on a rock in the woods?"

"Well, it could be," Lindenberg answered. "Depends on how fast she falls, whether she slipped on muddy ground or just fell over on her buttocks and then hit the brain, hit the skull . . . You can get the same injury just by falling backward, particularly if you glide on a banana peel or something, or ice."

A banana peel? Even a young trial lawyer couldn't miss an opening like that.

"Assuming she didn't fall on a *banana peel* in the woods, Doctor, you also saw these photographs?"

"Yes."

"Saw the injuries to the face, is that correct?"

"Yes."

"Now, is it your opinion this was caused by her *falling* in the woods?"

"This could be . . ." he answered, trying to explain himself.

Pulver picked up a picture showing Dawn Hamilton's face bashed in, her head partially crushed and bloody, her eye damaged. He showed it to the doctor, then held it up for the jury.

"Now, if I understand your testimony, Doctor, these injuries to Dawn Hamilton were caused by her falling in the woods?"

Despite his expert's stumble, Stein might have ended his case there. He'd skewered the state's witnesses and raised the issue of whether the rock was even a factor. Rather, he called Richard Gray to testify, trying to implicate him as the murderer. Stein went through Gray's story, trying to raise the questions that had bothered Detective Mark Bacon. He even followed up by calling investigator Sam Wallace who'd gone to Gray's house and seen a red carpet rolled up outside. But Gray and the state were both ready. Gray had answers to every question. And in rebuttal the state called police officers to further confirm his answers to those questions.

The defense case ended. Kirk Bloodsworth had produced no alibi witnesses, no character witnesses, and had declined to take the stand to deny that he was the murderer. Leslie Stein had put his eggs in just a few baskets. The jury would have to doubt the quality of the state's evidence, would have to understand and agree with Stein's suggestion that the rock was not the murder weapon, and that this fact exonerated the defendant; or the jury would have to conclude that Richard Gray was more likely the murderer. But where was Mr. Bloodsworth? Some of the jurors had been waiting for him to testify. Why didn't he tell us he didn't do this? several questioned afterward. And where was he that day? Wasn't he with *anyone* who could vouch for his whereabouts?

The jury heard closing arguments on April 6. Ann Brobst was calm, even-keeled, low-key. She told them that five eyewitnesses placed Kirk Bloodsworth at Fontana Village. Two of those who saw and identified Bloodsworth at the lineup were children who were terrified of him. Jackie Poling was too frightened of him to point him out at the lineup, she said. She asked the jurors to consider why. Why would little Jackie Poling be so terrified of this man if he weren't certain he was the killer?

Leslie Stein argued it wasn't the rock that killed Dawn Hamilton, and it wasn't Kirk Bloodsworth either. During his closing, he was solicitous of Detective Capel and praised his dedication to his job. Capel had just made a wrong assumption, Stein said. About the murder weapon, about the rock. And that mistake had led to the wrong man being put on trial. Stein tried to point the jury to Richard Gray. He went through an exhaustive critique of the evidence.

After the arguments concluded, Judge Smith instructed the jury on the law, on what they now were required to consider. Back in his chambers the judge was troubled. He had significant reservations about the reliability of the child witnesses' identifications. He told his staff that evening that if the verdict were up to him, he might very well find that there was a reasonable doubt.

Leslie Stein believed he'd tried a superb case. Still, he worried about the jury's take on the first conviction. Every day the Baltimore area papers had carried news reports on the developing trial. These stories referred to the "retrial," and the fact that the defendant had been "convicted" before, been previously "sentenced to death." The jurors had to know this. Obviously they knew that the police and prosecutors still believed Kirk was guilty. How hard would it be, Stein wondered, to overcome all this in addition to the photos of Dawn, the horrendous nature of this crime?

That night Kirk lay awake until first light. He thought he had a good chance, pinned to Stein's strategic calls. Stein should know, shouldn't he? He was the savvy professional. But Kirk couldn't fathom why it should be so close. Wouldn't the system clear him of this ugly crime? Perhaps deep in his gut he knew that he was in trouble. But no. He could win. He told himself this. He tossed on his bunk. This jury would see the truth.

The next day, Stein felt confident. The buzz around the courthouse was that Bloodsworth would walk. The courtroom clerk, anticipating a not-guilty verdict, began preparing release papers. Ann Brobst chain-smoked outside the judge's chambers. "If he's acquitted," she snapped at Stein, "I'm going to throw myself out the window."

"You should dismiss this case," Stein fired back. "To even go forward on the evidence you have is reprehensible."

For six hours the jury deliberated before reaching a verdict. Finally, they came back to announce their unanimous decision. Kirk's insides were churned when he rose to hear it. Six hours was much longer than before. Long enough to acquit, he thought. He faced the foreman and listened to the verdict. Kirk Bloodsworth was guilty on all counts. Guilty! Kirk was stunned. His face burned crimson. The words sheared through his brain. He couldn't believe it. Kirk hung his head and sobbed. He was nearly cried out. Once again, guards took him back to a cage; again he was a dead man walking.

TWENTY-FOUR

THE MENTAL HEALTH clinic director, Dr. Gene Ostrom, was surprised, two years after his phone call to Judge Hinkel, to receive a subpoena to testify in a posttrial hearing in the Dawn Hamilton murder case. Not only did he have to appear, but several of his staff were summoned to testify as well.

Leslie Stein had filed a motion for a new trial alleging once again that the failure of the state to turn over exculpatory evidence in a timely manner was a violation of *Brady v. Maryland.* Judge Smith agreed to hold an evidentiary hearing on the matter, set for June 12, 1987. If the motion were denied, Judge Smith intended to go forward with Kirk's sentencing immediately following the hearing.

Again, Kirk Bloodsworth had been forced to make the impossible choice of whether to be sentenced for a rape and capital murder he didn't commit by the jury that convicted him or by the judge who presided over his trial. This time Leslie Stein counseled him at length about this decision, though Kirk seemed distant, absent, off in some zone of trauma. Still, after repeated discussions, Kirk agreed that he'd been impressed by Judge Smith's manner. Smith seemed to be a gentle man. Kirk thought he might also be merciful.

Despite the mistake he made going with Judge Hinkel the first time, Kirk elected to be sentenced by Judge Smith.

Over the days following the verdict, Kirk's emotions careened from one extreme to another. He felt he was living in a world gone mad, chained inside some insane theatrical production that kept repeating itself. Days went by when he could hardly speak. He'd cry for hours, then get angry. Gradually, as his June hearing date approached, a flat obstinacy took root. He asked his dad to buy him a new sweat suit—pants and jersey—all black, and black tennis shoes to match. He would dress in black at his sentencing as a way to protest the court's injustice. Black, from then on, would symbolize his innocence.

At the posttrial hearing on Stein's motion for a new trial, Dr. Ostrom told the court that in July 1984 he'd been the director of a community mental health center near Rosedale. David Rehill had been well known to his staff as a patient of the center. Ostrom related how he'd called Judge Hinkel in March of 1985 and told him of his concerns about Rehill. Until recently, he told the court, no one had ever followed up with him about these concerns.

Ostrom related that on July 25, the day of Dawn Hamilton's murder, Rehill showed up at the clinic sometime after noon and asked to talk to a counselor. He was not scheduled for a visit that day and was willing to wait three hours to see someone. An employee of Ostrom's testified that Rehill wanted to talk about a relationship he had with a little girl that day. Ostrom's secretary remembered that Rehill was wearing some kind of shirt that showed off his muscles and that he had scratches on him. He had curly hair then, and she was pretty sure he had a mustache. Another employee remembered that he was wearing shorts, probably light colored.

Here was a man, similar to the portrait in the composite sketch, dressed like the stranger at Bethke's Pond, with curly hair and a mustache, who showed up unannounced at a mental health clinic, with scratches on his face, shortly after Dawn Hamilton was killed, asking for counseling over his relationship with a little girl. Yet he'd never been put a in a lineup and his photograph had never been shown to the eyewitnesses.

Leslie Stein had subpoenaed David Rehill to this hearing. He called Rehill to the stand. Rehill had a lawyer accompanying him. Rehill answered a few questions about his personal appearance back in July of 1984, but when asked where he was on July 25, his attorney objected. He raised Rehill's Fifth Amendment privilege against self-incrimination and refused to allow him to answer. Stein requested that the state give him immunity so that he would be required to answer the questions. The prosecutors declined. Stein argued passionately. He accused the state of bad faith if it refused to do so. If the state were at all interested in the truth, he argued to Judge Smith, it would grant Rehill immunity to find out what he knew before it would send a citizen to the gas chamber.

Ann Brobst and Michael Pulver had deaf ears. They declined to give Rehill immunity. They never seriously entertained it. The state already had its culprit. It had no interest in further prolonging the inquiry.

Leslie Stein then argued before Judge Smith that his motion for a new trial should be granted. Upon first learning of Ostrom's phone call to Judge Hinkel, Stein had sent out an investigator to interview people at the community health center, but the witnesses with the critical information were off work that day. Stein hadn't had sufficient time to follow up and conduct a thorough investigation in the few days before trial. He had no way of knowing how significant the evidence was. The state's conduct in withholding the information for two years was inexcusable, he argued. And the evidence was compelling that Rehill, not Bloodsworth, may have killed Dawn

Hamilton. Certainly this evidence deserved further study. A new trial was warranted.

Pulver and Brobst argued that Rehill was not exhaustively investigated because he didn't meet the description given of the suspect. Rehill was only five feet eight inches tall and weighed 180 pounds, as opposed to the six-foot-tall muscular man the child witnesses had described.

Judge Smith became agitated, then angry. He was outraged, he said, at the Baltimore County detectives for not following through with an investigation of Rehill, for not putting Rehill in a lineup. The discrepancy in the descriptions, given by children in the first place, was of little significance, and the decision to ignore David Rehill as a suspect was ridiculous, he said. Judge Smith further lambasted the state's attorney's office for waiting two years to provide the information to the defense. "I am disappointed in the state's attorney's office," he said. "I am disturbed," he said. "It isn't gamesmanship we are playing here. It is truth. You represent your position, that's true. But the ultimate is truth . . ."

For a moment, Leslie Stein thought Judge Smith was going to grant a new trial. As Smith vented his anger, Stein began poking Kirk in the ribs with his elbow. "He's going to do it," Stein whispered. "He's going to do it . . ."

But then Judge Smith changed tacks. He was also uncomfortable that Leslie Stein had not moved for a continuance of the trial date, even though he had learned of this new information just days in advance of trial. A continuance would have allowed the defense ample time to investigate the new information. Judge Smith thought that Leslie Stein was a smart and capable lawyer. He wasn't sure, but he wondered whether Stein had tried to play both ends. Smith did not feel the court could permit the defendant to sit on the new information, not request a continuance, and then after he lost the trial come forward and claim prejudice. The only fair analysis, Judge Smith reasoned, led to the conclusion that the evidence was not newly discovered *after* the trial. It was known to the defense *before* the trial. Hence, the motion would be denied.

Kirk once again was crushed. His hopes had come alive, only to be snuffed out again. Rehill and his lawyer were excused. This man, who might very well be guilty of the murder, was walking away, free. Judge Smith took a recess. Upon his return, the sentencing of Kirk Bloodsworth would go forward.

JEANETTE BLOODSWORTH HAD wanted to accompany Curtis to the sentencing this time. She wore a floral dress and held a handkerchief up to her eyes. She had come to lend support to her boy. Cindy Bloodsworth and several other cousins were also there in the packed courtroom. During the recess, Kirk turned and found his mother's eyes. He wanted so to go to her. All he could do was watch her, slightly nod, and mouth the words that he loved her.

Leslie Stein began the sentencing hearing by calling a security guard from the detention center to vouch for Kirk's good behavior while at the jail. Stein then pointed out to the court that Kirk's family members were all in the gallery. Stein then looked at the defendant, motioned his head toward the witness stand, and called Kirk Bloodsworth to testify. Since Judge Smith had never seen Kirk testify at trial, Stein thought it important that the judge hear from him at the sentencing.

Stein asked Kirk if he committed the crime, and Kirk answered no, that he did not. Stein asked him whether he'd admit to killing Dawn Hamilton if it would save him from the gas chamber.

"No sir" was Kirk's reply.

Stein asked Kirk if he wanted to say anything else to the court. Kirk indicated that he did.

One more time Kirk Bloodsworth tried to reach inside, tried to dig within himself, tried for once to find the right words, words that would ring true. "I feel very sorry for what happened to the child and for the family and what they must be going through," he began slowly. "There is no way in my conscience that I could kill a little child or anybody for that matter. I respect life too much and I just couldn't do it. And I didn't . . ." Kirk struggled to keep composed, to not break down before a courtroom filled with people. "If you sentence me to death, Judge, there is no way down the road we can pull it back. I have no idea who killed the child. All I know is I didn't do it. When they close the doors on that gas chamber, that's it. You can't call it back."

He heard his own words and trembled inside. He shut his eyes and opened them. He took a breath. He wanted his voice to echo loud. Clear. To somehow reach this judge. There in this hushed and crowded courtroom, this simple waterman, dressed in black as his only means of protest, railed against the injustice of his world. "I have been locked up for almost three years now trying to prove myself to this court, pursuing every avenue I know how. The death penalty just doesn't fit me because I am not the criminal. I can't tell you a lie, Judge. I feel sorry for what happened to that child, but I am not your killer. And if you kill me, you are never going to find out. I'm not speaking for myself but for the little child; that's doing her an injustice . . . I have nothing else to say."

The state again argued vehemently that Kirk Bloodsworth should be put to death. Judge James Smith, though, couldn't bring himself to do it. He'd had his own reservations about the quality of the evidence, and these continued to disturb him. He wasn't going to countermand the jury's verdict, but he wasn't going to sentence this young man to death either. Judge Smith, back in chambers, had reviewed the same criteria that Judge Hinkel had considered. The crime was the same and the defendant was the same. But he had decided to exercise his discretion differently. On the bench, Judge Smith went through a long colloquy addressing these various criteria in detail. Then he sentenced Kirk to two consecutive life sentences, one to follow the other. Kirk Bloodsworth's life, to whatever extent he would have one in the Maryland Penitentiary, was saved.

TWENTY-FIVE

It was the summer of 1987 when Kirk was sent back to the South Wing of the old Maryland Penitentiary. The place seemed even more dank and dim, even filthier, than before. Half the bulbs in the hallway ceilings were out. Corridors were murky; many of the cells were unlit. There was little ventilation. Roaches grubbed around everywhere. In the summer the upper tier was a hothouse, a sweatbox. The men in this dark world exuded heat. The stench of excrement and urine was pervasive. The place was a cauldron of pent-up hate, an incubator of violence. When Kirk returned, still only twenty-seven, this time facing the prospect of losing his whole life to such a place, he went into a tailspin, falling hard into a sea of self-pity.

He'd lie in his bunk and watch the roaches crawl on the floor. A colorless despair took root in his belly. He had no interest in anything. The food at the prison was still barely edible. Starches, mostly—overcooked noodles, Stroganoff, macaroni and cheese, stews, anything that could be bulked up with flour and watered down. A vague nausea plagued him. He'd lie for hours staring at the wall, unable to find a reason to get up.

For a while Kirk was put in a cell with Frankie Marrone, a Jersey loan shark with a pockmarked face. Marrone was the kind who waited for someone else's crumbs to fall off the table. He watched for weakness and tried to exploit it. Occasionally he ran drugs for one of the South Wing dealers. One afternoon late in the summer, Kirk lay in his bunk sweating and sick over his life, nearly comatose. Frankie asked him if he'd like to escape for a while. Frankie had that weasely grin on his face. *Escape*—what a sweet word. *Escape . . .*

Frankie had gotten a hold of two "sets"—the poor man's speed-ball—a combination of the narcotic Talwin and an antihistamine. Frankie'd also boosted two sterile needles from the nurse's clinic. He showed Kirk how to crush up the antihistamine, heat it with water in the concave bottom of an upside-down cutoff soda can, and mix it with the Talwin. Kirk watched, fascinated, as Frankie drew the solution up into the spike and gave Kirk his first mainline punch. Frankie was right. Kirk was transported immediately to a different place. He felt light, soothed out. For the first time in three years, the fear drained out of his chest. The world wasn't so dark. He rushed along in a flood of sweetness, riding a wave. Afterward, he wanted it again.

Every community has its rules. In the joint you could borrow, but the levy was severe. The rule was you paid one back with two. You borrowed a pack of cigarettes, you had to pay back two. Kirk began trading whatever he had for these sets. The high would last three, maybe four hours. He wanted it more and more. He got to where all he could think about was a set and a clean needle to fire it.

Initially Kirk used the money he got from Curtis for commissary to buy the drugs. But it wasn't enough. He'd met a woman named Anita Smith while at the detention center. Anita played the guitar for Catholic Charities at the church service there, and she began to believe in Kirk, believed he was innocent. Wanda Bloodsworth mostly disappeared after the first trial, but Anita began visiting Kirk, encouraging him, trying to offer him some solace. She'd also bring him money sometimes. They'd talk about their religious beliefs. Hold hands. After every visit, Kirk would be searched, a full body and cavity search. At first, he'd have Anita use a razor blade to slit open the edge of a Polaroid picture, then slip a folded up fifty or hundred inside the photo and reseal it. This worked for a while, until another inmate got caught doing it. Then Kirk had her bring him a balloon, and he'd swallow the money in the balloon and pass it later in his cell, so he could use it to buy his sets. Anita thought the money was to buy decent food at the commissary. She knew nothing of his growing drug addiction.

Kirk soon needed three or four sets a day. He traded his television, his radio, his typewriter, the care packages his mother would send every week; he traded his clothes. He'd still get up every morning and write at least one letter protesting his innocence to somebody. When he lost his typewriter, he began writing the letters longhand. When he finished the letter he'd get high.

Kirk still hung out some with Half and Bozo, though he'd been lifting less and less. The sets were a better way to hide from his life. He'd met the prison Islam leader, Abdul-Haleem, and often talked with him about religion. The Muslims tried to construct a separate way of living in the prison. Abdul always wore his kufi and carried with him his copy of the Koran. He prayed every afternoon, observed Ramadan and the other Muslim holidays. He refrained from eating pork, never touched the drugs, and never drank the jump steady—the prison wine. Few whites got along with the Muslims. But Abdul seemed intrigued with Kirk. There was something about him that was different. Kirk, in turn, liked talking with Abdul. He told him about his two convictions. Kirk had a knack for the country metaphor. He explained to Abdul how the state had turned an orange into a tomato. How from Jump Street he'd been put on the B&O express for that long railroad ride to prison.

Abdul asked him if he'd be interested in converting to Islam. Kirk declined. He was a solid Christian. Kirk told him he figured there was probably only one God anyway. He just went by different names for different people and allowed for different roads to get to him. Abdul liked this notion. Abdul was a large, very black man, with a commanding presence. And his word carried real juice in the joint. The Muslims were a unified and loyal group.

Whenever Kirk saw Abdul, they'd exchange the Muslim greeting that Abdul had taught him. "*Assalaam alaikum,*" Kirk would say, holding his hand over his heart. It was a blessing of peace. "*Alaikum assalaam*" was the reply—an acknowledgment of mutual respect.

When Kirk was high from his sets he relished talking about religion, music, prisoner's rights, his own innocence. Like any addict, though, he gradually became more and more preoccupied with his next score, how to acquire his next fix. Kirk got to know all of the drug runners and the dealers in his section of the penitentiary. He also learned how to cop clean needles from the infirmary. He kept a disinfectant in his cell so he could reuse his own works. Most of the time he bought his drugs from Little Mussolini—Moose—who had guards on the take, his "whores," as he referred to them. Moose was pleased to have another regular customer. Kirk was careful not to get too far behind in what he owed Moose, though. Moose, it was said, had shot a man's testicles off with a .357 magnum over a dart game.

Kirk tried to keep abreast of all the prisoners who were in his building. This was necessary just for self-preservation. An inmate named Kimberly Ruffner had come to the joint about a month after Kirk had arrived the first time. Ruffner had been convicted of the attempted rape and murder of a woman in the Fells Point area of Baltimore. He kept to himself most of the time in a single cell one tier below Kirk's. Kirk seldom saw him. Their paths rarely crossed. Whenever they did, Ruffner would turn and walk the other way.

Kirk broke one of Half's maxim's and started borrowing to pay for his sets. Demon lent Kirk cigarettes. So did Pepper and Angel, Dino, Black Smoky, Bull Starkey, and Rock from New York. Kirk used the packs to parley for his drugs.

Kirk's habit was running out of control. It began to destroy his health, to consume him. He'd become vulnerable, more of a target. He got to where he owed over five hundred packs of cigarettes. He knew the men he owed them to were vampires, looking for any excuse to hurt someone. Whenever Kirk staggered out of his cell, high on a jag, the inmates on his tier would look at him like he were already dead. And the sets no longer made him feel so good. It was just that he felt sick without them. He'd been obliterating himself for close to a year.

Kirk lost track of time. He'd been writing his lawyers. The public defender had again been working hard on his appeal. This time, since the death penalty was no longer involved, the case would be argued before the Maryland Court of Special Appeals. Kirk assumed that the David Rehill issue would lead to a new trial, just like the Richard Gray issue had done before. He couldn't have been more mistaken.

The case was argued in the spring of 1988. Julia Bernhardt again took up the gauntlet for Kirk. It was obvious to her, though, as the oral argument ensued, that the Court of Special Appeals was not interested in giving Kirk Bloodsworth a third trial. He'd had two chances and lost them both. The judges were simply not impressed with her arguments that he should get a third.

Kirk learned in July of 1988 that his appeal had been denied. He was shocked. He couldn't believe it. The public defenders promised him that they would petition the Maryland Court of Appeals to see if it would hear the case, but they were not optimistic. Kirk was frantic. He wrote everyone. The passion and commitment of his lawyers seemed to have waned. What was the next step, he wanted to know? How was he going to clear himself? But no one had an answer. The world out there was quiet. All this sent him farther down, deeper into the drugs, into debt, into a place where he could forget, where he could escape from his misery and hide from himself.

One morning in the fall, after he'd learned that his appeal had been denied, Kirk started out of his cell but found his way blocked by Bull Starkey. Starkey was a grizzled old lifer from the mountains in western Maryland. Word was he'd killed a man by whacking him forty-seven times with a ball peen hammer. A blue rose tattoo spread across his forearm. Starkey was a chicken hawk and as mean as men come. He held a shank tightly in his hand, his elbow bent and cranked back, his muscular arm coiled, ready to thrust. His mouth was tight, his facial muscles flexed. "I'm gonna' drive this right into your heart if you don't pay me the ten packs you owe me right now," he growled.

Kirk stepped back. A crowd quickly gathered. Out of the corner of his eye Kirk saw Abdul-Haleem. Abdul walked over to Fresco, an Italian bank robber from the docks area of Baltimore and a big dealer in smokes. Abdul took a carton from Fresco and threw it to Kirk. Kirk caught it. Starkey hadn't moved. Kirk tore open the carton and angrily threw the cigarettes at Starkey, two, three packs at a time. "Come on! Come on!" Kirk yelled in his face. "I'll fight you with or without your goddamn knife."

Starkey hesitated. He saw Abdul there and wasn't sure how involved he might choose to become. Starkey didn't want to pick a fight with the Muslims. And Kirk was large enough himself, and enraged. Starkey stooped over and picked up the packs.

"Come on!" Kirk shouted again.

"Debt solved," Starkey hissed, backing away. "Debt solved . . ."

Abdul looked at Fresco. Fresco turned to Kirk. "Shit," Fresco said. "You don't even have to pay me back. It was worth it, seeing somebody stand up to Starkey like that."

But Abdul wasn't smiling. He took Kirk back into his cell. "You don't have to be a Muslim," he said to Kirk. "But look what you're doing to yourself. I thought you were different. I thought you were innocent. That you stood for something around here. You're in a stupor. You're becoming a punk. You're going to die in here if you don't pull yourself together."

After Abdul left, Kirk began to shake. Then he got sick in his toilet. He retched up everything in his stomach and then continued to heave. He sat there on the cold floor, his hand on the filthy steel bowl to keep himself from falling over. Finally, he shakily rose and looked in the cracked piece of mirror he'd taped to the wall. A skull wavered in the reflection. It transformed itself into another face, the one he'd seen in that cell block behind Judge Hinkel's courtroom the day he was first sentenced. Then it became a skull again, dried up, devoid of flesh. His reflection was that of a changeling. He turned away. All of his possessions, all that had once decorated his cell, were gone. Only a small picture of his mother and father, taped above his bunk, remained. He was wearing a state-issued shirt, state-issued trousers, and state-issued shoes with no laces. He'd traded away everything he had. He had the chills. He was ill. That afternoon he told Sergeant Cooley Hall that he was sick and in danger from other inmates; he asked to be locked down in protective custody. For a week he lay under the bunk in his cell writhing with cramps, vomiting, wracked with the sweats, grasping on to the rails, holding on. He detoxed alone, with no one to help or even sympathize. After that he never touched the drugs again.

IT TOOK A WHILE, but Kirk gradually came back to feeling somewhat human, even healthy. He started watching his diet, trying to avoid all the starches fed to prison inmates. He tried to eat more protein, drink more milk. He avoided those prisoners who drank the jump steady and traded in drugs.

Anita Smith continued to visit Kirk regularly. He looked forward to spending time with her. The two thought they might have found a connection together. Anita was devout in her Catholicism. They'd sit in the visiting room holding hands. Kirk would describe the joy of working on the river, the sunlight and breeze playing off the water, the broad sky. He promised to take her crabbing some day. Anita would bring her Bible and they'd read from it and study it. She introduced Kirk to her priest, Father Al Rose. Eventually, Kirk decided to convert, to become confirmed as a Catholic. Anita helped him study, helped him regain a sense of hope and purpose.

Lifting weights every day also helped build his self-confidence. The lifters welcomed him back. Kirk was different, special. There was some quality about him that set him apart from the other cons in the joint.

With his recovery, Kirk renewed his efforts to gain his freedom. He recommitted himself to this more than anything else. He wouldn't rest until he could find a way out. He decided one day that he needed more access to the prison library, more opportunity to read and do research. He applied to Sergeant Cooley Hall for a job as a library assistant and got it. Because of the experience of having his first conviction overturned on a constitutional violation, other inmates considered him knowledgeable about the law. Some of them came to him for legal advice. He'd copy cases from the library for inmates. He'd write letters for inmates who couldn't write. After Black Smoky was found hanged in his cell by his shoelaces, Kirk wrote his family. Inmates forgave Kirk's cigarette debts or traded them for his help. He began to acquire back his belongings.

Kirk used his time in the library to read everything he could find about the law and to research his own case. And he kept on writing his daily letters proclaiming his innocence, asking for help, all signed "Kirk Bloodsworth—A.I.M.—An Innocent Man." His output was remarkable. He read and wrote tirelessly.

In March of 1988, Dan Rodricks, a reporter for Baltimore's *Evening Sun*, published an editorial about Kirk titled "Haunting Questions." "Too many questions still haunt the case of Kirk Noble Bloodsworth, who was recommended twice for execution by the Baltimore County State's Attorney's Office," Rodricks wrote. Others in the community remained uncomfortable about the Bloodsworth case. It hadn't quite been put to rest.

Kirk knew that there were advocates out there still trying, people who'd come to believe he was innocent, people committed to helping him. He prayed and wrote every day to somebody who might come through. He wrote Ronald Reagan, Donald Trump, Senators Barbara Mikulski and Paul Sarbanes, Governor William Donald Schaefer, Willie Nelson, Waylon Jennings. He wrote the public defenders who'd worked on his case. He wrote the prosecutors and the judges. Gary Christopher was one of the people who got letters from Kirk. Christopher was one who had not given up entirely.

Christopher realized that Kirk's chances had diminished to almost nothing. He'd had two trials, two appeals, and the constitutional issues were not strong. Postconviction habeas relief was unlikely. What Kirk needed was a miracle. If there was any lawyer in the country who might deliver such a miracle, Christopher figured, it was Bob Morin.

And so it was that he called Morin in early 1989, and told him about Kirk. Morin responded that he was just too busy with death cases to take on a matter where the death sentence had been commuted. But Christopher had also told Kirk about Morin. Kirk wrote Morin a letter pleading with him to come see him. Morin also received a letter from Kirk's father. Christopher tried to persuade Morin a second time to at least visit and talk to this kid. Reluctantly Morin agreed. It was the first step on Kirk's road to freedom.

PART VII

FREEDOM

To be on the water and free
is a glorious thing . . .

—KIRK BLOODSWORTH

TWENTY-SIX

IN THE EARLY 1970s when Bob Morin was in college at the University of Massachusetts, he'd volunteered to spend a semester in an offshoot of the VISTA program, working at a legal aid clinic as a low-income-housing specialist. The poverty and injustice he saw changed him. Young and idealistic, he decided he wanted to go to law school and figure out a way to use his degree to help people.

After graduating from Catholic University's law school in 1977, Morin went to work for a small Maryland firm that needed a litigator and that promised to provide him with the opportunity to do pro bono work. His two pleasures, outside of the law, were romancing his girlfriend, Marty Tomich, and long-distance running. He began training for marathons and ran his first one that year. He had fallen hard for Marty and looked forward to his evenings and weekends with her. But as his private practice developed, he became frustrated over how little time he had to devote to public-interest work. He felt he wasn't doing what he'd set out to do.

In 1981, Morin got a call from a law school classmate, Gerry Fisher. Fisher was the director of a Washington, D.C., program called Law Students in Court. The program taught third-year law students from area schools in a clinical setting, allowing them to handle civil cases on behalf of indigents. In the process of teaching, the program provided an important community service. Fisher had just been offered a position with the U.S. Attorney's Office and asked Morin if he would agree to take over the program as codirector with Stephen Bright. Bright had been a public defender in D.C., a young star of a trial lawyer. He'd been almost too aggressive. He'd rankled some of his supervisors and was ready to move on.

Morin and Bright met and hit it off. They talked of their mutual aspirations to expand the Law Students in Court program, to turn it into a real force for justice in the city. They not only agreed to come aboard as codirectors, but they also convinced Fisher to forego becoming a federal prosecutor and to stay on with them. They'd all split the available salaries and work together to build the program.

It wasn't long before they received an unexpected phone call from a civil rights lawyer in Georgia. There was an inmate in Augusta, they were told, on death row, awaiting execution, and the man didn't have a lawyer. Morin thought it was a joke. How could a man be awaiting execution and not have a lawyer? Bright flew down to meet with Garnett Cape. Cape had been convicted of killing his wife. Morin, Bright, and Fisher took on his case. After they agreed to take this death penalty case, they began getting call after call. There was a flood of people awaiting execution in the South, they learned, and few had lawyers. They discovered that there were men awaiting execution whose lawyers had been drunk or asleep during their trials. In some places, lawyers hardly got minimum wage to defend a death case. The racial issues were profound and complex. The representation of many of these people had been nonexistent, at best a travesty. Morin and his colleagues couldn't say no. They began having less time to devote to their program. Something had to give.

Stephen Bright learned that the Southern Prisoner's Defense Committee in Atlanta was relocating. It was low on funds. Its principal lawyers were leaving. It was almost a bust. He was asked if he'd be interested in taking it over. Bright was passionate, totally committed, and wanted to go. Morin was willing to go down for a while, but didn't want to be away from his fiancée, Marty, for too long. If he went, it could only be on a temporary basis. And someone needed to continue running Law Students in Court. The three finally agreed that Gerry Fisher would remain behind and continue to run the program. Morin would head south with Stephen Bright to help get the Southern Prisoner's Defense Committee—which they renamed the Southern Center for Human Rights—revitalized. "We went down there," Bob Morin later said, "and realized that there was this horrendous black hole—this absence of justice. I knew that at some time down the road, at some later point, historians would look back and ask, 'Where were the lawyers?' We just had to go . . ."

Morin's time in Georgia was a defensive blitzkrieg trying to hold back the dam of pending executions in nine southern states. They were overwhelmed with cases. The center had little money. They sent their petitions for stay of execution by Greyhound bus, because they couldn't afford overnight mail. They went to the small towns where the crimes had been committed, and when people learned who they were they were denied places to stay. Prosecutors and judges treated them with contempt. They worked around the clock. And they learned the art of postconviction advocacy in capital cases. They found ways to delay the executions, they won new trials for their clients, and they brought some dignity back to a process that had lost sight of equal justice.

Two years later, Morin got a call from Gary Christopher in Maryland. The dam was now giving way in his state, and Christopher needed the help of an experienced death penalty lawyer. Morin was overdue in coming home to Marty. He and Stephen Bright had begun to turn the Southern Center around. It was attracting idealistic law students from around the country, and Morin felt he finally could afford to move back. He accepted the job. Christopher said later that Morin was a godsend. "He brought to the Maryland public defender a whole new level of experience and expertise in defending death penalty cases," Christopher said. "He was a brilliant strategist. Bob Morin was just a great lawyer."

Morin helped Christopher build his unit into a well-organized and efficient state center for death penalty defense. He handled capital cases at all levels and taught and supervised the lawyers. After a while, though, Morin realized that there weren't enough death cases in Maryland alone to justify his remaining there. He went back to work with Gerry Fisher. They joined with David Kagan-Kans and opened a small law firm dedicated to handling death cases from around the country. Morin was immersed in this work when he got the call from Christopher, asking him as a favor to visit with this kid—this Kirk Bloodsworth.

THE FIRST THING Bob Morin did, after he agreed to represent Kirk Bloodsworth, was to draft and file a motion with the Baltimore County Circuit Court requesting an order that the state be required to preserve all of the trial evidence, including all of the physical evidence concerning the case. He knew that following the denial of a final appeal, the state would periodically dispose of the physical evidence in a case. Later, Morin wasn't quite sure what he'd intended to accomplish with that motion. He'd written it out of habit, on instinct. He'd just wanted some breathing room.

The motion was filed in March of 1989 and was granted by the court. Immediately thereafter, Morin wrote the prosecutors a letter, enclosing the court order, and demanding that they preserve everything. On a whim he also requested that any items containing the bodily fluids of the assailant be subjected to DNA fingerprinting, a very new and still experimental technique about which Morin and other trial lawyers were just learning.

Ann Brobst wrote him back. Her letter acknowledged that the state would preserve the evidence that remained. She advised him, however, that no fluids of the assailant existed: "The vaginal and anal washings and swabs referred to by you were inadvertently destroyed prior to submission for analysis," she wrote. "Additionally, time and nature may have contributed to further deterioration of certain of the items you have requested. . . ." She went on: "This office would agree immediately to have the assailant's body fluids examined for the DNA testing you have suggested. It is my understanding, however, that said fluids do not exist."

Morin read the letter and put it in a file. That same month, he'd contacted one of the leading DNA labs in the country, Cellmark Diagnostics, in Germantown, Maryland. Apart from there not being any fluid from the murderer to test, Cellmark would not even attempt to analyze DNA from smears on glass slides, he learned. The lab required identifiable semen or other biological material containing DNA in a sufficient amount to test before it would even undertake an analysis.

Morin decided he'd start from scratch. He began to study the case since its inception. He pored over the police reports, the tips, the transcripts, the previous investigations conducted by the public defenders. He followed up by pursuing leads that had been dropped. He sought out updated information on John Michael Anderson, Richard Gray, David Rehill, and W. F. Johnson. He hired an investigator to look into murders occurring in the mid-Atlantic area after Bloodsworth's arrest, murders where a similar crime scene pattern emerged. He researched and drafted a petition for postconviction relief and filed it in the state court, arguing that the evidence was too circumstantial to support a conviction and that

Kirk's rights had been violated because the state had destroyed the critical evidence that could have exonerated him. He began preparing for a habeas corpus collateral attack in the federal court. But he was stymied. After nearly three years of working for Kirk, nothing he'd found had succeeded or was likely to succeed. The case ate away at him. Here he had a young man he knew was innocent. He had helped so many guilty people. Why couldn't he help Kirk?

It was Kirk who rekindled Morin's interest in a DNA test, who pushed Morin into pursuing the analysis. Morin had been learning about the science, about the developing technology. He was preparing to deal with it in other pending trials. But with no fluid samples from the assailant to test, it had no utility in Bloodsworth's case.

But after reading Joseph Wambaugh's *The Blooding*, Kirk hadn't stopped pestering Morin about a DNA comparison. "What about getting the stuff tested?" he asked Bob for the umpteenth time one day at the prison. "Where are we with that? Let's just send whatever's there out and test it. What's there to lose?"

"To start with, the FBI found that there was no semen on the swabs," Morin reiterated. "There was no semen on the clothes. There is no fluid to test." Morin still understood that DNA testing methods at that time were unable to analyze preserved specimens off of slides and that any test risked destruction of the DNA samples on them. Morin explained to Kirk that even if a lab could be found that was willing to test the physical evidence, and even if trace amounts of semen existed that had been overlooked by the FBI, there was this other problem: the risk of destroying the samples in an unsuccessful, premature test. In fact, there might be a lot to lose.

"I want the stuff tested," Kirk insisted. "Test it. Please, for God's sakes, Bob, a DNA test. I'm dying in here . . ."

Morin reluctantly agreed to try. He began calling around to other laboratories. Dr. Edward Blake's small lab in California,

Forensic Science Associates, was clearly the best bet. It did polymerase chain reaction, or PCR, testing, the most advanced type of DNA fingerprinting then known, one that could, under some circumstances, amplify a miniscule specimen of genetic material into enough of a sample to analyze. Blake's lab was willing, though with reservations, to test the swabs and smears. Morin was warned again that glass slide specimens stained with a preservative might not lend themselves to DNA extraction and that the specimens could be destroyed in the testing process. Morin explained that he understood. He and his client wanted the testing done anyway.

Morin negotiated the release of the evidence directly with Ann Brobst. She agreed to release the vial of the victim's blood; the oral, vaginal, and rectal swabs in the possession of the FBI; and the hand scrapings taken from the victim. Morin wasn't satisfied. He sought and received permission to go to the evidence clerk's office to look through old files for the other physical evidence. It turned out that following the second trial, Judge Smith had retained in his chambers, in his closet, some of the items of evidence relating to Dawn Hamilton. Smith had been uncomfortable enough with the verdict that he had kept some of the trial exhibits in a box where they wouldn't be destroyed. He'd since returned them to the court's evidence room.

There, on a shelf, Morin found a cardboard box containing Dawn Hamilton's panties, shorts, and the stick. Morin also interviewed the medical examiner and learned that the medical examiner's office had kept frozen the glass smears taken at autopsy. Morin wanted all of this tested.

Brobst eventually agreed to the following terms, set forth in a letter: Morin could have these items sent and tested at the California lab if he paid the cost and if all oral and written reports from the lab were made known to the state. She wrote: "If a qualified laboratory determines with scientific certainty that there is sperm present on any of the items and the sperm is not that of the defendant, and the state has an independent opportunity to have an expert review the protocol and methodology used by the laboratory and agrees to the accuracy of the results, the state will agree to his release."

In August 1992 the various items of crime scene evidence along with a vial of Kirk's blood were all sent to California to undergo this new form of scientific identification and comparison, to be subject to this developing forensic technology capable, under some circumstances, of excluding someone as the perpetrator of a crime.

Morin also sent the lab $2,500 from his law firm as an advance toward the total cost. But he had little in the way of expectations.

TWENTY-SEVEN

THE CONCEPT OF forensic identification was probably first recognized in ancient times. In Babylon fingerprints were used on clay tablets for commercial purposes. The early Chinese were known to use thumbprints on clay seals. The first European to identify the value of fingerprints for forensic use was Sir William Herschel, an English magistrate in Jungipoor, India, in 1856, who used them on contracts with local citizens. Local government pensioners used their fingerprints to sign for their monthly payments, and landowners put their official stamp on transactions in this manner.

In 1878 a Scottish physician and missionary in Japan, Dr. Henry Fauld, discovered fingerprints on ancient pottery. Dr. Fauld was inspired to begin a study of "skin-furrows" and is credited as being the first European to suggest using fingerprints to assist crime investigators with identifications. Fauld began trying to classify fingerprints and contacted the noted British biologist, Sir Charles Darwin about his findings. Darwin passed along Fauld's research to his cousin, Sir Francis Galton, considered to be one of the great scientists of his century.

Galton was already a famous anthropologist, statistician, and explorer in the 1880s when he began studying fingerprint patterns. In 1892 he published a book that established for the first time that no two human being's fingerprints are exactly alike. Galton's goal at the time was the study of intelligence, heredity, and race, but he learned that none of these traits could be determined from a person's fingerprints. His research did prove that fingerprints could be used as a means of identification, and he developed a classification system based on pattern types that is still used today. Galton determined that the odds of one person's fingerprints matching those of another were one in sixty-four billion.

In the United States the use of fingerprints to make criminal identifications surged in the early 1900s, and by 1946 the FBI had over one hundred million fingerprints on file. This number had grown to two hundred million by 1971. No other method of personal identification matched the impact of fingerprints until scientific advances in the 1980s opened the door to genetic profiling through DNA analysis.

The modern story of DNA began in 1953 when an American scientist, James Watson, and an English scientist, Francis Crick, working together at Cambridge University, discovered the "double helix" structure of the chain of repeating molecules known as deoxyribonucleic acid, or DNA. Advances in understanding genetics and the workings of DNA would accelerate through the rest of the century. DNA is the molecular blueprint of heredity found in most living organisms. Almost every cell in the human body contains DNA. DNA molecules are found in hair, blood, saliva, skin, and even tears. The molecules are shaped like two strands twisted around each other to form a spiraling ladder, a double helix. The strands are made up of only four chemical "bases" that repeat millions of times in certain sequences. These bases pair up to form bridges between each strand, making up the rungs of the ladder. Just like the binary code used in computer language consists of zeros and ones in various positions and sequences to represent data, the four chemical bases pair up in specific sequences along the DNA ladder. These sequences constitute the genetic code.

Almost 100 percent (99.9 percent) of the genetic code is identical in all humans. The code carries the instructions that make us look and function alike. We all have two eyes, two ears, arms, and legs. We walk, talk, and breathe using the same physiological mechanisms. It's the remaining one-tenth of 1 percent, or about three million of the three billion rungs on each person's DNA ladder that varies from one person to the next. Along the DNA ladder, sequences of base pairs that make up genes are interrupted by fragments of noncoding DNA that represent breaks in the genetic code. These fragments, called repetitive sequences, are different for each person in their length and number, creating a pattern unique to that individual.

An English geneticist working at Leicester University in England first developed the concept of a DNA fingerprint. Alec Jeffreys began studying molecular genetics in 1975 at the University of Amsterdam as a postdoctoral student. In 1977 he moved to Leicester Univeristy and changed the direction of his work. He started exploring the variations in genes and the evolution of gene families. In the early 1980s geneticists had begun working with a technique dubbed RFLP, for restriction fragment length polymorphism, which enabled them to analyze the regions of DNA that differed from one person to the next. The technique used a chemical probe to find the DNA sequences to be analyzed. In 1984 Alec Jeffreys took this a step further and discovered a new method of locating these regions along the structure of DNA, enabling him to isolate many specific fragments of DNA at one time. Using X-ray film, Jeffreys developed images showing the length of these fragments in repetitive patterns that looked like the bar codes used on retail packages. He realized that these patterns, which represent the patterns of the base pairs along the DNA ladder, were distinct for each individual.

Alec Jeffrey's findings were published in the science journal *Nature* in 1985, the year of Kirk's first trial. Two years after his discovery, Jeffrey's new science was used to help solve the mystery of the two murdered teens in Narborough, England, recorded in Wambaugh's *The Blooding*.

Meanwhile in California, in 1983, a scientist named Kary Mullis was working on another problem associated with DNA analysis. His discovery, combined with Alec Jeffreys's work, produced the technology that would help save Kirk Bloodsworth.

Mullis was working on the problem of trying to analyze DNA when only a very small sample was available. He came up with the procedure, utilizing the enzyme that copies DNA inside a cell during DNA replication, for creating chain reaction reproductions inside a test tube, that became known as PCR. His technique enabled scientists to take a tiny section of DNA and replicate it very quickly so that there was a sufficient amount to test. Whereas the RFLP methodology required a biological specimen consisting of approximately ten thousand intact sperm cells to conduct a test, using the PCR technology an analysis could be conducted on a specimen consisting of as few as fifty to one hundred sperm. Mullis published his work in 1986.

In forensic identification, two samples of DNA, taken from different sources, can be compared by looking for matches in the repetitive patterns. The statistical certainty of an identification grows as DNA analysis is conducted on multiple genetic locations. The more locations that match, the more likely it becomes that the two DNA samples are from the same person. On the other hand, if two DNA samples are compared and there is no match at any single correlating genetic location, then the samples cannot have come from the same person. Therefore, it is easier to rule someone out than to identify positively a match.

Initially, PCR-based tests were not as definitive as RFLP because they did not detect as many matches at as many locations on the DNA ladder. But they were quicker and cost the same. By the early 1990s scientific advances improved the statistical significance of PCR-based tests to the point where they were as practical as RFLP. In 1993 Mullis won the Nobel Prize in chemistry for his discovery of the PCR technique.

In 1989, when Bob Morin first contacted Cellmark Diagnostics to inquire about a possible DNA analysis for Kirk, Cellmark was using only the RFLP technique, which required a substantial sample of fluid or other genetic material to conduct a test. In 1992, when Morin revisited the question of whether a DNA test could be performed on any trace of foreign blood or semen that might have been overlooked by the FBI, he turned to the scientist in the United States with the most experience in performing the advanced technology known as PCR. Kary Mullis had been an employee of the Cetus Corporation at the time of his PCR discovery. Cetus owned the rights to his technique even though Mullis's name was on the patent. Cetus initially authorized Dr. Edward Blake, exclusively, to employ its PCR technology.

At that time, there were many unanswered questions about the amount, age, and condition of a DNA sample that was necessary to conduct a valid test. It's been discovered since that DNA has survived from fifty thousand to one hundred thousand years ago in the remains of a woolly mammoth preserved in Siberian permafrost. DNA has been extracted from a bone of a Neanderthal human dating from forty thousand to fifty thousand years ago. Scientists know that DNA can be degraded or destroyed by environmental contaminants such as sunlight and detergent. Light, heat, moisture, and pressure may break down a DNA sample such that no DNA fingerprint data or only a partial fingerprint can be obtained. However, environmental contaminants will not alter the DNA to the extent that an analysis will yield an incorrect result.

Bob Morin, of course, didn't think he had any semen to examine. The FBI had so determined. A DNA test was probably a futile exercise. But Morin needed to know that he had done anything and everything to save this young man.

TWENTY-EIGHT

THE YEARS HAD been passing inexorably for Kirk Bloodsworth. Through half his twenties and now into his thirties he'd been buried alive. He'd miraculously survived two prison riots. Seven, eight, nine terrible years entombed. The world around him was changing. George Herbert Walker Bush had been elected president. The Berlin Wall had fallen. The United States had invaded and defeated Panama. Iraq had overrun Kuwait, and the United States had stormed into the Persian Gulf. The Soviet Union had collapsed. Bill Clinton defeated George Bush in the election and was waiting to be sworn in. All this while Kirk wasted away behind bars.

Meanwhile, the State of Maryland temporarily closed down parts of the old penitentiary for repairs. Most of the inmates in Kirk's building were moved to nearby Jessup to a newly constructed prison. The conditions were better. Kirk wrote his letters every day, kept the library organized, and lifted weights. Half was there, and Bozo. Kimberly Ruffner had shown his face a few times, and Kirk had spotted weights with him once, though Ruffner didn't say much.

Kirk thought he'd arrived at some kind of equilibrium, though he still cursed his existence, still hated what the state had made him.

That Christmas, 1992, Curtis and Jeanette visited him bringing cakes and cookies. In the new horseshoe-shaped prison visiting room, he was able to hold Jeanette's hand while they talked. She had aged since he'd been locked up. He knew the ordeal had ground her down. Her face was more wrinkled. She was frail. Her soft skin was loose. Some of her last words to Kirk were not to worry, that he was going to get out. "I've seen it in a dream, son," she told him. She patted his hand. "You *will be* a free man . . ."

Kirk was watching President Bill Clinton's inauguration in January when he got a note that Anita Smith and Al Rose were in the visiting room and needed to see him. They told him that his mother had died of a massive heart attack. Kirk sat and sobbed for hours.

The warden allowed prison guards to escort him in chains for a short private viewing of his mother's body. He was driven in a windowless van to a local funeral home in Cambridge. Kirk was shackled, wrists to ankles. He never saw anyone but his mother's corpse. The warden wouldn't allow him to attend her funeral. Kirk spent many days in his bunk grieving.

When Bob Morin called him that April to tell him the news about the DNA, Kirk knew for certain that his mother had a hand in it. He felt her presence. Her felt her smile and touch.

After Kirk had finished running up and down the tier signaling a touchdown and hollering that it was over, that the DNA had cleared him, he had come back to the phone. Morin had then tried to explain that there were still issues to confront. That the test didn't mean he'd walk free tomorrow. Once again, Morin was surprised by Kirk's response. "That's okay," Kirk answered. "I can wait now. What's important is that it tells the world that it wasn't me. That I didn't do this crime. What matters is that the test finally shows that it wasn't me . . ."

The morning after Morin and Kirk learned about the DNA results, Morin picked up the phone and dialed Ann Brobst. He told
her of the test results reached by Dr. Blake's lab. While no testable
sperm or DNA was found on the cotton swabs or the smears on
the glass slides, the stain of semen on Dawn Hamilton's underpants
had yielded enough genetic specimen to successfully employ the
PCR technology. The analysis had definitively excluded Kirk Bloodsworth as the donor of the sperm. When Morin told Ann Brobst
this, all that came through from the other end of the phone was silence. Finally, he heard a very shaky voice say, "You're kidding me . . .
You're kidding me. . ." That's all she could reply.

Later, during a subsequent call, Brobst told Morin that her office
would require a confirmatory test. Morin rarely lost his temper, but
this made him angry. The agreement they had reached earlier permitted the state to have the methodology and accuracy of the protocols reviewed, not to demand a second test. Morin wasn't even
sure if enough sperm sample was left over to conduct a second test.
Brobst was adamant. "The FBI needs to do its own test," she said.
Otherwise, we're not agreeing to his release."

When Kirk heard this, the color drained out of his face. It was
another ploy, another way to keep him in prison. The FBI had
screwed him the first time. It had failed to detect the sperm that was
clearly there. How could he trust the FBI? In the prison visiting
room, he screamed at the wall, pounded his hand against the table.
Morin tried to calm him.

Morin learned from Dr. Blake that his lab, in anticipation of
such a reaction from the prosecution, had designed the test protocol to retain and preserve a sufficient sample of sperm for a confirmatory test. This was a relief. Morin, still concerned though, called
Barry Scheck at the Innocence Project in New York. Scheck, a pio-
neer in the forensic use of DNA, had consulted with Morin about
the case previously and knew as much about DNA testing as any

defense lawyer in the country. Scheck agreed to review Blake's results. Afterward, he assured Morin that they were solid and that he shouldn't worry. A confirmatory test was standard procedure. Morin wasn't satisfied. He learned that an FBI agent named Jennifer Lindsay had been involved in developing the DNA protocols at the FBI lab. Morin called her to talk about Kirk's case and the state's insistence that the FBI confirm the test. Lindsay listened and responded sympathetically. She knew Ed Blake. "If Ed Blake did the science," she told Morin, "then the science is good. You can count on it." She said that obviously she couldn't promise anything. But she said it was extremely unlikely that Blake was wrong.

Morin felt better. He relayed this information to Kirk. There wasn't any choice anyway but to allow the FBI to run its own test. Two agonizing months passed by. Morin was home on a Friday night having dinner with Marty and their two sons when Lindsay called him. "I didn't want to bother you at home," she said, "but after we talked I told the lab to let me know right away what the results were."

"Yes?" Morin asked quietly.

"Well, the results won't be official for a couple of days. But the test confirmed what Dr. Blake found. Kirk Bloodsworth is excluded . . ."

WHEN HE HEARD the news, Gary Christopher considered Kirk Bloodsworth to be the luckiest man alive. To have Bob Morin as an advocate, for him to file a motion to preserve evidence that was supposedly of no value, to have this coincide with an emerging technology that could identify or exclude a person from a tiny sperm sample, to have a stain of semen discovered on discarded clothing after nine years, to have all this converge—it really was miraculous. Of course Kirk had been unlucky too. He never should have been caught up in the Dawn Hamilton case to begin with. Nor should he have been subject to such incompetence from those responsible for handling and examining the physical evidence in the case. According to Dr. Blake's examination and findings, the semen stain on Dawn Hamilton's underpants was not that difficult to detect, and it might very well have revealed the blood type of the murderer in 1984, saving Kirk Bloodsworth from the horror he endured.

After Blake's report was disseminated, carefully supported with footnotes, slides, and microphotographs, the FBI had taken an additional two months, but this time had definitively confirmed that Kirk Bloodsworth was not the man who raped and killed Dawn Hamilton. Upon receiving the news on a Thursday night, Bob Morin immediately set out trying to have Kirk released. He spoke to Ann Brobst early the next morning, then prepared a motion for a new trial, which would be unopposed by the state. He filed it early the next day. The plan was for Judge Smith to grant the new trial and then the state would dismiss the case for lack of sufficient evidence.

But that Friday Judge Smith was out of town and wouldn't be back until Monday. The press picked up the news. A Baltimore radio station, 98 ROCK—WIYY-FM—had a weekend "Kirk Watch."

"It's eight thirty on Saturday evening, and Kirk Bloodsworth is still in jail," the disc jockey announced. Radios blared it all over the prison. Two DJs, Lopez and Stash, sent Kirk a request list for his favorite songs. Every song they played was dedicated to "Kirk Bloodsworth, still in the prison . . ." Jayne Miller, a television reporter, ran a two-part series on Kirk. For the guys on Kirk's tier, it was a hoot. "And here is Snoop Dogg going out to Kirk Bloodsworth, who on this fine Sunday morning, June 27, is *still* behind bars . . ." The media frenzy had started.

Over that weekend Kirk happily gave away everything he'd acquired in prison. He gave Half his television and Bozo his cans of tuna and potato chips. Rock from New York got his cigarettes. They all congratulated him. Kimberly Ruffner even hollered down the tier to him. Ruffner had a lion's mane of dirty blond hair, combed back and parted in the middle. Shorter than Kirk by several inches, he'd grown a full beard when he first came to the prison, and it now covered most of his face. "Blood! Blood!" he said, "come here." Bloodsworth walked down to where Ruffner stood by the commissary window. "I heard about the DNA. Congrats, man." He still had trouble looking Kirk in the eye. "You out'a this shit now, man, ain't you? Man, I know where that area is," he said. "Where that crime was done." The statement came from out of the blue. Kirk thought nothing of it, nodded, and walked away.

Monday morning Bob Morin met with Ann Brobst and her boss, Sandra O'Connor, in the chambers of Judge Smith. O'Connor said something cryptic about how the DNA results had compromised the integrity of the conviction. All agreed that Bloodsworth had to go free. Bob Morin had prepared an order to that effect, and Judge Smith signed it.

On June 28, 1993, at just after noon, Kirk Bloodsworth was marched by Sergeant Cooley Hall through the Jessup House of Corrections to the departure room. Cooley took turns whistling and laughing all along the way. "You gone and done it, Mister Bloodmon," he said in that Calypso accent of his. "Good for you, mon. Good for you. Yes, yes, yes. The world it is waitin' for you out there. Go now and get it . . ."

Abdul-Haleem watched Kirk pass and put his hand over his heart. Kirk gave him a salute in return.

In the departure room, the warden gave Kirk the money he'd earned and accumulated over the nine years he'd been working in the prison. It came to just over a thousand dollars. Kirk passed some of it back to Bozo and Half, and some of it to Rock, who'd stood up for him a few times. They were all happy for him. Rock shouted from behind the steel bars, "See you later, big fellow. Don't let your ass back in here or I'll kick it myself."

Sergeant Cooley Hall unlocked the handcuffs. Kirk looked down the drive, through the prison gate. It seemed bright out there. People were milling around in the glare. Bob Morin, Stephen Harris, the state public defender, and Thomas Saunders, the district public defender, came up to the departure room to greet him. Kirk and Bob Morin embraced.

"You ready?" Morin asked him.

Kirk was leaning against a table studying a quarter, part of the change he'd gotten from the warden as his prison earnings. He was turning the quarter in his fingers. He looked up at Bob Morin. To Bob, Kirk seemed gentle at that moment. Almost childlike.

"It's smaller than I remember," Kirk said. He hadn't seen a quarter in nine years. "Have they made these smaller?"

Sergeant Cooley Hall nudged Kirk. Patted him on the shoulder. "Go ahead," Cooley said. "Go ahead, mon . . . It's time for you to go now . . ."

Kirk put the quarter in his pocket and straightened himself up. He could hear his name being yelled by inmates through some of the barred windows behind him. This time the yells were not catcalls. They were cheers of congratulations, of triumph. With his lawyers at his side, he strutted out through the prison gate, out into the day. He had to squint and shield his eyes as he walked out into the full sunlight.

Curtis and Anita Smith were there to meet him. Several cousins and friends were there. It was a fine summer afternoon. Reporters and cameras were everywhere. Each of the lawyers gave a brief statement at a makeshift podium. During that year, the governor of Maryland had convened a panel to study whether to shorten the time between conviction and execution. "I think this case will cause anyone with a conscience to pause before trying to expedite putting people to death," Tom Saunders said.

Morin had advised Kirk to keep his remarks short, but Kirk couldn't help himself. He blasted the state for what it had done to him. He thanked the people who had helped him. "Since my arrest, I've lost so much," he said, trying to control his emotions. "It's been a nine-year nightmare. The death of my mother is the most painful . . ." He couldn't keep the tears from flowing down his face. Reporters shoved cards at him. Microphones were everywhere. Before he stepped away, he added, "Even though this is a small victory for me, to have proved my innocence, the real killer is still out there. And all of this won't be completed until the real one is behind bars . . ."

One of the disc jockeys, Steve Ash, aka "Stash," arrived with a stretch limousine, handed Kirk a cigar and a beer, and accompanied Kirk, Anita, Curtis, and Kirk's cousin, Salmo, all over town, broadcasting live from the stretch. This had been prearranged. Kirk was taken to the 98 ROCK radio station for a lunch of champagne, pizza, and sandwiches. The station played Guns N' Roses, ZZ Top, Ozzy Osbourne, and all of Kirk's favorites throughout the afternoon. Kirk had the windows rolled down, and he waved to everyone. He felt like a celebrity.

When Kirk finally got home to Cambridge his family and friends had set up a party at the Suicide Bridge Restaurant, and they celebrated late into the night. Kirk ordered every crab dish he could think of: crab dip, crab cakes, steamed hard crabs, fried soft shells, and crab imperial. Later, back in his house for the first time in nine years, he couldn't sleep. He tossed and turned. He got up and almost urinated in the corner. He cried over what he'd become. He saw his mother everywhere. The house where he grew up seemed haunted, empty without her. He was frightened. He tried to make toast, then called Bob Morin and woke him up to tell him that he had used a toaster for the first time in nine years. He'd made his own toast. He wept again. The house seemed so much smaller than before. Like it had shrunk over the years. Later he realized that the trees outside had grown so tall that they now dwarfed his family home.

Kirk and Anita tried to become a couple. But once Kirk was out, Anita seemed more like a sister to Kirk. And right off, she began scolding him, urging him to walk the straight and narrow. The one thing he didn't need was someone telling him what to do. He needed space and time; he needed to blow off steam. He needed his freedom. After a couple of weeks they fought. Kirk was sorry, felt guilty; she had been good to him, had helped him, but it just wasn't going to work. Anita went back to Baltimore.

Kirk and his cousin, Salmo, went down to the beach. They stayed drunk for three days. When Kirk came back he reviewed the statement issued by the state's attorney's office concerning his release and what the prosecutors said to the newspapers. In her press release, the state's attorney described over three pages of detail the evidence against Kirk Bloodsworth. The statement then indicated that he was released because, as a result of the DNA test, his conviction now "lacked the necessary integrity." There was no longer enough evidence to hold him.

In her news conference, Sandra O'Connor declined to say that Bloodsworth was innocent and offered no apologies. "There are no other suspects at this time," she said. "Based on the evidence, our office did the right thing in prosecuting him," she said. "I believe he is not guilty," O'Connor added. "I'm not prepared to say he's innocent."

There is a strain of hubris that affects certain people in power, people with authority. It can be slow to develop, like a dormant infection. If not guarded against, it can breed an unhealthy arrogance, a cocksureness that their judgments are beyond fallacy. Such self-righteousness allows them to close their minds to new possibilities. It can cause right-thinking people to do terrible things. The devil has a long tail.

Few people in Kirk's hometown had any idea what a DNA test meant. These statements by Sandra O'Connor undercut everything he thought he'd accomplished. They left a bitter taste. That week some neighbor of Curtis and Kirk left an anonymous note on the pickup truck parked in their driveway. *Child killer!* was all it said.

TWENTY-NINE

HOW DOES A MAN recover from an experience like Kirk Bloodsworth's? How does he recapture the lost years, the lost dignity? How does a man forced to become an animal in order to survive in a vile and violent jungle reenter his community and find his way? How does a person get past being branded a monster for a crime he didn't commit?

Over the months and years following his release, Kirk felt as if he were riding a roller coaster. At times a speed trip was all he wanted, a manic headlong rip into alcohol, partying, girls, a desperate flail to make up for lost time, a lost life. At other moments, he found himself engaged in a private, quiet, and somber search for peace, for recovery, for a way to heal.

He found that he couldn't stand being in any kind of small enclosure. He'd get claustrophobic, dizzy, and sick to his stomach. Everywhere he went he needed someone with him. He was terrified to be alone. He needed at all times to have a credible alibi witness at his side, someone able to confirm his whereabouts twenty-four hours a day.

Kirk had walked out of prison directly into the spotlight of a national death penalty debate. A lightning rod, a face to put on a harrowing story of injustice, he went from no one listening or believing a word he had to say, to everyone clamoring to hear his story. His very first week back in Cambridge, he spoke to the kids at his church school about his experience. He found it calming and strangely satisfying. A U.S. House of Representatives subcommittee on innocence and the death penalty, chaired by Representative Don Edwards from California, invited him to testify. Kirk asked Bob Morin if he'd go with him. Morin helped Kirk write his speech. There he was, this Eastern Shore crabber, now speaking in the halls of Congress. Kirk followed the script Morin had prepared for him and told his story. During the committee hearing Representative Charles Canady, a Florida Republican, made a remark suggesting that the system must only balance the risk of executing an innocent man against the danger of letting a convicted killer go free on a technicality. Kirk couldn't restrain himself. He jumped to his feet. His face was red, angry. "Well, that's no consolation for me or you if it was your son sitting on death row," he shouted out.

"Well, I didn't mean to offend you," Canady said, taken aback.

"Well, you already did, sir," Kirk replied.

Kirk Bloodsworth would be no shrinking violet when it came to speaking out about the death penalty.

In those first months Kirk and Bob appeared on numerous television talk shows together, shows hosted by Oprah Winfrey, Connie Chung, and Larry King. They appeared before Congress, and Kirk addressed several state legislatures. Kirk made a compelling presence. His story was real and true. There was no denying the torture he endured. But fame can be short lived.

Bob Morin, meanwhile, pursued a compensation package from the state for Kirk. A Maryland statute provided the mechanism for compensation but first required that the inmate be pardoned on the basis that he was innocent of the crime for which he'd been convicted. If this occurred, then an amount could be paid, though how much was left entirely to the discretion of state officials.

The pardon itself was no easy accomplishment. Morin had to make a written request to Governor William Donald Schaefer. He then had to engage in an extensive lobbying campaign. Schaefer wanted to have his staff read from the trial transcripts. He wanted to hear from the state's attorney's office. The press, though, kept Bloodsworth's story alive. Public sentiment was in Kirk's favor. The process took six months to resolve. In late December 1993 Governor Schaefer issued a full and complete pardon, reflecting the State of Maryland's recognition that Kirk Bloodsworth was innocent of the crime for which he had been convicted. Only after it was granted could Morin begin negotiations for a monetary award for Kirk.

The state started off with a low figure. Morin countered. At one point Morin tried to arrange a side benefit for Kirk, that he be hired as a park ranger. Kirk decided he could never work for the same state that had tried to kill him. State officials raised their offer to $300,000, roughly $30,000 a year for each of the years Kirk had been incarcerated, they reasoned, typical of a waterman's income. Morin thought it was paltry. The state comptroller asked Baltimore County to kick in another $50,000 to make it $350,000. Baltimore County refused. It had done nothing wrong, it contended.

The state had reached its choke point, Morin was told. State officials claimed they wouldn't go higher. Morin remained dissatisfied with the amount. He didn't think it was nearly enough. But there was no precedent for challenging it in court. Morin and his partners had previously agreed that they would take no fee from Kirk for any of their work. And though they had been reimbursed for their expenses and some of their time by the public defender, Morin had been lending Kirk money for living expenses during the nine months since he'd been out, money that Kirk wanted to pay back. Not only was Kirk in debt to Morin and others, but his father had spent close to $100,000 over the years in trying to help Kirk and also was broke and desperately in need of a financial boost. Kirk wanted to pay off his debts and reimburse his father; he wanted to buy a car, to begin living again. He decided to accept the offer.

The money went fast. Kirk paid his father back. He repaid the Cambridge bank for what Curtis still owed. He returned to Morin what he'd borrowed from his firm. He paid Wanda Bloodsworth $5,000 to divorce her. He leased himself a new Corvette, his first new car. He threw a huge party at the Suicide Bridge Restaurant to celebrate his one-year anniversary of freedom. He found a new girl-friend, and when her brother got into some drug trouble Kirk paid for him to go through rehab. The relationship didn't last, but for a short while he was riding high. He took a vacation in Jamaica and blew ten grand in a week. And then one day he found himself broke again. He wrote a check and it bounced. The money was all spent. The finance company repossessed his 'vette. He needed a job. Reality was a cold slap.

Many of the people in Cambridge continued to shun Kirk. To them DNA was a technicality, just another legal quickstep that had sprung Kirk when he still should have been locked up. Mothers in the grocery store would steer their children clear of his path. A lady on the sidewalk crossed to other side of the street when she saw him coming. Other notes appeared anonymously on his wind-shield.

Brenda Ewell was one woman from Cambridge who felt differ-ently. She and Kirk met at an American Legion dance in 1996. Brenda was shy and quiet but a good listener. She knew Kirk's story and never doubted the truth. His courage and character impressed her. She was a steady girl. She worked at a local restaurant. She had a country wisdom about her, a kindness and grace that Kirk re-sponded to. They started dating. Kirk would come by the restaurant and she'd feed him. Over time Brenda helped open up a heart that had been badly damaged and sealed shut.

Brenda's nephew, Jay Jones, had his own workboat and offered Kirk a job tonging oysters that next winter. The weather was miserable. It was the toughest winter Kirk ever remembered. He was on the river every morning before sunup, in the sleet and icy water, the stinging wind, but he worked through it, even enjoyed it. He kept on with Jay into the summer, trotlining for crabs. Kirk got a second job working in a machine shop. He began saving money toward buying his own boat.

On June 26, 1999, Brenda and Kirk married at the Open Bible Church.

In early 2000 Kirk put a down payment on an old, beat-up, wooden, crab-scraping dead-rise with no motor. He took a small loan out from the bank, bought a wrecked '87 Chevy Blazer, took the engine out, and had himself his first workboat. He chinked and painted her. When he put her in the water she leaked pretty badly, but he managed. He named her *Jeanette's Pearl*, for his mother. She was a dream come true. "A man on the water can have a beer, even a cigar," he remarked. "No one's there to tell you what to do. The air is clean and open. It's just a wonderful feeling . . ."

It was around that same time that Senator Patrick Leahy called Kirk on the phone. Leahy was holding hearings on the Innocence Protection Act, a bill that would mandate testing of DNA for a wide variety of inmates who seek it, and asked if Kirk would appear and speak. Kirk hadn't spoken in public in a while, and Bob Morin was no longer available to accompany him. Morin had been appointed to be a Washington, D.C., Superior Court judge in 1996. Bob and Kirk talked and Bob encouraged him to go. Kirk agreed he'd appear on his own.

On February 11, 2000, Kirk traveled to Washington, D.C., and met with Senator Leahy. Flanked by the senator and Brenda, he strode into the Dirksen Senate Office Building to tell his story before an array of national legislators, dignitaries, and international media. The conference chamber was packed, reminding Kirk of being in the courtroom years before. But this time the people had come to listen to what he had to say. And his voice was clear and strong. During the statement he'd prepared, he referenced the fact that some writers in the press had pointed to his exoneration as an example that the system worked. As Kirk told his story, he answered this suggestion:

Did the system work? I was not released because the system was interested in what happened to me, but because my lawyer was interested. . . . I was lucky to have a lawyer who cared about my case, who worked hard for me, although I was not paying him anything. I was lucky that a laboratory found a semen spot that no one had seen before. If I didn't have Bob Morin as my attorney, and if the DNA had not been found, I would still be sitting in a jail cell. Still telling everybody that would listen that I was an innocent man. . . .

Did the system work? I was released, but only after eight years, eleven months, and nineteen days, all that time not knowing whether I would be executed or whether I would spend the rest of my life in prison. My life had been taken from me and destroyed. I was separated from my family and branded the worst thing possible—a child killer. I cannot put into words what it is like to live under these circumstances. . . .

Did the system work? My family lived through this nightmare with me. My father spent his entire retirement savings. As a result, he cannot retire and must work on and on. My mother, whom I loved and stood up for me—stood right beside me the entire time—died before I was released. Died of a broken heart. I was not allowed to go to her funeral. . . .

When I hear people say that the system works, that the system is fine, that we need to speed up executions, I say bull. You see these people who say such things were not there with me during those nine years. These people think they are talking about some hypothetical person. But they're not. They are talking about me. . . . And if it can happen to me, it can happen to you. It can happen to your child, your son, your daughter—it can happen to anybody.

Kirk's testimony was so moving that CNN invited him to be on television the next day. Shortly thereafter, Kirk got a call from Wayne Smith, executive director of the Justice Project, a Washington, D.C., nonprofit organization advocating for criminal justice reform. Smith offered to hire Kirk as a consultant, with a yearly stipend, if Kirk would assist in strategic planning, attend speaking engagements, and let the world know more about his experience. Kirk signed on.

The Justice Project soon realized that they had a powerful voice in Kirk Bloodsworth. Audiences were transfixed by his story. Kirk had a presence, a passion, an eccentric and country way with language that painted a spellbinding picture to drive home the horror of what had been done to him. His experience endowed his words with a moral authority. He began appearing at universities, law schools, before state legislatures all over the country, before Congress time and again, with the Innocence Project in Chicago, with Hurricane Carter's Association in Defense of the Wrongly Convicted, with Stephen Bright's Southern Center for Human Rights. Kirk spoke out eloquently and articulately against the death penalty. His words carried the weight of experience and truth. People listened. He rang the bell for a more humane way to treat prisoners. John Rago, law dean at Pittsburgh's Duquesne University, called Bloodsworth an "American hero." Kirk Bloodsworth wasn't the first inmate to make use of DNA. But he was the first to do it who'd been on death row. Other death row inmates, following in his footsteps, obtained exoneration through genetic testing. More than a few. A subtle shift in the national death penalty debate began to take place. Undoubtedly he helped stir a change in the wind.

Kirk has kept it up. Since 2000, he has continued to speak all over the country. He's been invited to appear abroad. Proposed bipartisan federal legislation, providing funds for the DNA testing of inmates, has been named after him. He has turned his life into a positive and powerful force for justice. He has become a national symbol and voice for reform.

ACCORDING TO INFORMATION maintained by Amnesty International, the United States is one of only a handful of industrialized countries that continues to execute its prisoners. Great Britain, Ireland, Portugal, Denmark, Norway, France, Germany, Spain, the Netherlands, Australia, Canada, New Zealand, Romania, Slovenia, Hungary, the Czech Republic, Switzerland, Belgium, South Africa, and many others have abolished the death penalty for all crimes. Many additional countries have abolished it for ordinary crimes.

In April 1999 the United Nations Human Rights Commission passed the Resolution Supporting Worldwide Moratorium on Executions, calling on countries that have not abolished the death penalty to at least restrict its use. Just ten countries, including Rwanda, Pakistan, Sudan, China, and the United States, voted against this resolution.

In the United States today thirty-eight states and the federal government continue to carry laws permitting capital punishment. Approximately thirty-five hundred people sit on death row.

In Maryland, 75 percent of the inmates awaiting execution in recent decades have come from Baltimore County. As governor of

Texas, George W. Bush oversaw the executions of 152 people. Clemency was granted in one instance.

In early April of 2002 an Arizona death row inmate, Ray Krone, after spending ten years awaiting execution, was cleared through the use of DNA and walked into the sunlight a free man. Anti–death penalty advocates heralded Krone as the one hundredth death row inmate proven to be innocent since 1973. Numerous people on death row have been cleared through the use of DNA testing since Kirk Bloodsworth paved the way.

In 1992, the year before Kirk Bloodsworth was freed, Barry Scheck and Peter Neufeld started the Innocence Project at Cardozo Law School in New York. Since its inception, spearheading the use of DNA testing for inmates, it has proven that over 140 people convicted of serious felonies were actually innocent. Today hundreds of other inmates across the country are asking to be subjected to a DNA test. Conservative lawmakers, however, resist the widespread use of DNA testing for convicted felons, claiming that it is too expensive and burdensome to preserve the evidence and pay the costs of the tests, that it promotes frivolous delays and allows inmates to "play" or "game" the system, and that it undermines the important concept of "finality."

When Kirk Bloodsworth appeared before Congress on behalf of the Innocent Protection Act, he argued that innocent people deserved to be protected. "I don't ever want this to happen to anybody else," he said simply.

The Justice Project doesn't take a position on whether capital punishment is right or wrong. It seeks to educate and to advocate for fairer processes in the criminal system. Peter Loge, previously the director of the Justice Project, suggests that in just the last few years the death penalty debate has taken on a new dimension. For two centuries the arguments centered mostly around questions of the morality of execution, questions of whether capital punishment is an effective deterrent, and questions as to whether capital sentencing was applied in a racially fair way. Recently, Loge suggests, a significant question has arisen as to whether the convictions that underlie capital cases are trustworthy. He believes Kirk Bloodsworth has put an important face on this new parallel debate. Will our society tolerate the executions of people whose underlying convictions may be suspect?

THIRTY

THOUGH HE ADORED her from day one, *Jeanette's Pearl* had been giving Kirk a fit on the water. While he continued to mend her, chink her, patch her, and fix her engine, she remained an obstinate and recalcitrant boat. When he wasn't traveling and speaking, Kirk had been trying to trotline regularly on Slaughter Creek off the Little Choptank River. But he could barely afford to keep her afloat. She was costing him more than he was making.

For a while Kirk had been eyeing a replacement, a thirty-five-foot beauty with an Evans fiberglass hull, a deep scag, and a Caterpillar diesel. She was a lot of money. He talked it over with Brenda. He had a steady paycheck from his speaking engagements. In early 2003 he decided to go for it. He bought her and spent the winter months readying her up for the season. For the first time in his life, Kirk Bloodsworth had the real thing, a first-class dead-rise fiberglass workboat. He painted her and polished her. When he first saw her, he knew the name he'd paint on her stern. He christened her *Freedom*.

The year 2003 started well for Kirk and Brenda and then got better. From the day Kirk walked out of prison, he'd been asking who the real murderer of Dawn Hamilton was. Since 1993 he'd called the state's attorney's office repeatedly, and since no one would take his calls he'd leave a message asking them to seek a match of the DNA sample with the other suspects. He called Judge Smith, who'd been elected as the Baltimore County executive, and left messages requesting that the DNA be put into the national database of criminal suspects called CODIS—Combined DNA Index System—to seek a match.

Kirk had become friends with Barry Scheck at the Innocence Project in New York, and Scheck had made several calls to Ann Brobst requesting that the DNA be put into CODIS. On one occasion Brobst told Scheck that her office and the police had limited funds, had other priorities. She told him that her office was still not convinced that Bloodsworth was innocent. She suggested that maybe the panties were tainted, that the sperm came from somewhere else. In late 2002 Scheck wrote a letter to Brobst demanding that the DNA found on Dawn's panties be run through the CODIS but got no response. Kirk called other times and left messages. Since 1993 the state's attorney's office had known Kirk was not the killer. For ten years it sat idly by while a child murderer might be stalking other kids, might be released any day into the community after doing time on some other charge. Why wasn't a DNA match being vigorously pursued?

In early 2003 Susan Levine, a *Washington Post* reporter, decided to write a lengthy piece on Kirk Bloodsworth. As part of her research she contacted the Baltimore County State's Attorney's Office and asked what had been done to follow up on Dawn Hamilton's killer. She received little in the way of a response. In June of 2003 the *Baltimore Sun* ran an article questioning why the DNA had not been compared to the state's DNA database of convicted felons, a database in place since well before Bloodsworth's release in 1993. Pressure on the prosecutors was mounting.

On September 4, 2003, following a long Labor Day weekend,

Kirk got a telephone call that scared him. After a morning spent crabbing on the river, he'd been watching television in his and Brenda's cottage in Cambridge. When the phone rang he picked it up.

"May I please speak to Kirk Bloodsworth?" he heard. He froze. He recognized the voice. His heart started racing.

"Who's calling?" he asked.

"Ann Brobst from the state's attorney's office."

Kirk could hardly speak. Then it came to him. They had to have found the killer.

"I need to meet with you, Kirk," Ann said. "It's about the Dawn Hamilton murder."

"You found him!" Kirk screamed into the phone. "You found the bastard!"

"I can't tell you that," she answered calmly. "I need to see you."

Kirk could feel the blood rushing to his face. His ears burned. "Well, goddamn it, don't tell me no," he cried out. "Don't you tell me no!"

Brobst heard the plea. "No, I won't tell you no," she softly answered. "I just want to see you and tell you in person."

"You haven't said a goddamn word to me or called me in twenty years and now you want to meet with me?" Kirk cried out.

"Calm down. Please calm down, Mr. Bloodsworth," Brobst said. "I want to talk to you in person. I owe you that. You pick the time and place. Anywhere you want. It's important."

Kirk didn't want Ann Brobst coming anywhere near his home. He agreed to meet her the next day in the Burger King parking lot, the one on the water with a small broken-down pier out back. He thought he knew what she was going to tell him, but he decided to take no chances. The parking lot had two different exits by car, and he'd have his boat anchored just off the pier. He wasn't going to let them take him back. That night he couldn't sleep. He knew something important was about to happen.

Kirk was nervous enough about the meeting to call his legal adviser in Washington, Deborah Crandall, and she drove to Cambridge to join him. Kirk's cousin, Cindy, came to the house also, and accompanied Kirk and Brenda to the Burger King parking lot. Kirk was dressed all in black. Brenda held Kirk's arm as they got out of the car and walked over to where Brobst and two detectives were standing.

Ann Brobst shook hands stiffly and introduced the two detectives to Kirk. Brenda, Cindy, and Deborah said hello. They all agreed to go inside. One of the detectives pushed two tables together where everyone could sit.

"So what's this about?" Kirk asked.

"We have a cold hit on the killer," Ann Brobst said. "We've found more evidence on Dawn's clothing. We put the DNA into CODIS. We have the man. The evidence is unequivocal."

Kirk started shaking. Tears streamed down his face. Brenda was crying and holding on to him tightly. The floodgates just burst. He couldn't stop himself. "Oh my God," he cried. "Oh my God." He began sobbing into his hands. "Who is it?" he asked. "What's the bastard's name?"

"Kimberly Ruffner," one of the detectives answered. "He was in the prison with you."

"No!" Kirk screamed out. "Kimberly Ruffner? I spotted weights for that man. Brought him library books."

"We know," Brobst said.

"There is no doubt whatsoever in our minds," one of the detectives said.

"We've gotten three separate hits on him," the other detective said.

It went unspoken, but everyone at that table knew that it happened only because of the persistence of Kirk Bloodsworth in trying to clear his name. Only because he and Bob Morin had refused to quit, had found that unseen spot of semen on Dawn Hamilton's clothing. The crime was solved because of them.

"Believe it or not, I've been pushing for this to go into the database for years," Brobst said.

Kirk made no reply.

"The database has been there, but we honestly didn't have the funds to test this DNA. We got a grant just a bit back," the first detective added.

"Kirk, I'm sorry," Ann Brobst said. "I wanted to come and tell you that personally. I am deeply sorry for what we did to you."

Kirk was still shaking, almost convulsing. He pointed a trembling finger at Brobst. "I have hated you for twenty years," he said in a loud, bellowing voice. He was almost shouting. "For twenty fucking years! You have called me a monster . . ." His words broke up. He was sobbing, choking back his heaves. It took some time for him to compose himself. "You have called me a child killer . . ." He could hardly continue. Brenda handed him some paper napkins and he tried to stanch his tears. "I am no angel, but I am not out killing little girls . . ."

Brobst sat there across from him. Controlled. Professional. Inside the Burger King it had turned stone quiet.

Kirk calmed some and studied her. It was just a gesture Brobst had made, coming to Cambridge. Not much after so much pain, so much arrogance. But it was something. "I don't hate you no more," Kirk said more softly. He heaved a sigh. He nodded to her. "'Cause of what you done in coming down here yourself to tell me this. I know it was hard. I know it took a lot. I forgive you."

Ann Brobst sat there. She didn't know how to answer.

The detectives told Kirk what would probably happen. Kimberly Ruffner was being charged for the rape and murder of Dawn Hamilton. He would be brought to justice. Later Kirk learned that one of the original tips in the Hamilton slaying, from back in 1984, concerned the fact that the composite resembled a man wanted in the Fells Point area for a number of child rapes. The lead had never been adequately chased down.

Before he got up from the table, Kirk asked Ann Brobst about Thomas Hamilton, Dawn's father. Word had it that he'd had a difficult time, had gone to prison himself. Brobst was surprised at Kirk's question. That Kirk would care enough at such a time to express concern for Hamilton. She told him the little she knew.

Outside the restaurant, Kirk excused himself for a moment, stepped away, and called his father on his cell phone. Curtis Bloodsworth shouted out loud when he heard the news.

As Kirk rejoined the group, the sun was high over the silver Choptank, winding wide and silent across the landscape. From the parking lot, Kirk could see his boat bobbing gently on the deep river. He inwardly laughed. Freedom was his.

Kirk asked one of the police officers, the one with the twang, where he was from, and Major Rufton Price told him: "West Virginia."

"Took an old country boy from West Virginia to finally catch the son of a bitch, didn't it," chuckled Kirk. "Figures. And thank you."

Later Kirk likened that moment to having a million-ton ball of pig iron on his back and then having someone just kick it off. He felt like he had just walked through Alice's looking glass, back into the world. As everyone got ready to leave, Kirk shook the hands of the detectives, and said good-bye to them. He then turned to Ann Brobst. She stood there unmoving, small, diminutive. Kirk opened up his large bearlike arms. Brobst waited, uncertain. Kirk smiled, walked up to her, put his large arms around her and said, "Thank you for coming." He squeezed her, and she tentatively raised her arms and then hugged him back. "It's over," Kirk whispered. "It's finally over. And now we both can find some peace . . ."

EPILOGUE

*Kirk Bloodsworth (far left),
with his lawyer, Bob Morin
(third from left), leaves the
Maryland Penitentiary
on the day of his release,
June 28, 1993.*

SPRING 2004

KIMBERLY SHAY RUFFNER had been twice charged with sexually assaulting children before Dawn Hamilton's slaying. He'd been accused of an attack on a young teenager in Baltimore City, a charge that was dropped, and then charged for sexually assaulting an eleven-year-old girl in November 1983. He was tried on that charge in the summer of 1984, but when the jury could not reach a verdict was set free. The date was July 12, two weeks before Dawn Hamilton was killed. Ruffner lived in East Baltimore, approximately six miles from Fontana Village. Six weeks after Dawn's death Ruffner was arrested for the attempted rape and stabbing of another woman in the Fells Point area of Baltimore. It was that crime that put him in the same prison as Kirk Bloodsworth. Following the match of his DNA with that from the Hamilton crime scene evidence, including semen recently identified on the sheet used to transport Dawn Hamilton's body to the morgue, charges were filed by the Baltimore County Police Department on September 4, 2003, against Ruffner for the rape and murder of Dawn Venice Hamilton. In November 2003 he was indicted for the crime by a grand jury.

The Baltimore County State's Attorney's Office initially indicated that it planned to seek the death penalty. Kirk Bloodsworth, while intent on seeing Dawn Hamilton's killer brought to justice, opposed this decision. During the months following Ruffner's indictment, and with the consent of Thomas Hamilton, the prosecutors decided to engage in plea negotiations with Ruffner's attorney. On May 19, 2004, Kirk was visited by several detectives, including Major Rufton Price, as well as a deputy in the state's attorney's office, Steve Bailey. They explained to Kirk that in order to avoid the wrenching ordeal of another trial the state had offered Ruffner a plea bargain that would allow him to escape a death sentence. Ruffner had agreed to accept it. In so doing he had acknowledged his sole responsibility for the crime, stating that he had smoked PCP and had drunk a large amount of rum the morning before he encountered Dawn Hamilton. He also admitted that he had slain Dawn with the rock that was found near her head. On May 20, 2004, almost twenty years after the murder, in Baltimore County Circuit Court, Kimberly Ruffner, standing about five feet eight inches tall, and with cropped dirty blond hair, entered a plea of guilty to the first-degree premeditated murder of Dawn Venice Hamilton. He was sentenced that same morning to life in prison, to run consecutively, or in addition to, the sentence he was already serving. In a press conference following the hearing, Steve Bailey told reporters that his office expected that Ruffner would never leave prison. He also said that it was absolutely clear that Kirk Bloodsworth was innocent of any involvement in the crime. He went on to acknowledge that the Bloodsworth experience had caused his office to reexamine its decision making in capital cases.

Judge Robert Morin, appointed by President Clinton to the Washington, D.C., Superior Court in 1996, continues to preside over legal matters. His prior law partner and friend, Gerry Fisher, was also appointed to be a judge in that same court and occupies chambers not far from those of Judge Morin. Stephen B. Bright remains the director of the Southern Center for Human Rights in Atlanta, maintaining the fight against death sentences and on behalf of equal justice nationwide.

Dr. Edward Blake continues his work in the field of DNA testing for forensic purposes. Dr. Blake recalls the Kirk Bloodsworth case well. When Dr. Blake received the panties of Dawn Hamilton for testing, black markings were on them, having previously been put there by the FBI. This is consistent with the testimony of Agent William McInnis at Kirk's first trial that he had made such markings. These markings included circles, some lettering, and an arrow pointing directly at the stain of semen that Blake's lab discovered, analyzed, and from which Blake obtained the DNA sample that freed Kirk Bloodsworth. Blake reports that at the time he received the panties, no fabric from the area of the stain had been removed. He concludes that the FBI, even though it drew an arrow pointing directly to the area where the semen stain existed, failed to test the stain to determine what it was. Blake has photographs of the panties vividly showing the markings and the arrow pointing directly to the semen stain.

William McGinnis, the FBI serologist who testified at the first Bloodsworth trial, has no specific recollection of the case. He reports that he would often make markings on evidence indicating the spot from where he intended to try and lift samples for identification and testing. If no spermatozoa were then found, he'd conclude that no semen was present. The fact that there were markings on the clothes, he posits, would indicate only that he probably attempted to identify blood or spermatozoa from those areas. The question thus remains, How could McInnis and the FBI have failed to find any semen on the crime scene evidence?

Sandra O'Connor has provided little in the way of a satisfactory explanation as to why her office waited ten years—from 1993 when

Dr. Blake discovered the semen stain until 2003—to try and match the DNA found on Dawn Hamilton's underclothing with a suspect. For all her office knew, the murderer of Hamilton could have been stalking other victims during those ten years or been pending release from a prison or a jail. The Baltimore County Police Department utilized dozens of officers and spent vast resources to investigate the crime. O'Connor's office also spent significant resources in prosecuting Bloodsworth twice, in vigorously resisting Bloodsworth's efforts to free himself, and in defending its convictions during two appeals. Yet after Bloodsworth's release, when it came time to appreciate that Bloodsworth was not the assailant, O'Connor's office delayed ten years before comparing the DNA retrieved from the actual killer's sperm with that contained in the state's database. It was short of funds, Ann Brobst explained.

Ann Brobst has been promoted to be deputy of the Circuit Court Division of the Baltimore County State's Attorney's Office. She was not assigned to the Kimberly Ruffner prosecution.

Robert Lazzaro presently works in a law firm in Towson, Maryland, primarily handling divorce matters. He and his partners did accept appointments in two cases to defend death penalty prosecutions brought by his old boss. "There's quite a difference being on the defense side," he remarked. "As a prosecutor, the crime has already been committed. As a defense lawyer, you actually hold someone's life in your hands. It's a sobering responsibility." In both cases, he was able to avoid a death sentence.

Steven Scheinin, David Henninger, and Leslie Stein all continue in private practice in the greater Baltimore area.

Judge William Hinkel sits occasionally as a retired judge but has no plans to ever again hear a capital case. Judge James T. Smith left the bench in September 2001 to run for office. He was elected as the Baltimore County executive in 2002.

In 1994 the State of Maryland abandoned the gas chamber as a means of execution, replacing it with lethal injection, considered more humane. In May 2002 Maryland governor Parris Glendening, citing continuing questions about the integrity of capital punishment, placed a temporary moratorium on death sentences in Maryland. In January 2003 Maryland's attorney general, J. Joseph Curran Jr. called for an abolition of the death penalty in Maryland citing flaws in the system and the real possibility that innocent persons could be executed. Maryland's newly sworn-in Republican governor, Robert L. Ehrlich Jr., however, has lifted the moratorium. He has done this despite a recent independent study by a University of Maryland researcher pointing out that of the twelve men then awaiting execution in Maryland, the vast majority were from one county—Baltimore County, eight were black, and all were convicted of killing white people.

Kirk Bloodsworth continues his work as a consultant with the Justice Project and regularly travels to speak on behalf of prison reform, access to DNA testing for prisoners, and against capital punishment. He has been the recipient of numerous awards for his efforts promoting civil rights and equal justice. In 2003 bipartisan sponsored legislation in Congress, called the Innocence Protection Act, contained a grant to prisoners providing funds for DNA testing. It was named in his honor—the Kirk Bloodsworth Post-Conviction DNA Testing Grant Program.

On March 15, 2004, Sir Alec Jeffreys was awarded the prestigious Pride of Britain Lifetime Achievement Award in a ceremony in the Grand Ballroom of the London Hilton attended by dignitaries and celebrities from all over the world. Kirk Bloodsworth, accompanied by his wife, Brenda, was secretly flown in to appear onstage as the special guest of Jeffreys before a televised audience estimated at over 10 million people.

Freedom, Kirk Bloodsworth's workboat, at least when her skipper's in town, can usually be seen plying the tributaries of the Chesapeake Bay, trotlining for hard crabs, occasionally trolling for stripers, a fine example of a waterman's craft, not particularly fast but stable and sturdy, steadily moving forward through the waves, a white gem on a river of blue.

Author's Note
and
Acknowledgments

WHEN I FIRST APPROACHED Kirk Bloodsworth with the idea of working on this project, he agreed enthusiastically to make it a collaborative effort. He generously provided his time, shared with me the intimate and often painful details of his life story, and encouraged his prior lawyers to speak with me and give me access to their records. My job was to research and write the book. Since then, Kirk and I have spent many days together, and I am sincerely grateful for the opportunity he gave me to undertake this project and for his enormous contribution to it. In working with Kirk I have gained a profound admiration and respect for his courage, his integrity, and his character. To endure what he endured and then to turn his life into a positive force for justice is both remarkable and inspiring. It is in keeping, of course, with the grit of a Chesapeake Bay waterman.

In addition to learning from Kirk, I interviewed many of the people who participated in or reported on this real life drama. These include Kirk's father, Noble Curtis Bloodsworth, Judge Robert Morin, Dr. Edward Blake, Judge William Hinkel, County Executive Judge James T. Smith, Robert Lazzaro, Ann Brobst, Steven Scheinin, Leslie Stein, David Henninger, Valerie Cloutier, Julia Bernhardt, George Burns, Gary Christopher, Ted Weisman, Peter Loge, Katy O'Donnell, Susan Levine, Judge Gerald Fisher, William McGinnis, Major Rufton Price, and Barry Scheck, among others. I was also assisted by Michael Tigar, Laura Burstein, Jayne Miller, Stephen Nolan, and Dr. Ravindar Dhallan. My thanks go out to all these people for their cooperation and help. Detectives Robert Capel and William Ramsey have both retired from police work. Requests for interviews were made to them through Major Rufton Price of the Baltimore County Police Department, but neither agreed to come forward.

In researching the events depicted in this book, I also relied extensively on the voluminous police and FBI notes and reports, legal correspondence and pleadings, trial exhibits, court documents, and trial transcripts concerning the Dawn

Hamilton murder investigation and Kirk Bloodsworth's trials, appeals, and exoneration. Additionally, contemporaneous news stories from the *Baltimore Sun* papers, the *Times* of Baltimore County, the *News American*, and the *Washington Post* became important secondary sources. I thank the reporters for these newspapers who wrote about the Dawn Hamilton murder investigation and the events surrounding Kirk Bloodsworth's convictions and exoneration. The police reports and notes, the legal pleadings and notes, and the correspondence that I've reviewed and relied on are too numerous to list. I have attempted in the bibliography to name all other sources as well as a selection of letters specifically referred to in the book.

I am in debt as well to my editor, Shannon Ravenel, for her confidence, encouragement and skill, and particularly to Kristin Curran Junkin, for her research assistance, her many readings and suggestions, and her consummate patience and support.

KIRK BLOODSWORTH WISHES to express the following sentiments: He dedicates this story to God, for without him no things are possible; to his mother, who will always be with him; to his dad, whom he loves for all he endured and has done in helping to free him; and to Dawn Venice Hamilton and the Hamilton family. He wishes to thank Al Rose, and Anita, who will always be friends in Christ; Dave Bloodsworth and his cousin Cindy for standing by him when he was down; Janet Taylor, Pat Ryan, and, particularly, Bob Morin for helping to save him; the Justice Project and Wayne, Laura, John, Peter, Cynthia, Cheryl, Kim, Penny, Grace, Bobby, Wendy, and Lynn; Dick Dieter at the Death Penalty Information Center; Ginny and all his friends at the Constitution Project; John Rago, Maria, and his friends at the Duquesne Law School; the Lancer's Club; Judge Hammerman; Kim Summers and Lynn; Shawn Ambrose; Larry Marshall and Rob Warden of the Northwestern Center on Wrongful Convictions; Barry Scheck and Peter Neufeld; Jayne Miller; Mike Tricky; Jayne Henderson; Senator Patrick Leahy; Congressmen Bill Delahunt, Ray LaHood, and F. James Sensenbrenner Jr.; Jesse Jackson Jr. for letting his voice be heard; Aunt Frances; and he especially thanks his wife, Brenda, whom he considers the most wonderful woman on earth, and her fine family.

Bibliography

Amnesty International. "Abolitionist and Retentionist Countries." Retrieved September 24, 2003, from http://www.web.amnesty.org/pages/deathpenalty-countries-english.

Amirani, Amir. "Sir Alec Jeffreys on DNA Profiling and Minisatellites." *Science Watch* (1995). Retrieved September 22, 2003, from http://www.sciencewatch.com/interviews/sir_alec_jeffreys.htm.

Archaeology Online News, Archaeological Institute of America. "Neandertal DNA." (July 29, 1997). Retrieved September 25, 2003, from http://www.archaeology.org/online/news/dna.html.

Bishop, Jerry E., and Michael Waldholz. *Genome.* New York: Simon and Schuster, 1990.

Blake, Edward T., and Jennifer S. Mihalovich. "Report to Robert E. Morin re: *Maryland v. Kirk Bloodsworth,* File No. 92-508. Forensic Science Associates, Richmond, Calif., 17 May 1993.

Bloodsworth v. State, 307 Md. 164, 512 A.2d 1056 (1986).

Bowerman, Sam, and Sa W. Hagmaier. "Criminal Personality Profile—The Dawn Hamilton Homicide–Sexual Assault." Report prepared in consultation with other members of the Behavioral Science Unit of the FBI Academy, Quantico, Va., 1984.

Brobst, S. Ann. Letter from the assistant state's attorney for Baltimore County to Robert E. Morin, re: *State v. Bloodsworth,* 17 April 1989.

Brown, Clarence. "Dawn's Father: Didn't Know of Camp Plans." *News American* (Baltimore, Md.), 28 July 1984, 1A.

Brown, Clarence. "Man Sought in Slaying of Rossville Girl." *News American* (Baltimore, Md.), 26 July 1984, 1A.

Brown, Clarence. "Police Seek Leads in Killing." *News American* (Baltimore, Md.), 27 July 1984, 1A.

Browne, Gary Lawson. *Baltimore in the Nation, 1789–1861.* Chapel Hill: University of North Carolina Press, 1980.

Butler, John M. *Forensic DNA Typing: Biology and Technology behind STR Markers.* San Diego, Calif.: Academic Press, 2001.

Carson, Larry, and Frank D. Roylance. "Man Held in Girl's Murder." *Evening Sun* (Baltimore, Md.), 9 August, A1.

Criminal Justice Legal Foundation. "Minority Views on Senate Bill 486, the Innocence Protection Act." Retrieved October 12, 2003, from http://www.cjlf.org/deathpenalty/Dpinformation.

Davis, Paul J. Letter of congratulations from the chairman of the Maryland Parole Commission announcing the pardon of Kirk Noble Bloodsworth by Governor William Donald Schaefer, 28 December 1993.

Erlandson, Robert A. "Bloodsworth, on Stand, Denies Murdering Child." *Sun* (Baltimore, Md.), 8 March 1985, 1D.

———. "County Detective Learns to Use Psychological Profile." *Sun* (Baltimore, Md.), 19 May 1985, 2B.

———. "Kirk Bloodsworth Gets Death Penalty in Child's Murder." *Sun* (Baltimore, Md.), 23 March 1985, 7A.

Evans, Martin. "Dawn Trusting, Guardian Says." *News American* (Baltimore, Md.), 27 July 1984, 8A.

Evans, Martin, and Joe Nawrozski. "Slain Girl Was 'Supposed to Be at Camp.'" *News American* (Baltimore, Md.), 27 July 1984, 1A.

Fridell, Ron. *DNA Fingerprinting: The Ultimate Identify.* New York: Franklin Watts, 2001.

Gans, Jeremy, and Gregor Urbas. *DNA Identification in the Criminal Justice System.* Trends and Issues in Crime and Criminal Justice, no. 226. Canberra: Australian Institute of Criminology, 2002.

German, Ed. "The History of Fingerprints." Retrieved September 16, 2003, from http://www.onin.com/fp/fphistory.html.

Goldstein, Louis L. *Louis Goldstein's Maryland.* Annapolis: Maryland State Archives, 1985.

Gove, Maureen. "Bloodsworth Denied New Trial in Hamilton Murder." *Essex Times* (Baltimore County, Md.), 20 March 1985.

———. "Bloodsworth Guilty in Hamilton Murder." *Essex Times* (Baltimore County, Md.), 13 March 1985, 1.

———. "Bloodsworth Sentenced to Death for Hamilton Murder." *Essex Times* (Baltimore County, Md.), 27 March 1985, 1.

———. "Testimony Begins in Bloodsworth Murder Trial." *Essex Times* (Baltimore County, Md.), 6 March 1985.

Hiaasen, Rob. "The Second Life of Kirk Bloodsworth." *Sun* (Baltimore, Md.), 30 July 2000.

Husdon, Elizabeth, and David Michael Ettlin. "Rosedale Girl, 9, Is Found Murdered; Police Seek Man She Reportedly Met." *Sun* (Baltimore, Md.), 26 July 1984, 1A.

Innocence Project Home Page. Retrieved September 24, 2003, from http://www.innocenceproject.org.

Jacobson, Joan. "Is the Death Penalty a Lottery? You Bet." *Washington Post*, 26 May 2002, B1.

Kent, Milton. "No Solid Leads Found in Girl's Killing." *Sun* (Baltimore, Md.), 27 July 1984, 1D.

Kimble, Vesta. "More than 200 Offer Tips about Girl's Slaying." *News American* (Baltimore, Md.), 1 August 1984.

Lazzaro, Robert W., Assistant State's Attorney for Baltimore County. Letter to Steven J. Scheinin, Re: State vs. Bloodsworth, February 11, 1985.

Levine, Susan. "Md. Man's Exoneration Didn't End Nightmare." *Washington Post*, 24 February 2003, 1A.

Levy, Harlan. *And the Blood Cried Out: A Prosecutor's Spellbinding Account of the Power of DNA.* New York: Basic Books, 1996.

Lion, John R., Clinical Professor of Psychiatry, University of Maryland School of Medicine. Letter to Neil Blumberg, M.D., relating to the criminal personality profile of the FBI regarding *State v. Bloodsworth*, 21 March 1985.

LoLordo, Ann. "Psychological Profile of Suspect Drawn by FBI." *Sun* (Baltimore, Md.), 10 August 1984.

Marck, John T. *Maryland, the Seventh State: A History.* 4th ed. Glen Arm, Md.: Creative Impressions, 1998.

Maryland Department of Public Safety and Correctional Services, Division of Correction. "Maryland's Gas Chamber." Retrieved September 19, 2003 from http://www.dpscs.state.md.us/doc/gaschamb.

"Maryland execution moratorium ends." *USA TODAY.* Retreived November 2, 2003, http://www.usatoday.com/news/nation/2003-01-22-death-warrant_x.

Maryland Historical Society. "The Great Escape of Tunnel Joe Holmes." Retrieved October 14, 2003, from http://www.mdhs.org/radio/md.

Masters, Brooke A. "DNA Testing in Old Cases Is Disputed; Lack of National Policy Raises Fairness Issue." *Washington Post*, 10 September 2000, A1.

McCabe, Deidre Nerreau, and Jay Apperson. "DNA Tests Could Be Key to Freedom for Many Convicts." *Sun* (Baltimore, Md.), 5 July 1993, 1B.

Meeker-O'Connell, Ann. "How DNA Evidence Works." Retrieved October 6, 2003, from http://www.science.howstuffworks.com/dna-evidence.htm.

Montgomery, Lori. "Maryland Questioning Local Extremes on Death Penalty." *Washington Post*, 12 May 2002, C1.

————. "A Stellar Witness for DNA Testing; Man Cleared in Slaying Testifies for Legislation." *Washington Post*, 23 February 2001, B4.

Morin, Robert E. Letter to S. Ann Brobst, State's Attorney's Office, 27 April 1993.

————. Letter to Governor William Donald Schaeffer Re: Kirk Bloodsworth Pardon Application, 19 November 1993.

————. Letter to Jennifer Mihalovich, Forensic Science Associates, 20 August 1992.

————. Letter to Michael Pulver, Esq., State's Attorney's Office, 6 April 1989.

National Academy of Sciences. "DNA Technology in Forensic Science" (1992, 2000). Retrieved September 17, 2003, from http://www.nap.edu/openbook/0309045878.

Paternoster, Raymond, and Robert Brame, "An Empirical Analysis of Maryland's Death Sentencing System with Respect to the Influence of Race and Legal Jurisdiction." Executive Summary. University of Maryland, College Park, 2003.

Pipitone, Anthony. "Bloodsworth Jury Didn't Doubt Guilt." *Evening Sun* (Baltimore, Md.), 25 March 1985, 1D.

————. "Ex-Officer Names 2nd Suspect in Girl's Death." *Evening Sun* (Baltimore, Md.), 19 March 1985.

————. "Man Seen with Slain Area Girl Hunted." *Evening Sun* (Baltimore, Md.), 26 July 1984, 1A.

Prewitt, Milford. "Man Arrested in Girl's Death in Rosedale." *Sun* (Baltimore, Md.), 10 August 1984.

Price, Joyce. "Essex Man Charged in Death of 9-Year-Old Girl." *News American* (Baltimore, Md.), 10 August 1984, 4A.

————. "State to Seek Death Penalty in Girl's Killing." *News American* (Baltimore, Md.), 11 August 1984, 1A.

Ridges and Furrows. "Early Fingerprint Pioneers." Retrieved September 17, 2003, from http://www.ridgesandfurrows.homestead.com/early_pioneers.

Rodricks, Dan. "Bloodsworth, the Suspect from Central Casting." *Evening Sun* (Baltimore, Md.), 29 June 1993, D1.

————. "Down Twice, Still Fighting." *Evening Sun* (Baltimore, Md.), 24 May 1989, D1.

————. "Haunting Questions." *Evening Sun* (Baltimore, Md.), 14 March 1988, D1.

Rollo, Vera Foster. *Your Maryland: A History.* 5th rev. ed. Lanham, Md.: Maryland Historical Press, 1993.

"Sandra A. O'Connor Biography." Retrieved September 14, 2003, from http://www.co.ba.md.us/Agencies/statesattorney/sabiog.

Scheinin, Steven J. Letter to Robert Lazzaro, State's Attorney, 27 November 1984.

Shane, Scott. "5 Place Man with Slain Girl, 5 Say He Was Home." *Sun* (Baltimore, Md.), 8 March 1985, 2D.

———. "Bloodsworth Denied New Trial Despite Report of Second Suspect." *Sun* (Baltimore, Md.), 19 March 1985, 1D.

———. "Murder-Rape Trial Starts with Gruesome Evidence." *Sun* (Baltimore, Md.), 5 March 1985, 3D.

Shapiro, Robert. *Human Blueprint.* New York: St. Martin's Press, 1991.

Shugg, Wallace. *A Monument to Good Intentions: The Story of the Maryland Penitentiary, 1804–1995.* Baltimore: Maryland Historical Society, 2000.

Skove, Cynthia. "Bloodsworth Convicted of Slaying Girl, 9." *News American* (Baltimore, Md.), 9 March 1985, 8A.

———. "Bloodsworth Gets Death Sentence for Rape, Murder." *News American* (Baltimore, Md.), 23 March 1985, 1A.

———. "Dawn Hamilton's Companions Testify in Murder Trial." *News American* (Baltimore, Md.), 6 March 1985, 1A.

———. "Footprint Tentatively Links Defendant to Slain Girl, 9." *News American* (Baltimore, Md.), 5 March 1985.

———. "Man Tells of Surprise At Arrest in Slaying." *News American* (Baltimore, Md.), 8 March 1985, B1.

———. "Relatives Testify Defendant at Home When Girl Was Slain." *News American* (Baltimore, Md.), 7 March 1985, B1.

Skowron, Sandra. "New DNA Testing Provides Hope for Some Inmates." *Los Angeles Times,* 4 July 1993, 26.

Small, Glenn. "Bloodsworth Testifies on Death Penalty." *Sun* (Baltimore, Md.), 24 July 1993, 1B.

———. "Nine-Year Prison 'Nightmare' Ends as Former Convicted Killer Is Released." *Sun* (Baltimore, Md.), 29 June 1993, 1A.

———. "Innocent Man's Ordeal Raises Many Questions." *Sun* (Baltimore, Md.), 9 January 1994, 1B.

Smyth, Dennis F. "Post Mortem Examination Record for Dawn Hamilton, Case No. 84-1043." Report of the assistant medical examiner for the state of Maryland, Baltimore, Md., 14 September 1984.

State of Maryland v. Kirk N. Bloodsworth, Case No. 84-CR-3138, Circuit Court for Baltimore County, Maryland, docket entries, trial transcripts, and presentence report. Transcript dates: February 25, 1985; March 1, 1985–March 8, 1985; March 18, 1985; March 22, 1985; March 23, 1987–April 6, 1987; April 22, 1987; June 12, 1987.

U.S. Department of Energy Office of Science, Office of Biological and Environmental Research, Human Genome Program. "DNA Forensics" (March 14, 2003). Retrieved September 17, 2003, from http://www.ornl.gov/hgmis.

Valentine, Paul. "Jailed for Murder, Freed by DNA; Md. Waterman, Twice Convicted in Child's Death, Is Released." *Washington Post,* 29 June 1993, A1.

Wagner, Dennis, Beth DeFalco, and Patricia Biggs. "DNA Frees Arizona Inmate after 10 Years in Prison." *Arizona Republic*, 9 April 2002, Retrieved September 24, 2003, from http://www.truthinjustice.org/krone.

Wambaugh, Joseph. *The Blooding*. New York: William Morrow, 1989.

Warren, Marion E., and Mame Warren. *Baltimore: When She Was What She Used to Be*. Baltimore, Md.: Johns Hopkins University Press, 1983.

Watson, James D. *The Double Helix*. New York: Atheneum, 1968.

WBAL Channel. "I-Team Uncovers New Details in Sexual Assault, Murder Suspect." Retrieved November 20, 2003, from http://www.thewbalchannel.com/11investigates/2506217/detail.